The Politics
of
John Dewey

The Politics
of
John Dewey

by

Gary Bullert

Prometheus Books

700 East Amherst St. Buffalo, New York 14215

Published in 1983 by
Prometheus Books
700 East Amherst Street
Buffalo, New York 14215

Printed in the United States of America

Library of Congress Card Catalog No. 83-62872
ISBN: 0-87975-208-4

Contents

Foreword

Gary Bullert's *The Politics of John Dewey* is noteworthy for several reasons, chief among them is that it contains the most complete documentary account of John Dewey's political thought and activities available to students of American culture. The measure of Dr. Bullert's achievement may be gauged from the fact that John Dewey's career spans the period during which the United States was transformed from a primarily agricultural economy to a primarily industrial one. Just as important is the fact that parallel to this shift was a change from the conventional religious consciousness that pervaded both private and public life to a secular and scientific outlook in practical affairs. Periodical revivals of religious sentiment do not gainsay this shift.

There is almost a symbolic significance in the dates that mark Dewey's life span. He was born in 1859, the year in which Darwin's *Origin of Species* was published, and on the eve of what turned out to be the fiercest and bloodiest conflict in recorded human history up to that time—the American Civil War. He died in 1952, while the Korean War was still raging, after two world wars that changed not only the course of age-old empires but the condition and quality of life of untold millions. It is unlikely that any comparable period ever witnessed such a variety and depth of social and political change. It is not surprising that the varying emphases in Dewey's political thought reflect these changes.

John Dewey's political philosophy does not consist in a set of formal propositions applicable to political problems at any time and place. It expresses some basic ideas and values brought to bear on the specific subject matter of man's organized social life. Political issues, therefore, are not distinct from sociological, economic, and legal issues. Pervading all of his discussions of the problems that confronted human beings are certain attitudes that he deemed fruitful not only for understanding these problems but also for their successful resolution.

Dewey had a profound sense of the historical dimension in human

3

experience. Whatever man is *as such,* however the human condition is defined, he and she are historically bound by their time. Even "the eternal" appears in a temporal context, which always makes a difference to the way it is interpreted. Men and women are creatures of tradition but, precisely because of that, they are confronted and challenged by the emergence of new experiences, of ideas, practices, and institutions. That is why history itself, although necessary for understanding the human predicament, is never sufficient in indicating what should be done.

Men and women are not only historically conditioned, they are creatures of culture. The individual mind or personality is not born with the biological organism but is made in the course of its development in a specific culture. Whatever moral and psychological traits are acquired reflect in some way the environing cultural and social institutions regardless of whether human beings accept them or revolt against them. That is why, for Dewey, even in the absence of formal schooling, the social process is an educational process. Because the individual is socialized and influenced as a rule more by what goes on beyond the school than within it, Dewey was concerned with the educational impact of all modes of human experience, by how men and women work, play, worship, and idle. Since education is a process by which on the basis of present experience the future becomes more accessible to us, Dewey was concerned to render that future experience both more secure and richly significant. Political decisions, he therefore urged, should be assessed for their educational effects.

Central to John Dewey's political philosophy is the concept of freedom. But freedom to him did not mean blind impulse, the power to do anything one pleases. To be sure, it is uncoerced choice, but choice informed by relevant knowledge and sustained by institutional opportunities to achieve reflective goals. Freedom does not exist in a state of nature in which human beings run wild, driven by need and passion. It is not a ready-made possession independent of social institutions. The counterposition of freedom and social control, of the individual and the community or state, is a false dichotomy, a consequence of a mistakenly conceived individualism. There never has been an association of human beings without some form of social control. The question is always of what kind, degree, and direction that control should take. Dewey was as aware of the evils of totalitarianism as he was of those of anarchic individualism. He feared the former more than the latter, which sometimes prepares the way for the greater evil, and condemned both. John Dewey was not a narrow partisan of the New Deal. He welcomed it as far as it went but criticized it on the ground that its concept of human welfare was not comprehensive enough.

Perhaps the most distinctive aspect of Dewey's political philosophy was his belief that the soundest political judgment is based upon reflective inquiry, whose basic pattern is exemplified in scientific method. He contended that at the heart of all policy is a value judgment, and that no important problem in human affairs is merely or purely technical. Values are not identical with facts. Nonetheless Dewey held that rational grounds can be found to justify some courses of conduct as more valid than others in the specific contexts in which human beings are required to act. For him the underlying logic is the same as that which determines what judgments of fact are warranted in the light of the evidence.

This view that, although judgments of fact do not entail judgments of value, the factual consequences of proposed courses of conduct have a bearing on their validity differentiated Dewey from the long line of empirical thinkers, from Hume to Russell, who believed that there could be no rational grounds for the choice of ultimate values. For Dewey all value judgments were penultimate.

Pervading all of Dewey's political philosophy was his rational commitment to democracy as a way of life. By this he meant a society whose institutions made it possible for its citizens freely to select careers and patterns of life that would enable them to achieve their desired potential in all areas of human experience. That is why Dewey stressed the processes of cooperative activity, self-determination, participation, and appreciation of diversity, not only in our political life, narrowly conceived, but in our education and economy.

These are some of the leading ideas of John Dewey that come into play in the development of his political thought and activity. The perceptive reader will find implicit reference to them in Dr. Bullert's fascinating chronicle of the political events, situations, decisions, and controversies in which John Dewey was involved. As humanist, pragmatist, and democrat, John Dewey's philosophy expresses the considered faith of a thinker who believed in the promise of American civilization.

SIDNEY HOOK

Acknowledgments

The author extends his sincere gratitude to the many individuals and institutions who have assisted in the preparation of this manuscript.

The generosity of the Earhart Foundation and, most particularly, the John Dewey Foundation enabled this project to be completed.

Special thanks are reserved for my teacher, Herbert Schneider, whose cooperation in revealing his insights about Dewey, in procuring grant support, and in giving helpful comments on the manuscript was invaluable.

George Blair, James Gouinlock, George Dykhuizen, Selden Rodman, and Robert Roth were extremely responsive to my inquiries.

Many libraries assisted in providing correspondence material, including the University of Wyoming Library, the Joseph Regenstein Library (University of Chicago), the State Historical Society of Wisconsin, the University of Oregon Library, the Ohio State University Library, the University of Michigan Library, the Morris Library (Southern Illinois University), the Suzzalo Library (University of Washington), and the University of Virginia Library.

The staff of the Center for Dewey Studies warrants commendation for their assistance.

Paul Kurtz, editor-in-chief of Prometheus Books, deserves my heartfelt thanks for both his perseverance and his support for the project.

Steven L. Mitchell, who spent many arduous days editing this manuscript, not only purified the text of many typographical and stylistic errors but, as a student of Dewey, he offered many penetrating comments about the book's argument. His cooperation has been indispensable in polishing the text.

Finally, I owe a great debt to Sidney Hook, who wrote the foreword. In addition, his encouragement and assistance is most singly responsible for the publication of this book on the politics of John Dewey. And like his mentor, Sidney Hook serves as an exemplary model of intellectual integrity who will, it is hoped, inspire scholars to the high standards of critical inquiry necessary for the maintenance of a free society.

The following list of abbreviations is used in the notes to refer to the most frequently cited sources.

Journals

CC	*The Christian Century*
CS	*Common Sense*
N	*The Nation*
NL	*The New Leader*
NR	*The New Republic*
PR	*Partisan Review*
PLB	*Peoples' Lobby Bulletin*
SRL	*Saturday Review of Literature*
SF	*Social Frontier*
WT	*World Tomorrow*

Books

CJA	*China, Japan, and the U.S.A.*
F&C	*Freedom and Culture*
GPP	*German Philosophy and Politics*
ION	*Individualism Old and New*
LCJ	*Letters From China and Japan*
L&SA	*Liberalism and Social Action*
P&IP	*The Public and Its Problems*

1

Introduction

Liberalism, Relativism, and Democracy

In 1940, Alfred North Whitehead remarked with some misgivings that America was living in an age subject to John Dewey's influence. Today, not even Dewey's staunchest admirers would make that claim. While acknowledging that Dewey seems presently to be in eclipse, Sidney Hook refers to him as "one of the most misunderstood writers of his age."[1] Perhaps, this was the inevitable penalty to be exacted for Dewey's attempt to popularize his thought and to shape the course of history. He remained at the center of heated intellectual and public controversy. Concerted attacks from a disparate legion of critics have finally rendered Dewey's pragmatic liberalism intellectually unfashionable. Unfortunately, his enduring insights into democratic politics might well suffer neglect.

Dewey's public career existed in an age of radical political upheavals and cultural dislocations. He underwent the trauma of World War I, the Scopes Trial, the Sacco and Vanzetti Trial, the Great Depression, the rise of totalitarianism, the Trotsky Trial, World War II, and the Korean War. Modern mass society's erosion of traditional beliefs and social bonds jeopardized both political freedom and cultural stability. Totalitarian movements challenged democracy's intellectual legitimacy and military survival. Throughout this perpetual crisis, Dewey maintained an unyielding commitment to scientific intelligence as an instrument that could remedy humankind's material insecurity and its spiritual homelessness. He inextricably joined the scientific attitude with a democratic political culture. Becoming America's preeminent public philosopher, Dewey tirelessly addressed himself to the public issues of his day. He served as an unofficial ambassador for democracy, was associated with countless liberal groups and unpopular causes, and gained notoriety as a chief spokesman for educational reform. He endeavored to reorient philosophy toward the concrete problems of humanity. He insisted that a philosophic faith could be tried and tested only in action.[2] By examining Dewey's political activities, the viability of pragmatic liberalism can be judged by its own standard. Historically, critics have not

9

accepted this challenge, preferring instead to discredit Dewey on theoretical grounds.

Amidst the rise of Nazism and Stalinism, Dewey responded by formulating his most sophisticated defense of democracy. In *Freedom and Culture* he recalled the inspiring message of America's founding fathers, most particularly Thomas Jefferson. Dewey described Jefferson as "the first modern to state in human terms the principles of democracy."[3] In the Declaration of Independence, Jefferson referred to certain "inalienable rights" and "self-evident truths." While Dewey discounted the theory of natural law, which was Jefferson's initial premise, he agreed that the ends of democracy and the rights of man were moral principles that are both universal and unchangeable.[4] Due to man's nature as a rational, moral being, these axioms ought never to be renounced. They circumscribe and supply ethical purpose to the institutions of government. Critical free intelligence is a distinctively human faculty that permits moral responsibility and human dignity. Reason is not a mere instrument to obtain pre-existing desires but the capacity to ascertain moral truths and guide behavior.[5] Dewey repudiated the tendency of psychologists to emphasize the primacy of subconscious emotions and appetites. Knowledge must influence actions; totalitarianism merely reduces ideas to a subhuman product of class or race.

When the Declaration of Independence proclaimed "a decent respect for the opinions of mankind," it assumed that the mass of people possessed the collective common sense to establish justice on an objective basis. These opinions are not arbitrary but informed by verifiable facts. This enables the community to strive for a consensus on both ultimate principles and specific social policies. Dewey recognized in this famous phrase not only a faith in human intelligence, but that all men were created equal as moral beings. While men differed in their natural abilities, they were all entitled to the rights of citizenship. No man should rule over others as master to slave. Dewey noted that all forms of intolerance emanate from one source: the denial of human qualities to certain despised groups of people.[6] These human rights involve equality under the law, the ability to participate in government, and a rough equality of opportunity. Dewey held that the world suffered more from power-mad leaders than from the masses. Experts should not determine policies but discover and publicize the facts necessary to formulate them. Social engineering, as proposed by the Technocrats, for example, obviated democratic participation. Dewey was convinced that a government by experts would degenerate into "an oligarchy managed in the interests of the few."[7]

Jefferson appreciated the role of surrounding cultural-economic conditions in sustaining democratic life. Democracy required more than mechanized institutional arrangements designed to ensure political liberty by preventing the concentration of power. Jefferson glorified the small farmer as the embodiment of the virtues of initiative, thrift, honesty, family solidity, and independence. These virtues were stimulated when individuals had a direct control over the scope of their lives. Small, local governing units maximized individual social responsibility. The grave problems of industrialism included the accretion of impersonal bureaucracy and the dislocation of local community life. The simple age of individualism, what Daniel Boorstin termed "the lost world of Thomas Jefferson," has been supplanted by an industrialized society with corporate control. These transformations necessitated, according to Dewey, a restructuring of democratic institutions toward group activity and more social control of the economy. When Jefferson advocated the right of each generation to recast government, he understood that the mechanisms of democracy must be responsive to historical change. Ironically, Jeffersonian principles were employed in the modern age as an apologetic for a *laissez faire* economics, which consolidated political-economic power in private hands.

While Jefferson desired a system that reinforced the pursuit of happiness, he realized that the roots of the American political tradition were moral and not a narrow utilitarian device to satisfy material interests. Likewise, Dewey contended that government is instituted among men to provide more than merely the material conditions for the general welfare. As he put it: "the founders of American democracy asserted that self-governing institutions are the means by which human nature can secure its fullest realization in the greatest number of people."[8] Dewey grounded his political ideals historically within the American democratic experience. He sought to adapt Jeffersonian idealism to the corporate-industrial age. The democratic values remained constant, while the means to maximize them were subject to historical change.

Dewey acknowledged that totalitarianism was successful in capturing the passions of the masses by generating constant excitement bordering on hysteria. The Nazis appealed to emotions more visceral than merely intellectual loyalties. Dewey was convinced that the scientific attitude and the democratic faith must permeate the dispositional level. In totalitarian countries, science was corrupted into an instrument of human regimentation. Dewey feared that a science of human nature might actually multiply the means of manipulation by the state. Universal literacy was not a protection against propaganda but merely enabled modern communications systems to engage more effectively in thought control. Science was perverted to serve sinister ends due to the absolute separation of facts and values—a position popularly espoused by positivism. Dewey strongly repudiated positivism, charging that any doctrine that eliminates or obscures the choice of values undermines personal responsibility in decisions and actions.[9] Rather than being the slave of pre-existing desires, science had intrinsic moral potentiality. Science must not only destroy old values but create new ones. Dewey's philosophy stands or falls on the ability of science to be applied to moral judgments.

Scientists and scholars inherited the social responsibility to propagate the scientific attitude, which manifested a moral standard for personal conduct. The scientific enterprise was motivated by the love of truth, which entailed the holding of beliefs in suspense, doubting the credibility of a claim until sufficient evidence is obtained to support it, the capacity to go where the evidence points rather than adhering to personally preferred conclusions, the implementation of working hypotheses rather than dogmas, and the exploration of new fields of inquiry.[10] By practicing such open-mindedness and rationality, scholars could elevate the level of political discourse for the entire community. However, in adopting the mantle of generalized social critics, scholars oftentimes judge the world through their peculiar tastes and sensibilities. Instead of practicing their professional discipline, political enthusiasms sweep away any elementary sense of caution and objectivity. Yet, Dewey recognized that a retreat from liberal education into narrow specialization held additional dangers. How could academics reconcile intellectual and political responsibility? This issue is crucial in Dewey's career. Insulation from political power could ferment alienation and political irresponsibility. Total immersion in government and competitive policies might undermine objectivity. A healthy democracy requires a sensitized equilibrium between scholars as a cloistered leisure class and servants of society. While initially optimistic that educational reform could function as the basis for social reform, Dewey gained the seasoned recognition that the mating of ideas and social action was an agonizingly protracted process.

He defended academic freedom as a primary loyalty. It provided the matrix for the discovery of truth, an essential for a rational social policy. On the eve of World War II, as chairman of the American Association of University Professors, Dewey warned scholars not to subordinate academic freedom to any partisan loyalty. Conceding that these remarks "seemed aloof," he reiterated that the university's supreme end was the preservation of free inquiry. Dedicated scholarship and research would benefit society most in the long run.[11] The scientific method promoted a genial orthodoxy, one that preserved standards of reasoned inquiry. Authority is not imposed; rather, it is consistent with the purposes of individual scholars who submit their findings for verification. Dewey guarded vigilantly the integrity of his profession. He strove to expose and discredit totalitarian influences that tended to lure intellectuals into a tragic self-corruption. He also warned that scientific research must retain its objectivity by being divorced from any operative framework imposed by special interests. Testing social policies by their consequences for the entire population provided the calculus for democratic problem-solving. Rather than abstract disputes, specific means and ends could be examined. For example, Dewey agreed with Trotsky that the proper ethical end was the liberation of humankind. However, Trotsky deemed class struggle to be the only means to arrive at such social justice. By imposing this absolutist law on history, Trotsky dogmatically refused to examine his policy of class struggle, along with others, according to its actual consequences.[12] In his lifetime, Dewey was quite capable of revising his viewpoint when new knowledge was revealed. Living in a world of probabilities, he did not presume to have all the answers in advance.

During the 1930s, an intense academic debate raged over whether democracy demanded an absolutist or relativist foundation. The menace of totalitarianism induced many to insist that a democracy in crisis needed a nontentative fighting faith in order to survive. As early as *German Philosophy and Politics* (1914), Dewey argued that philosophical absolutism led to political authoritarianism; scientific experimentalism promoted democracy. Critics charged that he merely offered a method of approaching social problems without advocating any detailed solutions.[13] For fear of appearing to be dogmatic or frozen, pragmatic liberalism lacked a galvanizing ideological vision. This resulted in numerous defections from liberalism during the thirties, these critics contended. Yet, Dewey argued that democracy was not merely a negative, mechanical system of checks and balances designed to prevent the concentration of political power. It was a way of life: "the only form of enduring order that is now possible."[14] Skeptics held that no moral judgments could be validated and that democracy could permit no agreement on fundamentals. Struck by the inadequacy of this relativism, Dewey developed a scientific foundation for ethical values, a means to arrive at a consensus on first principles. This consensus, like truth itself, was an ideal limit. During the interim, democratic institutions comprised a basis for cooperation short of full agreement.

The emergence of anthropology as an academic discipline gave rise to another species of relativism: cultural relativism. Ruth Benedict, in her classic *Patterns of Culture,* uncovered societies which adhered to an ethos diametrically opposite to the West. These explorations into the heart of darkness prompted her to conclude that no universal standards existed. Each culture contained its own moral code and therefore could not be judged objectively to be better or worse than any other. All values were culture-bound, resting upon assumptions that were ultimately arbitrary. Amid the rise of Nazism, many anthropologists were theoretically reduced to the viewpoint that no scientific basis existed for criticizing Hitler. Leading anthropologists, including Franz Boas, were sincerely convinced that cultural relativism would assist tolerance, racial understanding, cosmopolitanism, and equality. However, in a relativist quicksand, these values could as easily slip into their opposites. A clear contradiction emerged between the moral beliefs of anthropologists, grounded in sentiment, and the scientific posture assumed in their discipline. Some critics have also alleged that there are two Deweys: 1) a scientific skeptic and 2) a utopian social engineer.[15] If this contention is valid, then Dewey's whole effort to link theory with practice was an abysmal failure.

Dewey acknowledged his debt to anthropology for its concept of culture, which helped to transcend conceptually the dichotomy between the individual and social. He insisted that along with the demonstrated plasticity of human nature, some needs were inherent in men due to their constitution.[16]

For Dewey, the fact of human plasticity "does not prove that all these different social systems are of equal value, materially, morally, and culturally. The slightest observation shows that such is not the case."[17] Far from adopting cultural relativism, Dewey identified the critical issue in this way: Which culture is in fact the most desirable?

Dewey has been classified as the theoretical founder of that brand of historical relativism utilized by the New History School, whose prominent members included Charles Beard and Carl Becker. These scholars were indicted for reducing history to an instrument of propaganda. Subjectivist-presentist-relativism was alleged to contribute to the rise of Nazism by assisting in its conquest of the German universities.[18] Relativism bred both passivity and acquiescence toward Hitler's barbarism. Dewey was outraged by these allegations.[19] Though historical studies might be influenced by the prevailing climate of opinion, they were not simply random fabrications. During the Trotsky inquiry, Dewey concretely exhibited his approach to history. At the Moscow Show Trials, Trotsky was accused of specific crimes. After collecting and critically examining the evidence, Dewey concluded that the facts demonstrated Trotsky's innocence. The belief that history should be shaped in order to harmonize with the current Party line was a typical perversion of totalitarianism. Though commonly categorized as a relativist, Dewey rejected ethical, historical, and cultural relativism. This misnomer obscures the most substantive elements of his lifelong effort to defend and articulate the moral basis for democracy.

The neglect of Dewey's emphasis on first principles has resulted in the charge that pragmatism is a philosophical cancer eating away at the ethical foundation of Western civilization. In both "Ethical Principles Underlying Education" (1897) and *Ethics* (revised 1932), Dewey upheld the urgent necessity for establishing a universally applicable moral standard. He asserted that, "the attempt to discover a standard upon the basis of which approbation and disapprobation, esteem and disesteem, should be awarded has nothing less than a revolutionary effect on the whole conception of virtue and vice."[20] What is this ultimate standard, this compass to guide conduct? Dewey defined it as whatever conduces to the freedom and welfare of the entire community. In his numerous writings on ethics, Dewey delineated more specifically the elements that comprised the good life. Freedom, growth, and shared experience are its main constituents.[21] He praised interest in science, art, and literature. Participation in community life and social service were likewise rewarding. Dewey's utilitarianism was devoid of the dubious hedonism of earlier theorists. Society should do more than promote the material welfare; it should nurture the development of virtuous character in its citizens.

Dewey criticized absolutist philosophies that enumerate certain *a priori* principles, independent of experience, placing them beyond the province of rational criticism. General rules could not be applied blindly in order to meet every contingency. Like Aristotle, Dewey recognized that the virtuous man attained the ability to deliberate morally by experience and knew habitually how to cope with concrete situations. Such contextualism does not reduce Dewey's position to improvisation or expediency but provides for the capacity to check general principles against specific conditions. Though recognizing the importance of negative freedom (absence of restraint), he articulated a positive doctrine of freedom. Dewey contended that, "the democratic idea of freedom is not the right of each individual to do as he pleases, even if it be qualified by adding 'provided he does not interfere with the same freedom on the part of others.'"[22] Freedom of mind is the basic human freedom. By cultivating the individual's positive mental powers and his self-discipline, the capacity to solve problems with moral prudence would be realized.

People must be persuaded that the social order ultimately serves their long-range interests and that this interest harmonizes with the common good. Specific laws and customs are justified in so far as they provide for the common good. They are subject to continuous inquiry and revision. However, the general standard is constant because it provides the framework for a human community to exist in the first place. Dewey sought to reconcile the importance of critical inquiry with the requirements of social duty. Since human beings are naturally interdependent, the individual, as individual, does not establish the demands for moral action or the final principles of value. The community as a whole, through formal laws and customs, codifies behavior that ultimately commits individuals to a specific course of action. Such predictable actions are required for community life. The schools function as socializing agencies, internalizing the child's recognition of social duties and the will to carry them out.

Dewey insisted that social ties, like the parent-child relationship, are natural. The mutual responsibilities corresponding to these specific stations are therefore intrinsic and binding. By nurturing the social spirit of the child, an habitual disposition to act out of social service and for the common good will becomes manifest. Pursuit of self-advantage and infidelity to one's social responsibilities is a primary evil according to Dewey.

Freedom and social responsibility are not incompatible. Social authority is natural and inevitable, not a necessary limitation on personal freedom. Throughout his writings, Dewey retained the Hegelian insight that man achieves human qualities and fulfillment by participating in the enhancement of community life. Individuals should identify the social good as their own true good by perceiving the values and common interests that bind people together. Their freedom and happiness ultimately depend upon it. Individuals should obey the law even if they do not immediately desire to do so. Not fear of punishment, but a generalized altruistic sense should motivate a democratic citizenry. Dissenters should be tolerated, for they are a vital instrument of social progress. However, in advocating policy changes, they must persuade others voluntarily. The burden of proof is upon them to demonstrate how a specific law or practice fails to serve the common good.

Dewey's theory of democracy was designed to reconcile freedom with authority, social stability with the need for reform, and universal standards with specific circumstances. He substantively refined Lockean individualism, which is popularly associated with the modern liberal tradition.

Dewey comprehensively applied these insights to the reform of education. Once again, many critics mistakenly identify him with the radical, subjectivist approach of progressive education. Dewey denounced the progressive educator's romantic fetish for the "natural child." The child-centered school provided no standards at all; logically it culminated in anarchy. Proper teacher authority and a well-structured curriculum were indispensable. Dewey argued that, "to fail to assure them guidance and direction is not merely a permit to operate in a blind and spasmodic fashion, but it promotes the formation of habits of immature, undeveloped, and egoistic activity."[23] Indulging a child's selfish whims would lead to an arrest of growth and the disintegration of personality. The development of mental powers follows certain laws of growth. The fact that a child might desire something does not mean that it is in fact desirable. That judgment can be determined only after critical reflection.[24] The glorification of the spontaneous and immediately enjoyable also stunted the child's capacity to understand contemporary social life. These students were not socially responsible or cognizant of the forces of industrial civilization. While progressive schools might randomly stimulate artistic orientations, they were largely sandboxes for private consumption. Dewey castigated their students' impertinence and disrespect for the rights of others. Far from endorsing permissive education, Dewey's educational reforms provide a microcosm for his ideal democratic community.

The relationship between Dewey and modern American liberalism has continued to be a source of confusion and controversy. Arthur Schlesinger, Jr., credits Dewey with establishing the philosophical framework for twentieth-century American liberalism with its gospel of intelligence as the instrument of social progress.[25] Reinhold Niebuhr, Dewey's arch-nemesis, conceded that no one was better certified to speak in behalf of liberalism than Dewey. Indeed, Dewey was not reluctant to identify himself as a "liberal." He endeavored to explicate its specific agenda throughout his public career, most notably in books like *Individualism Old and New* (1930) and *Liberalism and Social Action* (1935). He noted its ambiguous legacy. Tracing the history of liberalism from its rational-economic and religious-humanitarian roots, he indicated how these older doctrines had outlived much of their utility in the corporate age. He firmly rejected the atomistic liberal doctrine of the British empiricists. Dewey defined the general ends of liberalism as "liberty and the opportunity of individuals to secure the fullest realization of their potentials."[26] Effective liberty is the function of social-economic conditions at a particular time. During the Great Depression, key issues focused upon relieving material insecurity and enabling the masses to participate fully in cultural pursuits. Liberals were (and are) confronted with the task of collectively formulating the specific means to relieve human oppression. Unfortunately, a continual tendency exists toward canonizing once successful programs, thereby insulating them from critical analysis. Sensitive to Santayana's charge that the reformer never knows how close to the roots of society he is chopping, Dewey sought to retain the traditional American ideals by creatively adapting them to meet modern contingencies.

What were the more general principles endorsed by Dewey? First, the scientific habit of mind must be applied to public life. Liberals must vigorously defend the freedoms of speech, inquiry, press, religion, association, and political participation.[27] A delicate tension should be struck between the individual and the group, allowing for criticism and experimentation but ensuring that they will be conducted in a socially responsible manner. Second, equality of opportunity should be the goal of public policy. Equality of opportunity, not equality of results, is primary.[28] A meritocracy stimulates individual initiative, which in turn energizes social progress. Equality of results imposes a stifling uniformity and ultimately fosters a bureaucratic tyranny. Third, the political should not be subordinated to the economic. Capitalism or socialism is justified not on the basis of absolute rights of property or ideological blueprints. Economic arrangements should be judged as to whether they weaken or strengthen liberal democracy, whether they promote both liberty and economic security. Fourth, methods employed should correlate means and ends. Class struggle within an existing democracy utilizes violent techniques, which negate the expressed ideals of the revolutionists. A strong preference is given to social reform through voluntarism and persuasion. Fifth, opportunities for citizen participation in community, industrial, and political life should be enhanced. Politics is a vehicle for community, the discovery of common goals, and the institution of collective programs structured to serve the common good.

In 1929, Dewey conceded that American liberal movements had experienced "temporary enthusiasms and then steady decline." He doubted whether the pre-World War I liberal optimism could ever be recovered. Has the belief in free government steadily lost its worldwide appeal during the twentieth century? One of the criticisms lodged against Dewey argues that his liberalism requires a tacit framework of moral assumptions, a consensus of values regarding human decency that permeates the community. It can neither create these values nor defend them effectively when they are under attack. Can a pragmatic political culture survive if its basic values are challenged?[30] Does pragmatic liberalism break down in times of crisis? Is it a milque-toast doctrine committed to sweet compromise and token reforms? Does not politics pivot around inexorable clashes of economic interests that cannot be assuaged by appeals for more facts? In an age of genocide and total war, don't calls for experimentalism fall remarkably flat?[31] Hasn't the ingrained human impulse toward radical evil proven its compulsive power over the sickly sentiments of human brotherhood and reason?

Dewey was fully aware of these challenges to his political philosophy.

He considered democracy to be both a means and an end. It is judged in relation to its practical consequences for human betterment. In addition, democracy provides the necessary conditions for free inquiry and consent, both of which are intrinsic to any legitimate human community. Dewey constructed a sophisticated defense of democracy. The crucial issue of whether he prudently applied these insights in practice remains unresolved. The rise and fall of pragmatic liberalism is directly related to the political positions that Dewey publicly adopted. By scrupulously investigating his career as a political activist, an educated judgment can be rendered. This investigation entails situating Dewey within the context of intellectual opinion during his lifetime, detailing his direct political activities, and analyzing his prescriptions for the major domestic and foreign crises of the twentieth century. This Dewey inquiry transpires at a time when liberalism is discredited and under siege. This is a condition quite similar to that of Trotsky in 1937, when Dewey himself decided to chair an investigation into Trotsky's alleged political crimes.

NOTES

1. Sidney Hook, "John Dewey and the Crisis of American Liberalism," *The Antioch Review* (Summer, 1930):218.

2. John Dewey, "What I Believe," *The Forum* (March, 1930):182.

3. John Dewey, *Freedom and Culture* (New York: G.P. Putnam's Sons, 1939), p. 155. (Hereafter cited as *F&C*)

4. Ibid., p. 156.

5. Ibid., p. 138.

6. Ibid., p. 127.

7. John Dewey, *The Public and Its Problems* (New York: Henry Holt and Co., 1927), p. 208. (Hereafter cited as *P&IP*)

8. *F&C*, p. 130.

9. Ibid., p. 172.

10. Ibid., p. 145.

11. John Dewey, "Higher Learning and the War," *American Association of University Professors Bulletin* (December, 1939):613-614.

12. John Dewey, "Means and Ends," *The New International* (June, 1938):163-73.

13. Morton White, *Social Thought in America* (Boston: Beacon Press, 1957), pp. 244-45.

14. John Dewey, *Liberalism and Social Action* (New York: G.P. Putnam's Sons, 1935), p. 54. (Hereafter cited as *L&SA*)

15. Morton White, *Social Thought in America*, pp. 244-45.

16. John Dewey, "Does Human Nature Change?" *Rotarian* (February, 1938):11.

17. John Dewey, "Does Human Nature Change?" *Rotarian* (February, 1938):59.

18. John Dewey to Merle Curti (July, 1950), Merle Curti Papers (Wisconsin State Historical Society, Madison, Wisconsin). While crediting Dewey with elaborating the conceptual scheme that fueled the progressive movement, Eric Goldman accused pragmatism of a "dangerous relativism." See Eric Goldman, *Rendezvous With Destiny* (New York: Vintage Press, 1956), pp. 158-59, 348.

19. Chester Destler, "Some Observations on Contemporary Historical Theory," *The American Historical Review* (April, 1950):525. Auriel Kolnai linked William Dilthey's historical

relativism with the particularism of Nazi culture. See Auriel Kolnai, *The War Against the West* (New York: Viking Press, 1938).

20. John Dewey, *Ethics,* revised ed. (New York: Henry Holt & Co., 1932), p. 280.

21. James Gouinlock, ed., *The Moral Writings of John Dewey* (New York: Hafner Press, 1976), pp. xxii–xxiii.

22. John Dewey, "Democracy and Educational Administration," *School and Society* (April, 1937):459. See Robert J. Roth, S.J., "John Dewey's 'Moral Law' Ethics," *International Philosophical Quarterly* (June, 1980):127–42. On the absolutism-relativism debate, see Edward Purcell, *The Crisis of Democratic Theory* (Lexington: University of Kentucky Press, 1973). Also see, James Gouinlock, *Dewey's Philosophy of Value* (New York: Humanities Press, 1972).

23. John Dewey, "How Much Freedom in the Schools," *The New Republic* (July 9, 1930): 205. See John Dewey, *Experience and Education* (New York: MacMillan Co., 1938), 91 pp.

24. John Dewey, *The Quest for Certainty* (New York. Milton, Balch & Co., 1929), p. 266.

25. Arthur Schlesinger, Jr., *The Crisis of the Old Order,* Vol. 1 (Boston: Houghton, Mifflin & Co., 1957), p. 130. Reinhold Niebuhr, "The Pathos of Liberalism," *The Nation* (September 11, 1935):303–4. See William Gerber, *American Liberalism* (Boston: Twayne Publishers, 1975), 308 pp.

26. *L&SA,* p. 54.

27. John Dewey, "Creative Democracy—The Task Before Us," in *The Philosopher of the Common Man: Essays in Honor of John Dewey to Celebrate His Eightieth Birthday,* edited by Sidney Ratner (New York: G.P. Putnam's Sons, 1940), p. 227. See John Dewey, "Justice Holmes and the Liberal Mind, *The New Republic* (June 11, 1928):210. (Hereafter the *New Republic* will be referred to as *NR*.)

28. John Dewey, "Individuality, Equality, and Superiority," *NR* (December 13, 1922):61–63. John Dewey, "Liberty and Equality," *Social Frontier* (January, 1936):105–106. (Hereafter cited as *SF*)

29. John Dewey, "*Commentary* and Liberalism," *Commentary* (November, 1948):485.

30. John Diggins, "Ideology and Pragmatism: Philosophy or Passion?" *American Political Science Review* (September, 1970):889–900. Diggins declared that Dewey's alleged failure to respond effectively to the crisis of World War II demonstrated the political bankruptcy of pragmatic liberalism. See John Diggins, "John Dewey in War and Peace," *The American Scholar* (Spring, 1981):213–30.

31. See Frederick Olafson, *Ethics and Twentieth Century Thought* (Englewood Cliffs, N.J.: Prentice-Hall, 1973), p. 21.

2

John Dewey's Guild Socialism

Dewey's vision of democracy assumes greater definition by examining his approach to economics. Escape from servitude was impossible unless man possessed economic control over his environment.[1] Though economics was not the exclusive determinant of a political culture, both Dewey and Charles Beard gave it much emphasis. In 1930, Dewey felt compelled to concede that "economic determinism is now a fact, not a theory."[2] Dewey historically analyzed the relationship between particular political philosophies and the ruling economic class. Dualistic philosophy reinforced the subordination of the working class by establishing a cultural cleavage between the spiritual and the material. He protested such rationalizations due to their potential for economic and political oppression. Though *laissez faire* capitalism was a force for human emancipation at one time, this theory served an ideologically apologetic role during the emerging corporate age. Seeking to inject humane values into the industrial process, Dewey fought against the nexus of big business and political power. His chief targets were the captains of industry and finance who established an oligarchic control contrary to democratic principles. In addition, he pointed to a structural incompatibility between science, technology, and the professed values of business enterprise. Technology was necessarily rational and required social planning and organization.[3] However, Dewey recoiled against the dangers of a totally planned society. His economic thinking evolved into support for a mixed economy that combined individual initiative and cooperation with social welfare. Most of all, cultural rather than purely economic interests should be primary for individuals.

At Chicago's Hull House around 1900, Dewey encountered an assortment of anarchists, communists, and single-taxers who stimulated his political imagination. The most affectionate and lasting acquaintance was his friendship with Jane Addams, pacifist and social worker. He became preoccupied with school, labor, and local civic reform in the Chicago area. As a member of the Civic Federation of Chicago, he favored government regulation of private monopolies, municipal ownership of utilities, and the enhancement of labor union power. However, support for union activity did not spell an endorsement of labor violence and lawlessness. Reform, not abandonment of the capitalist system, was Dewey's preferred policy.

After moving to Columbia University in 1904, Dewey met each week with the "X" Club whose membership included Hamilton Holt, Lincoln Steffens, Charles Edward Russell, James T. Shotwell, Charles Beard, and Walter Weyl. These individuals discussed and critically appraised various socialist alternatives to capitalism.[4] Dewey housed Maxim Gorky in 1906 and nearly lost his job in the process. Gorky was seeking funds for a socialist revolution in Russia. Joining the Intercollegiate Society of Socialists, Dewey voted for Eugene Debs, socialist presidential candidate in the 1912 election.[5] Afterward, Dewey became an active member of the League for Industrial Democracy, serving for a time as its president. He championed "economic democracy" but insisted that its precise formula would depend upon the specific social and economic circumstances currently in existence.

When he was forty-nine years old, Dewey collaborated with James Tufts to write the *Ethics* (1908). This book offered a brief but significant glimpse at how Dewey addressed economic problems.[6] Democracy was both a piece of political machinery, to be judged by its efficiency, and a moral ideal. This ideal consisted of bringing to fruition each individual's positive freedom and social capacities.[7] *Laissez faire* liberals and socialists had considerable room for compromise: the former need not abolish all social agencies, and the latter had no reason to be doctrinaire in abolishing all private property and free enterprise. Dewey noted that recent socialists, i.e., the British Fabians, did not advocate utopian social control of all production. Their belief was that the state should undertake such production only if free enterprise was less efficient or dangerous to the public welfare.[8] To subordinate the state completely to commercial interests was immoral, not to mention the fact that it might result in a public outcry for total ownership.

The American progressive revolt demanded increased governmental regulatory power over the particularism of vested interests and private monopoly. Herbert Croly's ringing declarations in *The Promise of American Life* (1909) called for more economic intervention by the government; he also employed the standard of efficiency. Dewey praised the Germans for constructively organizing the state for public welfare. They employed trained intelligence, social organization, and skilled technique to implement steady economic growth. The British Fabians were prompted to advocate national efficiency based upon social welfare for the workers, trade protectionism, and a gradual nationalization of the economy.[9] How consonant was Dewey with Croly's new nationalist statism? The evidence is not overwhelming, but Dewey stood somewhat to the left of Croly. Croly supported Theodore Roosevelt for president in 1912, while Dewey backed Debs. Dewey endorsed progressive election reform measures as a means of expressing the common interest while remaining flexible, and at the same time undermining conservative financial control. Employing Hegelian language, he stated that citizens should view themselves as public servants, "or organs through which society acts and moves forward."[10] Cooperation, not competition, was the vehicle for social progress. Competition could be crude and wasteful. Public service was the highest, most disinterested ideal. The "free" press should be removed from strictly commercial control with new federal agencies informing public opinion. The community required some expert guidance; the state must provide direction until the citizenry could be properly enlightened to cooperate voluntarily and efficiently.[11] Did Dewey's outlook imply an elite of social engineers? The First World War would become a testing ground for Dewey's theories.

With the founding of the journal known as the *New Republic,* and the outbreak of the war, Dewey's viewpoint was more precisely delineated as he addressed a much wider audience in his role as a political journalist. In *German Philosophy and Politics* (1915), Dewey attacked the absolutism of Hegelian philosophy, which offered a metaphysical reinforcement for "bureaucratic absolutism" in the form of Prussian statism and militarism. German workers were trained only in technical skills and were indoctrinated by their school system to adhere with total allegiance to a state adorned with a spiritualizing mission. The schools also implanted an ominous dualism between vocational and liberal arts training. Dewey held that human activities and loyalties were pluralistic. Democracy required a philosophy that could account for the proliferating variety of groups and interests within society. The artificial supremacy of the state was exacerbated by war. The role of the state should be analogous to that of an orchestra conductor who merely harmonizes group activities and fosters the growth of voluntary associations.[12] Harold Laski expressed the same approach, noting, "what the Absolute is to metaphysics, the State is to political theory."[13] A federalist social organization through democratically self-governing industrial and vocational groups was the path to political freedom and individual self-development. Social democratization, not a statism dependent upon enlightened capitalists, highlighted Dewey's reforms.

During World War I, one of Dewey's major goals was an enduring peace predicated upon the emergence of guild socialism in the industrialized states. Guild socialism emerged in Britain as a reaction to both the ruling Tory democracy and Fabian state socialism. Tory democracy attempted to emulate the mechanical efficiency of the Kaiser's Germany. It assumed a protectionist, militarist, and imperialist character while rallying the working classes around the banner of national patriotism. Domestic affluence was correlated with imperialistic exploitation. The workers were pacified by a welfare state that raised the standard of living while at the same time it provided the masses with mindless diversions. These reforms merely established control in the hands of the ruling captains of industry and finance. Competition would be stifled both at home and abroad. Fabian state socialism might alter the personalities in the ruling bureaucracy, but its implications for democracy would be just as elitist. The war mobilization stimulated the collectivization of industry and concentrated planning and production for use rather than profit. Dewey acknowledged that nationalizing industry would still enable clever capitalists to control state enterprises, thus manipulating public facilities for private advantage.[14]

J. A. Hobson's *Imperialism* (1903) provided a basic tract for international socialists, like Dewey, who defended free trade. Dewey contended that financiers and bankers encouraged overseas investment and stimulated deficit spending in a war economy as a means to obtain a stranglehold on national policy. Dewey was not innocent of the economic causes behind the World War. He believed that an unintended release of democratic-liberal forces would occur, multiplying the power of the wage-earning classes. The war offered a catalyst to awaken the people from drift, illustrating that genuine social planning and reform were possible.

Instead of organizing workers on a national basis, Dewey and other guild socialists argued that international harmony could be solidified only if workers formed international trade associations. Worldwide economic integration could be promoted. The proliferation and social control of science also could help establish a new type of democracy. Dewey was fearful of any paternalistic welfare state and centralized bureaucracy detached from the popular will. He remarked that the syndicalists had done most of the advanced thinking about how to mitigate elite control. The guild socialists advocated the autonomy of each industrial group within its functional sphere, thus decentralizing power. The workers are enabled to participate actively in directing their daily activities. Dewey forecast that workers would utilize their new power to increase their control over industry rather than abandon it to government bureaucrats. Political measures could democraticize industry from within. A federated league of nations would supply the breeding ground for "freely experimenting and self-governing local, cultural, and industrial groups." This diversity symbolized democracy just as autocracy required uniformity. Dewey thereby envisioned a simultaneous solution to both the domestic and international obstacles to democracy.

He kept abreast of British Labour Party activities, calculating that this worker's movement could be a forerunner of trends in the United States. Along with J. A. Hobson, Dewey criticized a Labour Party manifesto that predicted an automatic evolution of workers' control growing out of the war. Dewey derided Marxism as "unscientific utopianism" that obstructed the painstaking research necessary to solve particular problems. In 1918, Hobson outlined the coalition of reactionary forces mounted against any fundamental reorganization of industry. Dewey agreed with Hobson's appraisal, anticipating "a long period of struggle and transition."[15] The conventional view that Dewey was infected with a naive faith in progress is misleading. He knew what would constitute a viable international settlement, but he was also aware of the odds against it.

On both sides of the Atlantic guild socialism aroused considerable interest in liberal circles. Dewey had not formulated any comprehensive program on how to initiate guild socialism. He referred to "appropriate agencies of legislation, judicial procedure, and administrative commissions." Other liberals among the *New Republic* contributors made more specific recommendations. These British intellectuals and Labour Party officials included H. G. Wells, Harold Laski, J. A. Hobson, George Bernard Shaw, Norman Angell, G. D. H. Cole, Bertrand Russell, and H. N. Brailsford. Harold Laski was a faculty member at the New School for Social Research in New York, an institution that Dewey helped to found in 1919. Laski became a leading formulator of guild socialist pluralism during this period. Consent rather than coercion should be the basis for obedience. Centralized authority eroded local initiative and responsibility. Laski's federalist approach was reviewed sympathetically by the *New Republic* editors Walter Lippmann and Herbert Croly. They incorporated political organization on an occupational basis (industrial democracy) as part of their reform program. Instead of relying upon class conflict, the *New Republic* utilized the middle class as an instrument for social reform. The editors distanced themselves from the more statist Socialist Party. The journal endorsed efforts by the Reconstruction Committee of the British cabinet to promote workers' democracy after the war.[16] Attentive to the ideological differences between authoritarianism and democracy, these liberals stressed that power must be distributed and dispersed to remedy the effects of state socialism.[17]

Among guild theorists, G. D. H. Cole was by far the most prolific and influential. He propagated his views in America by contributing to the *New Republic,* the *Dial,* the *Nation,* and the *Freeman.* When Dewey became an editor of the *Dial,* along with Thorstein Veblen in May 1918, Cole commented regularly on guild socialism and the war. Cole considered the State to be an organ of coercion, and he proposed to eliminate it entirely. By abolishing the wage-profit system, social service could reign as the supreme standard. Society would collectively own the tools of production, parceling them out to individual guilds acting as trustees. In addition to occupational guilds, consumer groups would also organize. They would be permitted representation at the guild congress. As president of the People's Lobby, Dewey followed Cole in attempting to organize consumers as an effective political force. The guild congress would mediate inter-guild relations, while enabling (ideally) each guild to retain autonomy over its own immediate affairs. Through this congress, a genuine participatory industrial democracy would prevail.[18]

Guild socialism appeared too exotic and complicated for popular appeal and mass implementation. Yet, in Dewey's mind it constituted an ideal, long-range model toward which piecemeal reforms and voluntary organizations would be directed. Guild socialism avoided the evils of governmental centralization and bureaucracy, while stressing social cooperation and participation. One could have voluntary planning without dictatorship. This effort to graft a medieval structure onto modern industrial society was hindered by a complex economy that would stifle total social planning. Labor unions were suspicious of efforts to break down the dualism of owner and wage-earner upon which their existence depended. Dewey refused to term himself a "socialist," due to the alien and statist connotations of the term. He groped for a unique brand of social democracy that would be expressive of American conditions.[19] He sought to unify farmer-labor groups with an advanced middle class in order to reconstruct the economy. During the Great Depression, Dewey demanded specific reforms that would temporarily increase state activity. Even during this statist period, he would espouse the ideal of local community and voluntary groups.

The writings of Henry George and Edward Bellamy exercised a substantial influence on Dewey. Describing Henry George as "one of the world's great social philosophers," Dewey reaffirmed George's condemnation of unearned income.[20] Dewey was honorary chairman of the Henry George School of Economics. Surprisingly, in 1935, both Dewey and Charles Beard listed Edward Bellamy's *Looking Backward* as the second most influential book of the past half-century.[21] Dewey praised Bellamy's advocacy of peaceful change, the translation of democracy into economic terms, and the founding of socialism on an ethical basis instead of the speciously scientific terms of dialectical materialism.[22] Human rights and morality should not be discarded as epiphenomenal to political power. Dewey categorized socialists in two ways: (1) moral versus scientific and (2) anarchic versus statist. Sympathizing with what Marx derided as "utopian" or "sentimental" socialism, Dewey believed, in 1919, that people were returning to the pre-Marxist ethical socialism.[23] The origins of Dewey's economics were rooted in Henry George and Edward Bellamy, not Karl Marx.

Dewey's two closest associates among academic economists were Wesley Mitchell and Thorstein Veblen. Veblen's analysis of the leisure class, absentee ownership, workmanship, conspicuous consumption, and the relation between the technological and business aspects of industry clearly shaped Dewey's approach to economics.[24] He adopted Veblen's social-psychological critique of capitalism. Neither workers nor businessmen were motivated exclusively by lust for private gain. Workers actually desired security with an occasional spree to relieve the tedium of life. Businessmen were absorbed in the adventure of profit-making. That many businessmen thrived on insecurity and risk was far different from the textbook model of economic man as a rational, calculating intelligence.[25] This romance was being undermined by the organization man of the corporate age. Dewey prophesized that economic activity should be reduced to the purely mechanical routine so that even businessmen would clamor to pursue higher creative, cultural activities. He rejected the attempt to divide labor into physical labor and mental labor. Such a model reduced workers to mere appendages of their machines. Little satisfaction could be derived from this dull routine. Production was made merely instrumental, a question of quantity. Only those who determined the ends (goals) of production had any real control. Money rather than concern for individuals' lives or world affairs animated this system. Dewey argued that the workaday world could be more than just instrumental; it could be impregnated with human values and meaning. The attainment of excellence was impossible if the multitudes were prevented from utilizing thought and emotion when at their jobs. Exercising control over one's work signified a freedom of mind that rendered superficial the periodic right to vote. Economic security provided the necessary foundation for the emergence of a dynamic, humane civilization.

During his visits to China and Russia, Dewey reaffirmed his commitment to a guild socialist approach. Witnessing the birth of the Chinese nation in 1920, he was excited about the possibilities of a radical social experiment. Chinese village life was basically self-sufficient; little notice was paid to the largely ceremonial centralized government. Untouched by politics of the Western variety, the Chinese people were attuned to moral considerations. Dewey envisioned a new China structured on the foundations of guild organizations. China might emerge as a hybrid democracy, more advanced than European political institutions. Americans and Europeans placed too great a dependence upon government; they were victimized by excessive organization and institutionalization.[26] Mirroring his guild socialism, Dewey advocated a gradual, decentralized, and apolitical approach to China's future.

When he toured the Soviet Union in 1928, Dewey didn't perceive a police state; instead, he saw before him an emerging guild socialist society.[27] In sanguine dispatches, the spirit of revolution—the organization of society according to a unified social purpose—was emphasized. Downplaying the significance of Marxist ideology, Russia's authoritarian practices were little more than a "transitional stage." The democratic revolutionary spirit would triumph. Dewey maintained that the Soviet experiment was tangible proof of the possibility that a society could be organized on "cooperative" principles. He was impressed by the psychological transformation of the masses from egoism to selfless dedication. The intellectuals also were mobilized by a "united religious social faith."[28] Rather than simply promoting pluralism, Dewey reveled in a unity of ultimate aims that could be accomplished in a society organized, not by the capitalist ethos, but by social cooperation. Unfortunately, more traditional Russian cultural habits would predominate.

The Great Depression intensified Dewey's political activities. He advised the implementation of radical economic change to alleviate the crisis. Socialist economic planning became a popular intellectual theme with books like *New Republic* editor George Soule's *Planned Society* and Stuart Chase's *Man and Machines*. Charles Beard desired economic planning that was respectful of American traditions of individual liberty and self-government. Rather than adopting a Russian model, he sought a native American radicalism consistent with democratic customs.[29] Dewey viewed the collapse of capitalism as inevitable and wanted no compromise with even a humanized and controlled capitalism of the New Deal.[30] Arthur Schlesinger, Jr., criticized Dewey's rejection of the New Deal as ideologically motivated. Dewey had made socially directed planning the sole agency for economic reform. He preferred a systematic program to experimentalism. Schlesinger also accused Dewey of belittling liberal commitments to individual freedom and parliamentary politics.[31] Dewey did not forsake his commitment to individual freedom, though he did prefer a comprehensive program to that of a floundering "ad hoc" approach. According to Dewey: "the government as the representative of the whole people is the sole agency that is capable of taking the necessary measures. The obvious beginning is for the people through their government to take over the basic agencies upon which industry and commerce depend."[32] Corporate capitalism resulted in pervasive unemployment in the midst of material abundance. But with the liberation from the profit motive, a new type of socialized man could be forged.

As president of the People's Lobby and the League for Independent Political Action, Dewey sponsored a unifying philosophy that could serve as a basis for effective political action and power.[33] Dewey and Beard proposed a permanent Economic Council, including labor representatives, which could coordinate industrial development. Rexford Tugwell of Columbia, one of Roosevelt's leading braintrusters, offered a similar proposal; it was later amended into the National Industrial Recovery Act. Dewey's program included public ownership of the basic agencies of industry: banks, railways, power companies, mines, oil companies, and so on. Heavy taxes would be lodged against business and wealth. The redistribution of this income would give purchasing power back to the consumer. Dewey campaigned to (1) reduce credit rates, (2) liquidate debts, (3) provide immediate relief and unemployment insurance, (4) tightly monitor investments overseas and domestic war industries, and (5) supplement parliamentary government with institutions representing consumers and producers. Money was the great issue for Dewey. He condemned Wall Street financiers, creditors, and bankers. In the short run, government had to adopt temporarily the role of provider, though he still appealed for voluntary action.[34]

During this period, Dewey considered corporate capitalism to be the fundamental corruptive force in American culture. The League for Independent Political Action designated the elimination of capitalism as its central political goal.[35] However, Dewey supported gradual and largely voluntary means despite his fiery rhetoric regarding capitalism. He held that "those who control the giving and holding of credit govern the country, whoever controls the country in name."[36] The press functioned as a propaganda "henchman for big business." Free speech was a mere safety valve to vent antagonisms; real power was maintained by corporate capitalists. In 1935 the Hearst press ran an exposé on communist influence at Teachers College, Columbia University. A statement issued by George Counts, William Kilpatrick, Charles Beard, and John Dewey condemned this frame-up.[37] Dewey insisted that both political parties were captured by vested money interests. Complicating his scenario of democracy as an empty shell, Dewey argued that coercive force was utilized by the capitalist order as a means of social control.[38] When threatened by radical change, Dewey surmised that the property interests would jettison the constitution and rule by overt violence and dictatorship. Though capitalism was energized in part by fear of starvation, and the law protected some private property rights, Dewey's severe indictment seemingly conceded too much to the advocates of class struggle. If democratic-capitalism is maintained by force, violent revolution would appear as the only viable method of change. How could Dewey succeed in his educational campaign to rally progressives into a third party if the capitalists would seize power when threatened?

During the 1930s, Dewey's concerns about a centralized, planned economy intensified. Walter Lippmann had identified socialism exclusively with statist collectivism, precluding democratic guild socialism. This oversight enabled Lippmann, like Frederick Hayek, to advocate capitalism as necessary for democracy. Dewey termed this notion "an absurdity."[39] He repeated his claim that private property rights and the quest for profit should be subordinated to the public good. During periods of economic crisis, the government would violate property rights out of dire necessity. The door would be opened for the disposal of other sacred civil liberties with less hesitation. By defending democratic freedoms not on the basis of natural law but rather on their contribution to the social welfare, Dewey attempted to establish such liberties on a more secure foundation. As early as 1933, he distinguished between a planned society and a "continuously planning society." Planned societies, like Russia and Italy, utilized a fixed blueprint to stamp uniformity upon its citizenry. Dewey advocated a continuous re-evaluation of social policy and experimentation that could enhance individuality.[40] By 1938 he conceded that he had shifted his emphasis to highlight the role of individuals as "the finally decisive factors of the nature and movement of associated life." The rise of totalitarianism reinforced the idea that "only voluntary initiative and voluntary cooperation can produce social institutions that will protect the liberties necessary for achieving development of genuine individuality."[41] The protection of civil liberties, with or without socialism, was primary.

He endorsed no relapse to *laissez faire* liberalism. The government should still offer positive social programs, but the standard now became how well such programs encouraged voluntary choices and activities. After the activism of the early Depression years, Dewey now stressed nonpolitical, voluntary organization—again praising "functional socialism." In *Freedom and Culture* (1939), he acknowledged that modern economies were so complex and intricate that government policies were certain to have unforeseeable and often counterproductive results.[42] The transfer of industrial control to government officials without guarantees that it would benefit the general public was dangerously irresponsible. The socialist myth that the collectivization of industry would spontaneously usher in a new and humane order was discredited as utopianism. Dewey had not yet witnessed any functioning example of melding democratic methods and a fully socialist economy.

Skeptical of both socialism and capitalism, Dewey had moved much closer to New Deal style of reformism. He recognized that a political experiment was "very different" from one in natural science. It was "a process of trial and error accompanied by some degree of hope and a great deal of talk." Legislation improvised patchwork policies, implemented, hopefully, by an intelligent civil service that did not degenerate into an oligarchic bureaucracy. Dewey concluded that "conditions in totalitarian countries brought home the fact, not sufficiently realized by critics, myself included, that the forms which still exist (democratic capitalism) encourage freedom of discussion, criticism, and voluntary associations, and thereby set a gulf between a country having suffrage and popular representation and a country having dictatorship, whether of the right or left—the differences between the two growing continually less as they borrow each other's techniques."[43] State capitalism and state socialism would become identical in practice.

Still critical of the excesses of modern capitalism, Dewey discovered a patron-saint of democracy in Thomas Jefferson. He termed Jefferson, "the first modern to state, in human terms, the principles of democracy."[44] Jefferson implicitly upheld personal rights above property rights, fearing encrusted government officialdom and business tycoons. He advocated small, self-governing communities (wards), which were a precursor to Dewey's guild socialism. Charles Beard was similarly impressed with Jefferson, who recognized that democratic traditions were based upon the popular will and were not a "front for capitalism."[45] Voluntary associations, person-to-person relationships, and the quality of local community life were the lynchpins of democracy. C. Wright Mills charged that Dewey was actually a defender of agrarian smalltown America, which had become an historical anachronism. Dewey accepted the irreversibility of technological-industrial life, but he sought to extend Jefferson's democratic ideals to the industrial environment.

Dewey's wholesale condemnation of capitalism subsided during the 1940s, but by no means did it collapse into an embrace of the status quo. He insisted that economic progress was dependent upon the growth of scientific (cooperative) knowledge rather than the growth and accumulation of capital. If capitalist financiers had a creative function, then Dewey believed that one must accept a capitalist economy as "the price of progress."[46] Economic growth does require both individual initiative and cooperation. Unearned income offended Dewey's elemental sense of justice, but democracy could partially remedy the effects of such exploitation without imposing collectivist socialism. In the midst of the calamitous Great Depression, he indicted capitalism for: (1) poisoning the free press, (2) co-opting the party system, (3) stimulating wars, (4) utilizing public schools as vehicles for indoctrination, (5) destroying the roots of community life, (6) capturing scientific research for private gain, (7) cultivating money materialism at the expense of culture and social cooperation, and (8) leading the country toward economic ruin. These perceived deficiencies stimulated his political campaign to abolish capitalism altogether.

At times, Dewey's indictment focused more on the logic of capitalism than on its practical consequences. Corporate economic concentration and elite power is dangerous, even more so because of its collusion with government to nullify the effects of a capitalist market system and popular democracy. Corporations are becoming less rather than more concentrated. Capitalism has also promoted a high degree of voluntary cooperation through free trade. The anti-social, selfish, and philistine attitudes of some Americans are not a necessary consequence of capitalism. Efforts to regiment good tastes have resulted in the destruction of democratic liberties. The pure profit motive is balanced by a multiplicity of other human interests. Furthermore, the market system has created a means for promoting economic rationality, affluence, and political liberty. Production for use and production for profit may well be identical as individual consumers freely determine which products they want to use. Once capitalism is not instinctively identified as a sinister force, a realistic balance between the public and private economic sectors can be drawn.

Along with many other disillusioned social democrats, Dewey shifted from an outright rejection of capitalism to a grudging recognition that the available alternatives were much worse. He accepted the viability of a mixed economic system.[47] In 1948, Sidney Hook also endorsed a mixed economy as "securing the goals of democracy without the inefficiency, bureaucracy, and evasion of responsibility that seem attendant upon a completely planned system of production."[48] Hook and Dewey agreed that democracy took precedence over socialism. A mixed economy allowed for a high degree of diversity, experimentalism, and flexible decentralized control.[49] Consumer organizations, cooperatives, and labor unions could check centralized bureaucratic power. No doctrinal compulsion existed to socialize small businesses and farms. Economic arrangements could be judged as to whether they strengthened or weakened liberal democracy, whether they promoted both liberty and economic security. Social reforms should remain limited and piecemeal. The formula between government interference and free enterprise could be reconstructed depending upon specific circumstances.

Though Dewey tailored his economic policy to manage particular circumstances, the tendency toward voluntary cooperative or guild socialist organization remained strong. His emergency support for government socialism during the Great Depression was both temporary and atypical. Four identifiable shifts of emphasis occurred in Dewey's economic thinking. (1) Up to 1918 he advocated a capitalist system controlled by progressive governmental reforms. (2) From 1918 to 1927 he defended the orchestra leader theory of the state. In order to combat centralized political power and nationalism, the power of government should be distributed over a vast complex of economic groups (guild socialism). (3) In *The Public and Its*

Problems (1927), Dewey moved from a minimal state conception toward the notion that government was a flexible instrument to provide for human wants. During the Great Depression, an expanded role for government was necessitated. At no time did Dewey justify dictatorial measures in the name of public welfare.[50] (4) After 1936, Dewey's enthusiasm for the possibilities of social engineering waned. He still sought democratic controls in the economy, but during this period he emphasized a mixed system with voluntary cooperation.

The effort to humanize the economy by injecting it with moral values and social justice was a paramount concern. That Dewey revised his policies is a testimony not to his expediency but to his ability to incorporate new knowledge. The mature espousal of a mixed economy subordinated ideological fixations to the recognition of the complex mechanisms of a democratic social order.

NOTES

1. John Dewey, *Human Nature and Conduct* (New York: Modern Library, 1930), p. 280.

2. *ION,* p. 119.

3. Charles Beard, "A 'Five Year Plan' for America," *Forum* (July, 1931):1.

4. James Weinstein, *The Decline of Socialism in America (1912-1928)* (New York: Monthly Review Press, 1967), p. 80. George Dykhuizen, *The Life and Mind of John Dewey* (Carbondale: Southern Illinois University Press, 1973), pp. 50-51.

5. John Dewey, "Wallace vs. A New Party," *NL* (Oct. 30, 1948):1. Charles Forcey mistakenly described Dewey as a strong supporter of Roosevelt. See Forcey, *The Crossroads of Liberalism* (New York: Oxford University Press, 1961), p. 256.

6. John Dewey and James Tufts, *The Ethics* (New York: Henry Holt & Co., 1908), p. 537. (Hereafter *Ethics*)

7. Ibid., p. 474.

8. Ibid., p. 543.

9. See Bernard Simmel, *Imperialism and Social Reform* (New York: Doubleday Inc., 1960), p. 33.

10. *Ethics,* p. 534.

11. Ibid., p. 485.

12. John Dewey, *Reconstruction in Philosophy* (New York: Holt & Co., 1920), p. 202-203.

13. Harold Laski, *Studies in the Problems of Sovereignty* (New Haven: Yale University Press, 1917), p. 6.

14. John Dewey, "What Are We Fighting For?" *Independent* (June, 1918):474, 480-483. William Y. Elliott correctly identified Dewey's guild socialist tendencies. However, Elliott criticized pragmatic pluralism for being anarchic, thereby undermining the legal sovereignty of the state. He linked it to the rise of fascism. William Y. Elliott, *The Pragmatic Revolt in Politics* (New York: McMillan Co., 1926), pp. 60, 64. This book was written before *The Public and Its Problems,* in which Dewey endorsed law as "embodied reason." Law canalized action to enable individuals to act correctly in accordance with long-range social consequences, an area where shortsightedness might otherwise prevail. Law was absolutely required for social order. Again, Dewey stressed the public nature of morality in the creation of proper social habits. *P&IP,* pp. 53-57.

15. John Dewey, "A New Social Science," *NR* (April 6, 1918):294. J. A. Hobson, *Democracy After the War* (New York: McMillan Co., 1917), p. 230.

16. "Towards Industrial Democracy," *NR* (Sept. 1, 1917):121-3. J. A. Hobson, "Representative Government in British Industry," *NR* (Sept. 1, 1917):130-32. "Labor and the New Social Order," *NR* (Feb. 16, 1918):3-12. Herbert Croly, "The Future of the State," *NR* (Sept. 15, 1917):179-83. "Supremacy of the State," *NR* (Sept. 15, 1917):192-3.

17. Walter Lippmann and Harold Laski, "Authority in the Modern State, *NR* (May 31, 1919):149-50. Walter Lippmann, "A Clue," *NR* (April 14, 1917):316-17.

18. G. D. H. Cole, *Guild Socialism Re-Stated* (London: Parsons, 1920), pp. 224.

19. John Dewey, "The Future of Radical Political Action," *The Nation* (Jan. 4, 1933):8. (Hereafter *N*)

20. John Dewey, introduction to *Significant Paragraphs From Henry George's Poverty and Progress,* edited by Harry Gunnison Brown (New York: Doubleday, Doran & Co., 1928), p. 3.

21. "Savants Select Most Influential Volumes," *The English Journal* (June, 1936):497-8.

22. John Dewey, "A Great American Prophet," *Common Sense* (April, 1934):6-7. (Hereafter *CS*)

23. John Dewey, *Lectures in China (1919-1920)* (Honolulu: University of Hawaii Press, 1973), p. 118.

24. John Dewey, "The Collapse of a Romance," *NR* (April 27, 1932):292-94. For Dewey's acknowledgment of his great debt to Veblen see Joseph Dorfman, *Thorstein Veblen and His America* (New York: Viking Press, 1934), p. 450.

25. John Dewey, "Freedom of Thought and Work," *NR* (May 20, 1920):316-17. *ION,* p. 133. Dewey was also a member of the Arthursdale project, in which the government bought land and built houses. These were given over to homesteaders for repayment over a long period of years. The homesteaders set up their own cooperative corporation with local self-government. Dewey helped design the educational program for the Arthursdale experiment.

26. Dewey, *Lectures in China* (1919-1920), pp. 117-22.

27. John Dewey, *Impressions of Soviet Russia* (New York: New Republic, Inc., 1929), pp. 34, 116, 123.

28. Ibid., pp. 120-21.

29. Charles Beard, "The Myth of Rugged Individualism," *Harper's* (Dec., 1931):13-17.

30. John Dewey, introduction to *Challenge to the New Deal,* edited by Alfred Bingham and Selden Rodman (New York: Falcon Press, 1934), p. vi.

31. Arthur Schlesinger, Jr., *The Politics of Upheaval* (Boston: Houghton Co., 1960), p. 155. For a favorable response to Dewey's radicalism see Edward Bordeau, "John Dewey's Ideas About the Depression," *Journal of the History of Ideas* (January, 1971):67-84. Also Frank Warren, *An Alternative Vision* (Bloomington: University of Indiana Press, 1974), pp. 8-10.

32. John Dewey, "America's Public Ownership Program," *People's Lobby Bulletin* (March, 1934):1.

33. John Dewey, "The Future of Radical Political Action," *N* (Jan. 4, 1933):8. *P&IP,* pp. 61-2.

34. *ION,* p. 118, *L&SA,* p. 86.

35. "Our Enemy and Our Goal," *CS* (Jan. 1934):2-3.

36. John Dewey, "What Hope Is Their For Politics," *Scribner's* (May, 1931):406.

37. James Wechsler, *Revolt on Campus* (Seattle: University of Washington Press, 1973), p. 232. John Dewey, "Our Un-Free Press," *CS* (Nov. 1935):6-7.

38. *L&SA,* p. 64.

39. John Dewey, "Liberalism in a Vacuum: A Critique of Walter Lippmann's Social Philosophy," *CS* (Dec. 1937):9-11. Dewey, "Education, Democracy, and a Socialized Economy," *Social Frontier* (Dec. 1938):71-2. (Hereafter *SF*)

40. John Dewey and John Childs, "The Social-Economic Situation and Education," in William Kilpatrick, ed., *The Educational Frontier* (New York: Century Co., 1933), p. 72.

41. Dewey, "What I Believe," revised statement in *I Believe,* edited by Clifton Fadiman (New York: Simon & Schuster, 1939), pp. 347-48.

42. *F&C*, p. 62.

43. Ibid., pp. 93–94.

44. Ibid., p. 155. See Dewey, "Thomas Jefferson and the Democratic Faith," *The Virginia Quarterly Review* (Jan., 1940):1–13.

45. Charles Beard, "The Rise of Democracy Depends on Faith of American People," *NR* (April 10, 1937):4.

46. John Dewey, "The Theory of Economic Progress," *Saturday Review* (Oct. 14, 1944): 29. (Hereafter *SRL*) Dewey, "Letter to Editor (praise of Daniel Bell and Karl Polanyi)," *Commentary* (March, 1947):289. Dewey, "The Crisis in Human History," *Commentary* (March, 1946):1–9. Dewey, "Liberating the Social Scientist," *Commentary* (Oct., 1947):378–88.

47. John Dewey to Boyd Bode (September 16, 1950), Boyd H. Bode Papers, Ohio State University Library, Columbus, Ohio.

48. Sidney Hook, "Freedom and Socialism," *NL* (March 3, 1945):4–6. Hook, "The Future of Socialism," *Partisan Review* (Jan.–Feb., 1947):25.

49. See Lewis Corey, "Economic Democracy Without Statism," *Commentary* (Aug. 1947): 137–149.

50. See Saul Padover, *The Genius of America* (New York: McGraw-Hill, 1960), pp. 283–84. Padover detected a dangerous relativism in Dewey's thought about the elastic role of government.

3

A Pragmatic Approach
to the Great War

The outbreak of the First World War dramatically intensified Dewey's political activism. His prior public career was largely confined to the editorship of Franklin Ford's aborted "Thought News" (1892) and his association with Jane Addams's Hull House.[1] In addition, Dewey was a founding member of the National Association for the Advancement of Colored People (NAACP) and he joined the Men's League for Women's Suffrage.[2] The *New Republic,* launched in November 1914, functioned as a platform for publicizing Dewey's political views while he also came in contact with other prominent, progressive liberal thinkers including Herbert Croly, Walter Lippmann, and Walter Weyl. Many British writers were regular contributors to the journal. A number of these liberals, most notably Norman Angell and H. N. Brailsford, were members of the British Union for Democratic Control. This group formulated war aims that were quite similar to what later emerged as Wilson's Fourteen Points. Dewey and the *New Republic* soon became preoccupied with the war issue. This constituted the first concerted effort to apply the pragmatic outlook to politics.

As editor-in-chief, Herbert Croly exercised a pivotal influence on the journal's policy toward the war.[3] His book, entitled *Progressive Democracy* (1914), reflected more of an evolution toward Dewey's social democracy instead of Croly's earlier elitism. In *Drift and Mastery* (1914), Walter Lippmann championed the pragmatic emphasis upon science as the methodology for democratic practices. Dewey established the controlling world view within which political problems were approached by these progressives. While Dewey's specific political doctrines were not identical with the other editors on all points, his articles corresponded with the *New Republic*'s outlook. With some justification, Dewey's pragmatic liberalism has been evaluated historically in relation to the collective approach of the *New Republic* toward the war. This approach warrants careful scrutiny.

In 1909, Croly wrote the influential *Promise of American Life,* which outlined an American foreign policy bearing a striking resemblance to the posture subsequently taken by the *New Republic*. Declaring an end to American isolation, Croly argued that the national interest of the United States was intrinsically connected to the promulgation and success of liberal political institutions throughout the world. Democracy and nationalism could be effectively merged. Imperial Germany was the chief threat to peace, followed closely by Russia. If a European war broke out, Canada and the United States should lend their naval forces to Great Britain in order to protect food cargoes. Direct military intervention was mandated if Germany appeared on the verge of victory. American power could tip the scales in favor of a comparatively pacific settlement of international complications. A policy of neutrality would be cowardly and irresponsible, fostering a "democratic degeneracy." If Americans wanted genuine peace, they had to be "spiritually and physically prepared to fight for it."[4] Only the righteous use of superior force would enable democratic powers to triumph over warlike autocracies. An alliance with democratic European powers could serve as an instrument for world peace. Military and economic strength were a prerequisite for survival. Though accused of being a fascist "Bull Moose" nationalist, Croly was actually a romantic democrat who desired an eventual world government.[5] He neatly synthesized world peace, democracy, and America's mission.

In the *Ethics* (1908), Dewey acknowledged the constructive role of nationalism in welding together larger social organizations and common purposes among peoples. However, nationalism and warfare could not be an ultimate principle of political organization. He hoped that an international federation might emerge. The necessity for military preparedness must be balanced by the recognition that such power could be employed thoughtlessly. The idea that war was necessary to prevent moral degeneration was "unmitigated nonsense." In a 1909 lecture to the National Herbart Society, Dewey stated that

> force efficiency in execution or overt action is the necessary constituent of character. In our moral books and lectures we may lay all the stress upon good intentions, etc. But we may know practically that the kind of character we hope to build up through our education is one which not only has good intentions, but which insists on carrying them out. Any other character is wishy-washy; it is goody, not good. The individual must have the power to stand up and count for something in the actual conflicts of life. He must have initiative, insistence, persistence, courage, and industry.[6]

Dewey would adopt this vigorous Rooseveltian, progressive posture in criticizing the pacifists during World War I. His anti-pacifism was not wartime expediency; rather, it sprang from the conviction that power must be utilized for any good to be attained. Force must be applied intelligently and for righteous ends. "Resort to war in order to prevent the triumph of a greater evil" would lay the basis for true international harmony. Like Croly, Dewey's attitude toward the war was consistent with his earlier pronouncements.

In its initial issue, the *New Republic* announced an end to America's traditional isolation. American interests would be compromised regardless of who won the war. Instead of avoiding European entanglements by an innocent pursuit of material prosperity, the United States must clarify the relationship between its democratic national ideal and its international responsibilities.[7] The journal rebuked Wilson's "timid neutrality," which acquiesced in Germany's cynical invasion of Belgium. Ridiculing any American effort to settle the war without assuming risks and obligations, the editors insisted that the peace would be determined by those nations whose strength and sacrifices had produced the world balance of power.

Dewey approached the war issue at first from the high road of philosophical criticism. In *German Philosophy and Politics* (early 1915), he wedded transcendental-absolutist German philosophy to its political culture. He remarked that German philosophy was the most foreign to the American experience; no people were as "hostile to the spirit of pragmatic philosophy" as the Germans.[8] The book review in the *New Republic* seemed expressive of Dewey's particular intent: "the service John Dewey performs in these three lectures in this little volume is to trace the cartography of modern German idealism and to show how the stream which came from Kant could so appropriately float the submarine that torpedoed the *Lusitania.*"[9] However serviceable Dewey's discussion might have been, the book represented an honest expression of his basic philosophical approach. Stressing both environmental causes and false dogmas, Dewey's critique of German life did not seek to inspire nationalistic hatreds. He hoped that Germany, when freed from an environment of fear and autocratic administration, could discover itself in a dynamic democracy. He also criticized the British and the French. Throughout the war, Dewey continued to discuss national ideals. No matter how concerned he became about the war, Dewey remembered that he was primarily a philosopher. He did not indulge in backseat generalship by discussing immediate military strategy.

Immanuel Kant characteristically embodied the German mind. Kant bifurcated the world into two realms: (1) sense and mechanism (Nature) and (2) supersensible freedom and purpose (Spirit). Since morality could not be the work of mechanistic nature, Kant argued that human freedom must spring from an *a priori* law of duty. Men possessed no empirical knowledge in moral matters; he merely responded to the empty call of the Categorical Imperative in the spiritual realm. Dewey maintained that this vacuum of specific ends could be readily filled by state propaganda. Kant held that nature was firmly opposed to man's higher moral purposes. Natural desires aspired to an illegitimate control over human reason. Germans generally deemed the pursuit of happiness to be a slavish enterprise, a selfish materialism suitable for British shopkeepers. Dewey noted that those who did not regard happiness as a test of action unfortunately tended to make other people unhappy.[10]

Pragmatism employed concrete consequences rather than *a priori* rules to govern human behavior. By situating morality in a transcendental realm, the possibility of collecting contrary empirical evidence was removed. Philosophical absolutism led invariably to political absolutism since such doctrines become strongholds whereby authority shields itself from critical questioning. A hierarchical society mirrors a philosophy based upon fixed categories; a pluralistic, democratic society strives to be consistently experimental. Any philosophy not rigorously experimental would traffic in absolutes no matter how well disguised. The traffic was "without mask" in German philosophy.[11] Depicting Kantian morality as the "logic of fanaticism," Dewey contended that "weapons forged in the smithy of the Absolute become brutal and cruel when confronted with merely human resistance."[12] He conceded that Kant's political thought was individualistic and cosmopolitan. Kant was the author of *Perpetual Peace*. However, Kant's personal politics bore no logical relationship to his philosophy. Dewey was concerned with the historical impact of Kantianism.

Kant's empty categories were a convenient starting point for Hegel's philosophy. Systematically rationalizing the movement of history, Hegel sanctified the state as the well-spring of ethical being. An individual became rational, virtuous, and free by assimilating society's rational order. Terming Hegel a "brutalist," Dewey asserted that "no philosopher has ever thought so wholly in terms of strife and overcoming as Hegel."[13] War was the measure of a nation's spiritual fitness and vitality: patriotism assumed religious dimensions. As the state prescribed ethical imperatives, the military epitomized the ideal of obedient service.

Dewey did not find it surprising that General Friedrick von Bernhardi would reinforce appeals for military preparedness with allusions to *The Critique of Pure Reason*. Bernhardi's book *Britain as Germany's Vassal* was commonly employed by allied propagandists as proof of Germany's war conspiracy. While its impact upon German military strategy was dubious, Dewey utilized Bernhardi to illustrate the continuity between philosophy and politics in German popular thought. Dismissing any notion of international federation, Bernhardi claimed that the sublimation of nationalism rested upon a utopian error because it excluded life's essential principle— struggle. World history was the ultimate arbiter. Germany merely desired its "day in the sun." Wars should not be fought for material gain alone but for the highest spiritual principles. The self-sacrifice demanded in wartime indicated the vanity of merely finite interests. Private ends were engulfed by a collective cause that exacted the highest potentialities from each individual. The brutalities of war disappeared before the manifestation of higher idealism. Bernhardi was a caricature of those tendencies in German culture which combined blind idealism with technical efficiency. Dewey was not reluctant to formulate generalizations about national character, though they might be quite impressionistic. Instead of employing a pluralistic analysis, Dewey centered upon the general culture. He sought to bring to fruition the American mind or culture.

Dewey criticized Anglo-French empiricism, which was founded upon a narrow, egoistic doctrine of utility. This atomistic *laissez faire* philosophy circumscribed any positive function for the state in acquiring the goods necessary to obtain personal happiness. Basing judgments upon precedent, this historical empiricism could only muddle through by repeating the past routinely. English education was literary and humanistic, which perpetuated the classical view of education as a leisurely pursuit divorced from the practical affairs of men. Literary humanism generates a pretentious cultural snobbishness undergirding a class society. In comparison to Germany's trained obedience and technical skill, England's incapacity for scientific training and organization resulted in wartime weakness. However, Dewey left little doubt that he preferred cooperating with a nation of aristocratic gentlemen rather than drill sergeants.

Dewey synthesized in Hegelian fashion the German and Anglo-French world views. Humanistic civility could be combined with comprehensive training in scientific method. While Americans could learn from Germany's efficient social order, such efficiency could be employed for different ends. Whereas Britain was committed to the past and Germany the present, America's democratic destiny offered a compelling ideal for itself and the world's future. The real intent of Dewey's book was not to mobilize for war but to assist Americans in the process of self-discovery. The crisis of Europe exemplified a breakdown of the whole system of political nationalism. In America, this stimulated a cultural, nationalist movement that feverishly struggled to "articulate and consolidate the ideas to which our social practice commits (thereby) clarifying and guiding our future endeavor."[14] Dewey entertained this theme throughout the war.

Reaffirming Croly's expansive dream, Dewey asserted that America was uniquely situated to broaden the accident of its inner composition into an idea upon which to construct a domestic and foreign policy. Americans accepted national sovereignty only by accident because they were interracial and international in composition. Unless Americans were willing to forego national sovereignty and submit their affairs to an international legislature, they had no right to criticize warring nations.[15] Mere peace was simply a negative idea. There were ideals "more important than keeping one's body whole and one's property intact." What were these ideals? Dewey affirmed that

> any philosophy which could penetrate and articulate our present practice would find at work the forces which unify human intercourse. An intelligent and courageous philosophy of practice would devise means by which the operation of these forces would be extended and assured in the future. An American philosophy of history must perforce be a philosophy for its future, a future in which freedom and fullness of human companionship is the aim, and intelligent cooperative experimentation the method.[16]

Dewey's pragmatic liberalism could serve as an instrument for world redemption. World conflicts could be reconciled by the universal appropriation of democratic scientific experimentalism. Mere pluralism or mere relativism was insufficient.

Dewey's classic *Democracy and Education* (completed in 1915) detailed the social and political as well as the educational implications of democracy as a way of life. The educational system is the key to comprehending the fundamental values of an entire national culture. The isolation of classes or nations ferments antipathy and fear in addition to a rigidity of customs. Every expansive period in history has coincided with influences that reduced distances between peoples. Even war enforced communication between combatants. Genuine education is international in quality: the method for science, commerce, and art transcends national boundaries. European educational systems were captured by national interests who corrupted the educational process by harnessing it for nativist aims. Such national rivalries institutionalized incipient conflict. Dewey and Croly proposed a national system for American public education, which was cemented to the democratic ideal. National loyalty must be subordinated to a higher devotion to the common ends of mankind. This sense of cooperation and unity must be instilled as a "working disposition."[17] Whatever their pre-existing sympathies, Americans should approach the war crisis by carefully analyzing probable consequences. Dewey's cultural nationalism was actually international liberalism.

Dewey opposed efforts by business interests to regiment technical training in the public schools. The splitting of the school system would deprive laborers of the political knowledge necessary to maintain themselves in modern industrial society. Immigrant workers in the United States were particularly susceptible to manipulation by employers. The public schools should function as a means to liberate immigrant families from perpetual labor serfdom and a rigidified class society. At no time did Dewey favor exploitation of immigrant workers by regearing them for mindless assimilation into the industrial process.[18]

Dewey and the *New Republic* favored a program of preparedness by the year 1916. However, it involved more than merely military preparation.[19] The editors reasoned that "nations do not avoid war by preparing for war, but neither do they avoid war by being unprepared for war. Lack of preparation means merely that when war comes the disarmed nation is either more likely to be beaten, or if successful is successful at a heavier cost. The way to avoid war is not to disarm, but to adopt any means necessary to eradicate the causes of unrighteous war."[20] When Secretary of the Treasury McAdoo proposed to burden the lower and middle classes with the heaviest taxation in order to pay for preparedness, Dewey opposed it as a member of the Association for an Equitable Income Tax.[21] Dewey refused to offer a blanket endorsement for every military scheme.

He particularly opposed a plan developed by General Wood and Theodore Roosevelt for universal compulsory military service. Wood hoped to employ the military as a melting pot to ensure the loyalty of America's ethnic groups. Dewey had no desire to reduce the American population to drilled homogeneity. The real source of the divided loyalty stemmed from the localism of the school system. Reliance upon military training to supply the national ideal was an "unalloyed Europeanism" incompatible with American practices. A year before Wilson's declaration of war, Dewey announced prophetically: "I can, for example, imagine the American people arming universally to put an end to war. I cannot imagine them doing it to defend themselves against a possible and remote danger."[22] National unity purchased by instigating fears of foreign invasions was a "remedy of despair." Dewey testified before the Senate Committee on Military Affairs. While opposing compulsory military training as contrary to American ideals, he did endorse a voluntary plan.

The schools could perform a significant role in social preparedness. Refusing to blame Woodrow Wilson for the aloofness of America toward the war, Dewey held that the entire tradition of no entangling alliances reflected an educational curriculum that isolated America from European affairs. The United States and Europe were part of the same world that now was becoming more tightly connected due to industry and commerce. A new way of teaching history could become "an infinitely greater factor in national preparedness than a few hours of perfunctory drill."[23] American history was largely a reflection of European movements and problems. Critical thought, not eulogized mythology, would assist democratic control over social problems both at home and abroad.

After the United States formally entered the war, Dewey outlined one means through which students and teachers could aid the war effort. In the first of his Columbia War Papers written for the government, Dewey proposed that students and teachers serve their country by joining the depleted work force on the farm to increase the nation's food supply. This constructive patriotism would conscript the young in the universal battle against nature. It was not a product of European militarism but distinctively American. According to Dewey: "all can join without distinction of race and creed or even previous sympathy. It is service not only for our country and for countries on whose side we are fighting, but a service to the whole world when peace shall again dawn."[24] This proposal seemed designed to attract alienated peace groups to a common cause. Earlier Jane Addams had advocated similar measures.

The *New Republic* considered pacific sentiment to be a major obstacle to active and responsible American participation in world affairs. Isolationism was also reinforced by Jeffersonian liberalism and agrarian regionalism. Walter Lippmann insisted that the authentic peacemakers were those who grasped the grim nature of world conflict and offered concrete plans for improvement. Habituated to moralism, democratic peoples were peculiarly susceptible to pacific propaganda. Those loyal to democracy should be most influential internationally. A peace-at-any-price policy signifies a moral abdication, which leaves world affairs to "harder men." To preach weakness and submission to all of the opponent's points does not result in the abandonment of force, but the concentration of force in the most tyrannical hands.

Peace could not be obtained by the impotent policy of nonconfrontation. Lippmann and Dewey acknowledged that a democrat's possession of power may undermine his democratic faith. If democrats remained obsessed with the fear of power's temptation, then the world had little hope. If American democratic values had not been assimilated by the people, and if they would revert to barbarism as soon as they touched worldly affairs, then continued isolation was plausible.[25] Old liberals retained their moral purity by purchasing an innocent integrity at the price of impotence and political irresponsibility. The common denominator of the anti-war groups consisted of the view that war as such reduced all participants to the same savage level. The *New Republic* liberals denied that this retreat was inexorable.

The anti-war movement effectively mobilized isolationist sentiment at the beginning of the war. However, the peace ranks split when the Carnegie Endowment for Peace withdrew its subsidy of groups engaged in pacifism, which amounted to seventy percent of their funding. In 1915 the New York Peace Society was transformed into the League to Enforce Peace. It wanted to end war by defeating Germany militarily. The *New Republic* editors conscripted Norman Angell, British anti-imperialist, for the purpose of converting American pacifists to a more interventionist foreign policy. Despite difficulties with the British censor, Angell did arrive in America and contributed to the journal.[26] Since Dewey associated cordially with numerous pacifists and socialists, he was also ideally suited to persuade pacifists of their folly. Both Dewey and the *New Republic* did criticize the international police force approach for not constructively eliminating the root causes of war. They reproached the League to Enforce Peace for unconditionally supporting the *status quo* powers.[27]

Dewey discredited pacifism by demonstrating how its good intentions could not be accomplished by the means employed. The desperate tactics of pacifists to avoid war at all costs stultified their hopes of realizing lasting peace through international organization. Dewey specifically disputed Jane Addams's Tolstoyan position. He praised her efforts to promote international cooperation but deemed them insufficient. He did not, as Randolph Bourne charged, ignore the arguments of "realistic" pacifists that the war was an absolute evil. War did not necessarily destroy the possibility for intelligent action. Tolstoy simplistically held that all force was violence and violence was evil. The state was an archcriminal because it had recourse to violence on the largest scale. Though Dewey denied that coercive force constituted a legitimizing foundation for modern society, he was convinced that nothing could be accomplished without the use of force.[28] All energy was brute force doing work and therefore justified by its results. Violence, however, was energy running wild—force gone amuck. Violence was wrong, not because it employed force, but because it wasted force and used it destructively.[29] Dewey did not imply that he advocated a doctrine of efficiency; ends were never ignored. Squeamishness about force was not high idealism but "moonstruck morals."[30]

Instead of transforming existing conditions to assure less coercion and more harmony, pacifists resorted to moral incantations. "Belief that war springs from the emotions of hate, pugnacity, and greed, rather than the objective causes which call these emotions into play," Dewey argued, "reduces the peace movement to the futile plan of hortatory preaching."[31] The tactic of nonresistance could be justified only on the grounds that passive resistance would be more effective than overt force. Otherwise, one reverted to an "oriental absolutism," wherein the world is deemed to be intrinsically evil. Dewey observed that many pacifists were associated with Christian conservatism. Attributing native instincts to an antecedently given mind, they conceived human conditions in static terms thereby nullifying social reform programs. By concentrating on the individual soul's depravity, religious traditionalists were absorbed with meting out moral praise and blame. The world was conceived as an arena wherein mankind passes before the judgment of God. The most hostile and corrupting circumstances provided the best crucible for testing the human will. Both pacifists and seekers of vengeance were consumed by the immediate situation and failed to survey the long-range consequences of the war.[32] Conscientious objectors were victims of a moral innocence cultivated by their religious training rather than cowards or spoiled egoists.[33] The evangelical tradition emphasized emotions rather than intelligence and abstract rules instead of specific purposes. Morals were located in their private consciences and not objective social results. Disembodied moral forces and feelings could not alone produce justice. The purity of conscience was largely a "self-conceit."

While the other *New Republic* writers charted a specific war policy, Dewey applied his philosophy to condemn both absolutism and pacifism. He also analyzed the role of education in reconstructing democracy in America. Worldwide democracy was the only panacea to the present crisis.

NOTES

1. Neil Coughlan, *Young John Dewey* (Chicago: University of Chicago Press, 1975), pp. 82–112.

2. Warren Kuehl, *Hamilton Holt* (Gainesville: University of Florida Press, 1960), p. 60.

3. Charles Forcey, *The Crossroads of American Liberalism* (New York: Oxford University Press, 1961), pp. 230–1. Unfortunately, Forcey neglected Dewey's role almost entirely. (Hereafter cited as Forcey)

4. Herbert Croly, *The Promise of American Life* (New York: MacMillan Co., 1909), p. 312.

5. William Leuchtenberg charged, "no writer better demonstrates the close link between progressivism and imperialism, with the concept of the Hamiltonian state and democratic mission than Herbert Croly, whose *The Promise of American Life* influenced the progressive movement more profoundly than any other work." William Leuchtenberg, "The Progressive Movement and American Foreign Policy, 1898–1916," *Journal of American History (1952–3):* 501.

6. John Dewey, *Ethical Principles Underlying Education* (Riverside Educational Monographs), edited by Henry Suzzallo (Boston: Houghton-Mifflin Co., 1909), p. 21.

7. "The End of American Isolation," *NR* (Nov. 7, 1914):9–10.

8. John Dewey, *German Philosophy and Politics* (New York: Henry Holt & Co., 1915), p. 71. (Hereafter *GPP*).

9. "Traffic in Absolutes," *NR* (July 17, 1915):323. Max Eastman considered this book to be more of a contribution to war propaganda than the history of thought. See Max Eastman, *Einstein, Trotsky, Hemingway, Freud and Other Great Companions* (New York: Collier Books, 1959), p. 201.

10. *GPP,* p. 91.

11. Ibid., p. 113.

12. Ibid., p. 80. In 1924, Dewey maintained that the Great War was a day of reckoning for Kantian thought. He hoped that interest in Kant's thought would become increasingly antiquarian. Dewey, "Kant After Two Hundred Years," *NR* (April 30, 1924):254–256.

13. Dewey's critique of German idealism did not go unchallenged. William Ernest Hocking contended that Dewey didn't object to absolutes but only that Germany maintained the wrong one. Germany's ruling class was radically experimental in practicing "realpolitik." Dewey replied that German leaders were not controlled by idealistic philosophy but utilized it to disguise their political designs. See Dewey's "Political Philosophy in Germany," *NR* (October 2, 1915):234–36. Dewey also reviewed George Santayana's timely attack on German philosophy. *NR* (Dec. 9, 1916):156.

14. *GPP,* p. 143.

15. Ibid., p. 144. Alan Cywar's contention that Dewey was a nationalist until America's formal entrance into the war is misleading. Neither was Dewey swept away by patriotic emotion. See Alan Cynwar, "John Dewey in World War I: Patriotism and International Progressivism," *American Quarterly* (1969):578–594.

16. *GPP,* p. 145. See Dewey, "Our Educational Ideal in Wartime," *NR* (April 15, 1916): 283.

17. John Dewey, *Democracy and Education* (New York: MacMillan Co., 1916), p. 98.

18. Ibid., p. 318.

19. "Preparedness—For What?" *NR* (June 26, 1915):188–90.

20. *NR* (Dec. 19, 1914):1.

21. Arthur Link, *Woodrow Wilson and the Progressive Era* (New York: Harper & Row, 1963), pp. 193–4. Benjamin Marsh, the executive secretary, went on a speaking tour in the Midwest to place the cost of war preparedness on big business, its major booster.

22. John Dewey, "Universal Service as Education, I," *NR* (April 29, 1916):309–310. Dewey, "Universal Service as Education, II," *NR* (April 29, 1916):335.

23. John Dewey, "The Schools and Social Preparedness," *NR* (May 6, 1916):15–16.

24. John Dewey, *Enlistment for the Farm* (New York: Division of Intelligence and Publicity of Columbia University, 1917), p. 5.

25. Walter Lippmann, *The Stakes of Diplomacy* (New York: Holt, 1915), p. 222.

26. Norman Angell, *After All* (London: H. Hamilton, 1951), pp. 217–220.

27. John Dewey, "Force, Violence and the Law," *NR* (Jan. 23, 1916):396. Dewey, "The Future of Pacifism," *NR* (July 28, 1917):359.

28. John Dewey, "The Motivation of Hobbes' Political Philosophy. In *Studies in the History of Ideas,* Vol. I (New York: Columbia University Press, 1918), pp. 88–115.

29. John Dewey, "Force, Violence, and the Law," *NR* (Jan. 22, 1916):296.

30. John Dewey, "Force and Coercion," *International Journal of Ethics* (April, 1916):359–67. Norman Thomas later criticized Dewey's "insensitivity" to the plight of the conscientious objector. Norman Thomas, *The Conscientious Objector in America* (New York: B.W. Huebsch, 1923), pp. 262–63.

31. John Dewey, "Force, Violence and the Law," *NR* (Jan. 27, 1916):296.

32. John Dewey, *"Fiat Justitia, Ruat Coelum,"* *NR* (Sept. 29, 1977):238.

33. John Dewey, "Conscience and Compulsion," *NR* (July 14, 1917):297.

4

The *New Republic*
on the Eve of War

Randolph Bourne identified World War I as the first major test of Dewey's pragmatic liberalism.[1] The *New Republic* war liberals framed policies designed to maximize the possibilities for liberal democracy at home and abroad. They echoed Dewey's appeal to evaluate war policy rationally by examining probable consequences.[2] Their attention was attuned to the political settlement after military hostilities ceased. A liberal peace would require a new international order rooted in world federation and democracy. They were not narrow nationalists but internationalist liberals. In fact, Herbert Croly referred to himself as an "internationalist democrat."[3]

The *New Republic*'s war policy has been maligned by numerous critics who followed Bourne in pronouncing an epitaph on pragmatic liberalism. The indictment contains the following charges: (1) the war liberals were nationalists and were swept away by patriotic emotion; (2) they had a naive faith in progress and were sublimely optimistic; (3) they sacrificed principle to become servants of power—their intellectual objectivity was corrupted by support for Wilson's war effort; (4) these relativistic liberals escaped their agonizing uncertainties by a blind commitment to war; and (5) war provided them with an opportunity to engage in wholesale social engineering. Sympathizing openly with Bourne's indictment, Charles Forcey suggested that these cosmopolitan liberals were influenced by economic motives, since the founder of the *New Republic*, Michael Straight, was staunchly Anglophilic. Forcey considered the editors to be products of and spokesmen for the pro-British educated classes of New England.[4] Vilifying Dewey's role in the war, Christopher Lasch argued that the war liberals sought to enhance their virility by association with the powerful. Lasch characterized the war liberals as follows:

> It was a long time before the social planners were able to formulate a reply to the questions raised by the war. Badly shaken by the events of Europe, they groped uncertainly for answers, contradicting one week what they said the week before. Not until the third year of the war did they recover their poise.[5]

45

He termed the *New Republic*'s support for the war "a collective fantasy." Forcey found the 1930s isolationism of Charles Beard to be an appropriate American policy for the First World War. If these attacks on pragmatic liberalism hold, Dewey's political credibility would indeed be irreparably damaged.

The *New Republic* initially endorsed a policy of nonbelligerence with respect to the war. The editors criticized both parties in the conflict while seeking a negotiated settlement and defining the proper conditions for American involvement. They chided British partisans who pontificated about the criminal violations of German militarism, while praising the British destruction of neutral rights through its monopolistic control of sea power. They refused to charge Germany with full responsibility for the war.[6] Identifying with the forces of liberal Europe, the *New Republic* hoped to both undermine German autocracy and internationalize the seas as a basis for world federation.

The editors condoned both the German declaration of a submarine zone and arms traffic from America to Britain. The circumstances were unprecedented. They could not condone the eternal maintenance of British sovereignty over the seas, no matter how benign. The *New Republic* employed the defense of neutral rights as a lever against Britain.[7] The editors sympathized with the German proposal to neutralize the oceans and straits. Meanwhile, the United States and Britain might temporarily exercise joint trusteeship of the seas. This plan would solidify democratic America's ascendency in the counsel of nations. Cooperation between Britain and America was so essential for democracy that a war between them was virtually unthinkable. The British Empire was "the best existing experiment" in international political organization, a framework around which to construct a new world order.[8] After a *modus vivendi* with the British Empire, world power would be gradually transferred to the United States. The world must be made secure because American security ultimately depended upon it.

Woodrow Wilson had lost a great opportunity when he acquiesced to the Belgian invasion, a gross violation of neutral rights. The *New Republic* also advised that the United States should assume leadership in founding an international league of neutrals that would also seek cooperation with the British on sea power. If neutrals had been organized earlier to defend their rights, Germany's calculations would have altered. Such defensive measures were necessary to afford neutrals international influence.[9] A league of neutrals could both accommodate isolationist American public opinion and lay the basis for a world community.

The *New Republic* advocated far-reaching goals but realistically assessed their prospects. Mere moral suasion would not determine the outcome of the war. In November 1914 the editors prophesied that a peace conference headed by the president of the United States would reflect the balance of power at the war's conclusion. The nations of Europe would not sacrifice their men and resources only to let the United States decide the issue while maintaining its comfortable neutrality. The United States could assist in mediating a settlement but it could not determine the outcome.

The editors rejected the idea of a defensive alliance with the British and French as proposed by the League to Enforce Peace. The league's members included Hamilton Holt, Franklin Giddings, Theodore Marburg, and William Howard Taft. Since the league excluded the Central Powers, it was designed to preserve and extend the privileges of the *status quo* powers. The *New Republic* persistently differentiated its position from that of the League to Enforce Peace. As late as January 1917, the editors invoked a quotation by Dewey that a League to Enforce Peace ran the risk of becoming "a league to perpetuate war."[11] The *New Republic* was not to become the captive of either camp in this conflict. Their policies paid heed and were responsive to the emerging events of the war.

After seven months of stalemate on the western front, the journal declared that the war had lasted long enough to demonstrate that neither side could destroy the other.[12] Hopes for a negotiated peace were thwarted by Allied war aims of imposing indemnities that would have necessitated a military occupation of the Central Powers. The luxury of revenge should not be an object of policy. The destruction and defeat of Germany was not advisable.[13] Germany should be a full party in a reconciling peace settlement. At this time, the *New Republic* seemed willing to entertain the possibility that the Central Powers could reorganize *mittel Europa* under a federalized democratic system instead of enabling each quarreling nationality to struggle for its own sovereign state.[14] The British were on the verge of accepting this agreement before the war. Such a settlement could have had the eventual effect of undermining the control of the military-autocratic classes by allowing emerging democratic forces to reform these decrepit monarchies from within. The genuine security and economic interests of Germany would be accommodated.

The sensational sinking of the *Lusitania* and other passenger vessels prompted the editors to call for a policy of "differential neutrality." Did the journal capitalize upon such incidents in order to push America toward a British alliance, force Germany to abandon submarine warfare, and thereby aid an Allied victory? Could the United States have remained neutral by banning passenger travel on belligerent ships and embargoing all exports of munitions to the Allies?[15] But if this action aided the Germans, how could it be termed "neutral"? Strict neutrality was impossible. The *New Republic* was maneuvering to prevent a total military victory for either side. The editors warned Germany that such provocative sea attacks would precipitate public outrage and present a case for active belligerency.[16] Germany had to be told what actions it must avoid taking if America was to remain out of the war. Germany threatened anarchy on the high seas, and it was only the success of British sea power that had enforced the Monroe Doctrine thus protecting American interests. While desiring to force concessions on the Germans, the editors reiterated that America should fight Germany only if it could not avoid a military confrontation.

The *New Republic* quickly tempered the anti-German fervor. With Italy's entrance on the Allied side, the editors strove to justify a position of influence at any war settlement negotiations that might confront a doomed Germany. "If the Germans are beaten," they argued, "their defeat will be the result of an assistance rendered to the Allies by neutrals, acting under the protection of a legal rule which converts neutral nations during war into the handmaidens of sea power."[17] Italy entered the war only to profiteer and the editors predicted a frenzied scramble for booty. Though initially the Allies united to curb German ambitions, later additions to the alliance, like Japan and Italy, were themselves determined aggressors. Italy's entrance severely jeopardized the prospect for a positive peace. The Allies were stimulating exclusive nationalistic ambitions in order to defeat the Central Powers. This policy would incite future dangerous conflicts.[18] Furthermore, the *New Republic* conceded that passengers should not be allowed on ammunition ships, though the penalty for such misjudgment should not be death.[19] Forcey maintained that "any questioning of the right of Americans to travel on a munitions-carrying British liner would have lost the editors leverage toward a British alliance."[20] The *New Republic* asked just such a question.

The hardening of American public opinion would force the German government into a diplomatic corner, thus provoking war. Understanding that the Allies were not presently in danger of being overwhelmed, the editors admitted that it was "not our war."[21] The end of American isolation should involve participation in the post-war reorganization. A million or so American troops should not be sacrificed in order to have a voice over the disposition of Trieste or Constantinople. Effective American participation demanded a heavy human price plus collusion in secret deals that would contaminate the peace settlement. One great power, the United States, ought to stay disinterested.[22] With the very dim domestic and international prospects for positive American participation, the editors supported neutrality with the hope of exercising some economic influence during the war settlement. The editors were confronted with a perplexing dilemma. If the Allies could win without the United States, conditions for an American role were absent. If the United States did enter, how could it sufficiently transform the war aims of the Allies in order to justify the loss of blood and treasure?

The *New Republic* crystallized its war policy by the end of July 1915. The editors affirmed Norman Angell's approach, which declared that neutrality had become an anachronism in international law due to modern economic and military interdependence.[23] Angell outlined a policy of "limited war" that sought to reconcile America's divergent interests. A new international law of the seas could be developed during wartime with cooperative control among the Allies, the United States, and with the unofficial compliance of other neutral states. Britain would no longer exercise arbitrary control. An embargo on Germany could be transformed into a world organization that could establish conditions for German re-entrance and deter future recalcitrants without direct military force. The United States would hold a crucial position due to its relative self-sufficiency. Sea power was an ideal weapon for international policing. Concentrated in the hands of liberal powers, it could protect against the anarchy of the Balkans, Africa, and Asia where weakness tempted foreign exploitation and rivalry. Weak and decomposing nations were a threat to the integrity of the entire system. Therefore, international commissions should be established to oversee these and any other potential crisis spots. Human freedom could not be secured merely by the refusal of great nations to intervene.[24] Out of such collective cooperation, genuine world government could emerge.

If the Allies were successful in crushing Germany militarily, the price would involve "Prussianizing the whole continent." To exact indemnities would require the military occupation of Germany for fifteen years. Since wartime alliances usually disintegrate after the immediate threat is eliminated, the dangers of war would merely be transferred to a different arena. The military alternative to the complete subjugation of Germany consisted in allowing her to regain strength and thus strive again for world domination a generation later. Angell and Lippmann insisted that Germany must be integrated into a new economic order. Western civilization should be reunited in order to prevent its collective suicide. Germany should not be destroyed as a great power; it should be offered a reconciling peace that allowed for internal democratic stability.[25]

The editors advocated a policy of diplomatic and economic nonintercourse with Germany. The Germans would not declare war, because they wanted to avoid direct American belligerency. Likewise, the United States should not formally join the Allies, because it would be entrapped by Allied war aims. As a nonbelligerent, the United States had room to maneuver. It could re-establish full diplomatic relations with a reformed Germany and mediate a peace settlement. Attention could be directed to an international economic organization that would eventually aid in reconstructing a prostrate Europe. Landing troops in Flanders would abolish Germany's last incentive for moderation. While the United States might have to intervene militarily, only "the most terrible necessity" could justify it.[26] America should not drift into war merely to protect neutral rights. Not the submarine, but fear of German world conquest was sufficient. The war party in Germany must be discredited. Moderate peace terms would enable the liberal opposition to build a strong base of support. While condemning Germany as unfit for the society of nations, America must not be a co-conspirator in the predatory policies of Russia, Japan, and Italy. Attaining a frank and full understanding with the British was the keystone of American policy.[27]

The *New Republic* could reconcile itself to German hegemony over Central Europe. According to the editors:

All Germany would win would be a practically impregnable military position; establish the basis for a broader and more cosmopolitan industrialism than the world has yet seen. . . . And what will this victorious and invincible combination do about the British Empire and the Monroe Doctrine? Probably nothing. It will be occupied for a generation in cultivating its own garden.[28]

A congress of neutrals, pressing both sides equally, could promote a treaty of compromise and adjustment better than the ruthless subjugation of Germany. An acceptable compromise would consist of abandonment of the occupied areas in Western Europe in exchange for German hegemony in Bulgaria and Turkey. The war originated over conflicting claims in the Balkans between Russia and the Central Powers. The defeat of Germany was conceivable only by appeasing the aggressive ambitions of Czarist Russia, which was more dangerous in the long run. The editors preferred a German to a Russian dominated Balkans.[29] Russian control of Constantinople would radically shift the European balance of power, thus fomenting future wars.[30]

The Allies were resolved not to accept a German controlled Central Europe. The editors exclaimed that all Germany really wanted was *mittel Europa*. The organization of Central Europe was necessary for a peaceful world. Though such a "peace without victory" would undermine the British balance of power on the continent, this role would be inherited temporarily by the United States. A Germany dominant in Central Europe would not necessarily utilize this base to gain mastery over all of Europe and the world.[31] By restoring the *status quo ante* the war would reveal that Germany had simply conquered her own allies. Serbia and Rumania would eventually come voluntarily within its orbit. Germany wanted recognition of this empire as its price for approving a league of nations.[32] "Peace Without Victory" also became the theme of a Wilson speech in which he proposed a negotiated settlement based upon the *status quo ante*. Earlier the editors had called upon Wilson to mediate the war settlement after the Germans had made concessions in submarine warfare.[33] What peace conditions did the *New Republic* propose? Germany would renounce submarine warfare against commerce; evacuate Belgium, France, and Serbia; and accept a collective security pact against future aggressors. In return, the United States would become guarantor of the new European security system.[34]

The *New Republic* reminded its readers that Germany was composed of many conflicting socio-political groups. The German people should be separated from the ruling government, which consisted of a military-professional-bureaucratic elite. Before the war, Germany contained over four million social democrats, many of whom might have been amenable to a negotiated settlement. Unfortunately, a peace treaty could not be urged on a militarily ascendent Germany. After the collapse of Rumania, the editors proposed that the military balance be redressed to prevent the German elite from reinforcing its prestige.[35] If this elite was humbled, maybe the liberal democratic forces could reassert themselves. Even in July 1917 the German Reichstag passed a resolution renouncing annexations under the leadership of the social democrats. The Germans requested American mediation in

December 1916. Though the *New Republic* editors believed that they might be accused of betraying the Allies, they seized upon this opportunity as a means to capture the initiative from the narrow-minded nationalists in Europe.[36]

Wilson followed by asking the belligerents to state their peace terms. In 1916, John Dewey and the *New Republic* endorsed Wilson for president.[37] By January 1917, Croly and Lippmann were having weekly meetings with Colonel House, Wilson's advisor. Though the *New Republic* gained the reputation as a semi-official administration organ, it retained its independence throughout the war crisis. The degree of its influence is problematic, due more to parallel thinking than direct influence. Accused of a pro-British bias, the *New Republic* remained very balanced in its judgments. Wilson's peace campaign was aborted when the Germans adopted a reckless policy of unrestricted submarine warfare on February 1, 1917. Von Bethmann-Hollweg, German chancellor, had been defeated by the von Tirpitz faction, damaging severely the prospects for liberal influence on German war policy. Gambling on total victory, the Germans knew that their menacing naval stance meant war with the United States. The early success of the submarine and the collapse of Russia in March seemed to vindicate their decision. The Zimmerman telegram demonstrated how an imperialist Germany challenged America's interests. The Germans believed that they could starve out the British in five months. Neither the balance of power nor the preservation of the Atlantic highway alarmed Wilson, but the danger of a German peace by conquest did concern him.[38]

The *New Republic* greeted Germany's desperate gamble with the call to initiate a naval war.[39] However, sending land troops to Europe was another matter. Retaining freedom of action, the editors advised that land troops should be provided only after the Allies had defined specifically their war aims so that the United States could be assured of a just settlement. Sea power must be internationalized.[40] Political aims should not be subordinated to military strategy; nor should democracy at home be undermined.[41] An editorial composed by Walter Lippmann entitled "The Defense of the Atlantic World" established the basis for American entrance, not as a violation of neutral rights, but as the preservation of the Atlantic highway and Western civilization. With the Pan-Germans controlling policy, Germany as mistress of the seas would malign commerce throughout the world and spread autocracy. The real danger to a positive peace was the high price Western nations might have to pay for Russian and Japanese loyalty. American entrance into the war, coupled with the collapse of Tsarist Russia, reduced this danger. The war could be clearly defined as a battle between liberalism and autocracy.[42] America should not fight a war to conquer Germany but to return it to Western civilization. War should be waged only for an honorable peace.[43]

On April 2, 1917, Woodrow Wilson announced his agonizing decision to enter the war. The conditions for belligerence had been created by the failure of mediation efforts. Germany had revealed its aims by subjugating Belgium and part of France while destroying merchant shipping at will. Its government was the center of political reaction. Wilson's policy of waiting for the issue to ripen, to become unambiguous, was confirmed. The editors praised Wilson's use of this period to educate Americans in their international responsibilities.[44] Though liberals world-wide needed to accomplish much in rearranging their domestic politics, the New Republic proclaimed that "the cause of the Allies is now unmistakably the cause of liberalism."[45] Democracy was infectious and the editors prophesized that American and Russian participation would dissolve the war into a democratic revolution. Such honeymoon exuberance at the outset of a war is not surprising. However, the New Republic quickly returned to a more restrained mood. The United States had entered the war, not for selfish interests or territory, but for ideals consonant with liberal internationalism. Americans should closely monitor the internal politics of the Allies. Contact with liberal labor groups in Britain was particularly crucial. The editors praised Wilson's refusal to declare war on Austria-Hungary. This distinguished American war aims from those of the Allies and also could exploit latent rifts between the Central Powers.[46] Hopes for a reconciling peace depended upon the emergence of a liberal hegemony, which was far from a reality. Wilson's outstanding leadership could invigorate liberal forces throughout the world. The New Republic exclaimed that "no other statesman has ever so clearly identified the glory of his country with the peace and liberty of the world."[47]

John Dewey's thoughts on the war also revealed much agonizing. Complimenting the New Republic's editorial entitled "The Background of American Hesitation," Dewey wrote an article in Bourne's Seven Arts just prior to Wilson's declaration of war in which Dewey strove to mediate between the pro-war and anti-war Left. Explaining the genesis of the national hesitation about the war, Dewey rejected the popular explanation that America's reluctance was due to cowardice, ignorance, slothful materialism, or a lack of leadership. America had hesitated because it had undergone a process of self-discovery. Despite its traditional sympathies with France and Great Britain, an American culture had emerged that was vaguely but nonetheless discernibly different from that of the Old World. In Dewey's words:

> That the gallant fight for democracy and civilization fought on the soil of France is not our fight is a thing not to be realized without pangs and qualms. But it is a fact that has slowly disclosed itself as these long last years have disclosed us to ourselves. It was not ours, because for better or for worse we are committed to a fight for another democracy and another civilization. Their nature is not clear to us: all that is sure is that they are different. This is the fact of a New World.[48]

This message must have been welcomed by the cultural nationalists of the Seven Arts. America had integrated its national mind; it was no longer an appendage of Europe.

Did this appraisal signify a continued neutrality toward the war? Dewey recognized that America would have to confront the German challenge by overt war. America could not aid by its "passive compliance" the victory of a warrior nation that would employ any tactic to accomplish its imperial ends. The United States could not tolerate such a "future neighbor," which might supplant Britain as the dominant naval power surrounding its coastlines.[49] American entrance was primarily defensive; full participation would not remove the deeper hesitation that Allied war aims did not harmonize with American ideals. It would be a partially fulfilling event, designed to thwart an external, aggressive threat. "Not until the almost impossible happens," Dewey proclaimed, "not until the Allies are fighting on our terms for democracy and civilization will that [end of hesitation] happen."[50] Dewey hoped that some convulsion might occur to enable liberal forces to triumph, enabling America to identify completely with the cause. However, he doubted that this would happen. Moral perfectionism must be tempered by stern realism. Victories were partial and attempts to preserve moral innocence were ultimately futile. Quite possibly Dewey was more skeptical about the war than either Croly or Lippmann.

The *New Republic* advocated an independent role for America. It indefatigably called for a clarification of Allied war aims. For example, on April 28, 1917, the editors warned that "to put it bluntly America will not carry on the war a single day to dismember Austria-Hungary, to establish Russia in Constantinople, or to make the Adriatic an Italian lake."[51] Instead of blindly charging for military victory, they reserved judgment. "Whether war against Germany was wise will not be finally settled until the peace conference is over. The decision to enter the war is a decision to embrace a great opportunity."[52] The United States should not be asked to guarantee a military victory for the Allies, while closing the door to a German victory. Total defeat of Germany would play into the hands of the European ruling classes who would utilize the victory for anti-democratic purposes.[53] Carthaginian peace terms would weld the German people haplessly to their military war lords. The *New Republic,* like Wilson, wanted to stimulate the same kind of domestic revolution in Germany as occurred in Russia. The German people would grow convinced that their real enemy was the military power structure.[54] By imploring the Allies to begin acting on a higher level of political principle, the *New Republic* was actually indicted by the *Outlook* for being "seditious and disloyal."[55] The editors were never mouthpieces for the war machine.

Dewey and the *New Republic* editors were very concerned with the poisoning of domestic public opinion. The battle for democracy had to be won at home if the proper conditions for democracy abroad could emerge. Newspapers, the League to Enforce Peace, and the Creel Committee on Public Opinion resorted to evoking fear and hatred.[56] The traditional political psychology combined flowery idealism with appeals to immediate profit. Instead of frenzied patriotism, Dewey urged Americans to adopt a "businesslike" attitude toward the war. They should respond earnestly to duty with the sense of a job that must be done, though it was itself distasteful. America was in no immediate danger of invasion. The people generally knew what results they desired. The president should take the American people into his confidence, appealing to their intelligence, in designing a workable program for peace. Besides stifling an international nuisance, Dewey upheld a "genuine possibility" for world organization and the beginnings of public control as an additional war motivation. These goals were not "idealistic glosses" but "objects of fair adventure." If a democratic upheaval arose in the Allied countries elevating war aims beyond narrow nationalism, then a crusader's zeal would be added to the necessary labor on behalf of an unpleasant task.[57]

Alarmed about a derailment of American ideals on behalf of a total military victory, Dewey persistently criticized the outbreak of bigotry and the circumscription of democratic freedoms. The *New Republic* warned that the American propaganda campaign seemed to be defeating its own initial aims.[58] Dewey condemned emotional appeals for retributive justice. He cautioned that a pragmatic regard for the future required a reconciling peace.[59] Though social unity was particularly important in wartime, the attempts to dragoon dissenters were counterproductive and "gratuitously stupid." It resulted in breathing vitality into obnoxious beliefs by enabling them to assume the aura of martyrdom. The employment of brute force did not inspire unity but instead incited hysteria about spies and enemies everywhere. Critical discussion of the war issue should not be sacrificed in order to subdue a few dissident sects whose impact was minimal. Even if Wilson's leadership could formulate the wisest of peace proposals, the opportunity for maturing democracy would be missed. Americans would not realize how their national ideals could be utilized to remake the world and unify America.[60]

By November 1917, Dewey conceded that the erosion of civil liberties had become much more serious than he originally anticipated. Earlier, he had remarked that democratic freedom of speech had survived greater obstacles in the past than the current war crisis. However, this should not be taken to mean that Dewey impatiently disregarded the problem.[61] Anything that offended the majority of citizens was the popular working definition of treason. For Dewey this was analogous to a "psychological lynch law." The socialist press was persecuted and even the *New Republic* was investigated. The *Wall Street Journal* proclaimed that "we are now at war, and the militant pacifists are earnestly reminded that there is no shortage of hemp or lampposts."[62] Anti-war socialist Max Eastman was almost hung by a group of soldiers. Though Dewey disagreed with the violent tactics of the International Workers of the World (IWW), he and Thorstein Veblen defended them against government persecutions. The National Civil Liberties Bureau tried three times to place an advertisement (signed by Dewey) in the *New Republic* to solicit for the IWW. After the second refusal, it was learned that government agents had threatened to drop the magazine's second class mailing privileges if the ad was printed. As a leading member of the American Civil Liberties Union (ACLU), Dewey sponsored the ad in print. The alleged bedfellow relationship between the *New Republic* and the Wilson administration was suspect.[63]

What was responsible for this hysteria? Dewey contended that: (1) the ethnic populations were not well assimilated, (2) small signs of German intrigue aroused wild suspicions, (3) "peace" leagues fanned intolerance by questioning the loyalty of all who disagreed with them, (4) America's unfamiliarity with war caused a temporary disequilibrium. The *New Republic* noted scornfully that the detestable practice of categorizing every German as "assassin and Hun" was finding favor.[64] Dewey urged liberals to oppose aggressively reactionaries who threatened civil liberties. It was not necessary "to establish Prussianism at home in order to defeat it abroad."[65]

Dewey was alarmed at the erosion of academic freedom on the campuses of America, particularly at Columbia University. As early as 1915, he protested the political firing of Scott Nearing.[66] Later Nicholas Murray Butler, president of Columbia University, sensed that the campuses were popularly considered to be havens for disloyal citizens. A pacifist till it came to fighting Germans, Butler warned the faculty that free thinking would not be permitted. He purged Columbia of dissenters by charging them with sedition and treason. Leon Fraser, who had formerly worked for Butler as a peace propagandist, made the tactical error of continuing his peace activities after the declaration of war. He was summarily dismissed. The student editor of the *Columbia Jester* was expelled for protesting the campus ban on allowing pacifist Leo Tolstoy to speak. The *New York Times* reaffirmed Butler's approach, holding that, ". . . freedom to teach is correlative to the freedom to dispense with poisonous teaching. . . that universities were responsible to the same public opinion which holds them accountable for errors of indulgence to the teachers of false doctrine sheltering themselves behind the shibboleth of academic freedom."[67] The Columbia University trustees appointed a committee of nine faculty members, including Dewey, to cooperate with the loyalty investigations. The trustees dismissed two professors, James McKeen Cattell and H. W. L. Dana. One was dismissed over the committee's objection, while the other was fired without the committee even being consulted. Dewey was outraged and resigned from the committee. Charles Beard resigned from the university.[68] These events typified Dewey's forthright defense of academic freedom. He was active in founding organizations to defend this right, notably the New York Teachers' Union and the American Association of University Professors. He would not expediently compromise principle in order to prosecute the war.

In addition to protecting against abuses of democratic freedoms, Dewey held out hope that some gains could be derived from the conflict. The war had pinpointed weaknesses in the social system, while demonstrating that organized planning could be applied to broad areas of public life. One force released by the war was the rise in power of the wage-earning class, a group that could secure international cooperation among liberals. The Russian Revolution exemplified this rise to power. A lasting peace depended upon the unity of liberal forces throughout the world.[69] The use of science for collective purposes through the development of steam and electric power had transformed the life of the ordinary citizen. Air travel obliterated national boundaries. Technology had contributed to a much closer intercommunication, which could result in solidifying political and economic groupings. Joint planning in agriculture and industry strengthened mutual interdependence in the world economy. The growth of scientific knowledge, if it were employed for democratic ends, held the prospect for a new type of government. In each warring country, consumer production subordinated private profit to social demands. Even conscription in the United States reinforced the supremacy of public needs to individual pursuits.

Writing in the pro-war *Independent,* Dewey retained his intellectual autonomy even in this most buoyant of his articles. He recognized that the war had built up centralized governments that were militaristic in structure. He predicted that either a small number of great powers would emerge to compete with one another or there would be a federated concert of nations with political and administrative powers. Only a federated world government could secure democracy, but Dewey conceded that this result would require "a long period of struggle and transition." The *New Republic* agreed: "both democracy and international organization are requisite to the security of mankind. This is our belief. And Americans can use the war as a means to its realization. This is our faith."[70] Dewey anticipated no millennium but rather a long period of "drifting and social unrest."[71] While committed to Wilsonian ideals, Dewey remained aware of the immense obstacles that inhibited their realization.

The *New Republic* liberals tirelessly examined the issue of national self-determination for the peoples of Eastern Europe. This constituted the central question in any peace settlement. With the rivalry of various ethnic groups, this area was a powder keg that could stymie even the most dedicated of diplomats. The Wilson Administration supported self-determination for three reasons: (1) to maintain domestic support from ethnic populations in America (especially the Poles), (2) to spread dissension within territories controlled by the Central Powers, and (3) to reinforce democratic idealism by combining nationalism and democracy. Although it did not initially support this war aim, the *New Republic*'s policy shifted as the context of the war evolved. Instead of a largely defensive war to protect the Atlantic Highway, the editors feared German hegemony in Europe. The animating motive of *mittel Europa* was a political effort to increase manpower for war. German ambitions were in the east and southeast, which offered a base to seek world dominion. By August 1918 the editors supported the liberation of the Slavic peoples.[72] Even a closed German economic league violated Wilson's proposals for free trade and proved obstructive to international amity. If the destruction of German power was the ultimate aim, the opportunity for a compromise settlement would vanish.[73]

H. N. Brailsford, the *New Republic* columnist, continued to promote the maintenance of the Austro-Hungarian Empire. Dismemberment would destroy any basis for a negotiated peace. How could Germany accept the destruction of its chief ally? Hopes for peace in Eastern Europe were predicated upon a League of Nations. It was impossible, however, to satisfy the virulent ambitions of the hodgepodge of nationalities in the area.[74] Brailsford argued that the Russian Revolution had destroyed the dread of Pan-Slavism among Austrians, liberating them from dependence upon Germany. Emperor Karl of Austria had adopted a moderate program, renouncing all conquests. He sent out peace feelers indicating a tacit opposition to German ambitions. Brailsford contended that Austria, an agricultural nation, was on the verge of collapse, like Czarist Russia. The Allies should accommodate the Austro-Hungarian Empire as a means to end the war.

The editors of the *New Republic* responded to Brailsford's argument with an extended treatment indicative of their sophisticated approach to the war.[75] Reaching this decision "only after profound hesitation and utmost reluctance," they rejected the federalist alternative for Austro-Hungary, which previously appeared plausible. The German ruling class would still dominate in foreign and military policy. No federalist plan under the Hapsburgs could alleviate the unconscionable evil of Slavs being forced to fight in German uniforms. Before the Russian Revolution, a tolerant policy toward the dual monarchy was advisable in order to check the reactionary czarist aggrandizement in the region. However, the Carthaginian Brest-Litovsk Treaty fully exposed the German aim of subjugating the Slavs and fulfilling the wild dreams of Pan-Germanism. Emperor Karl accepted this treaty, remaining a tool of the German military. The *New Republic* realized that their policy would necessitate a longer war and a more substantial military victory. They further acknowledged that resentment would be aroused among Germans, even resulting in another war. Yet, the alternative contained "more injustice and insecurity." How could peace be assured under the continued German oppression of the Slavs? How could a League of Nations contain a slave state anymore than the United States could condone a Confederate South?

The *New Republic* admitted the existence of secret treaties but insisted that the execution of these treaties depended upon Czarist Russia. The Russian Revolution had obviated this danger. Despite their hostility to the Bolsheviks, the editors defended a hands-off policy for Russia. They were hopeful that a chaotic Russia would gravitate toward a liberal democratic regime. If Italy and France failed to accept the league's security measures, which depended upon American armies, then the United States should isolate itself. A predatory settlement would not long endure. Worried again about French war aims, the editors wanted these aims fully publicized. They did not underplay this danger. A vindictive treaty perpetuating the politics of force would be handled when it arose.[76] Germany was the more immediate threat. Under the leadership of Ludendorff and Hindenburg, a defiant Germany refused to negotiate. They carved up Russia and hinted at much broader imperial ambitions.

The *New Republic* rested its ultimate hopes on a genuine League of Nations. Only when democrats had defeated the reactionary forces in the Allied nations could a true peace conference and league be convened. The editors warned prophetically: "we hope and believe that such a conference will eventually be called, but that the delegates which the existing governments will appoint to discuss terms of the peace will live up to any such specifications as we feel sure is pathetic and baseless an illusion as any idealist shall cherish."[77] The subject peoples of Eastern Europe might build democratic momentum through their liberation. Such small nations would have to federate in order to maintain themselves economically and militarily. The editors had already drawn the terms upon which they would support the Allies and reasons sufficient to withdraw that support.

Dewey feared that future wars would be provoked by fulfilling the ambitions of ethnic groups for their own sovereign nation-states.[78] Economic dependence would constrain these nations to form military alliances with larger nations, thereby perpetuating an unstable balance of power. Destroying Germany to promote ethnic political goals should not become an end-in-itself. The absolute sovereignty of nations had to be subordinated to an international federation; peace demanded it, and it was necessary due to the impossibility of economic self-sufficiency. The "cultural emancipation" of nationalities with local autonomy within a federation was mentioned by Dewey as a primary objective of the war.[79] Separating cultural from political nationality, he held that cultural diversity was a positive good. However, it was hopeless for each ethnic nationality to serve as the foundation for a stable political organization. While denying the Irish the right to political self-determination, for example, Dewey granted it to the Zionists.

> If I do not mistake it the cause of Zionism has great claims upon those who are interested in the future organization of the peaceful intercourse of nations because it not only guarantees freedom of cultural development in that particular spot in which the new nation is formed, but because it gives a leverage for procuring and developing cultural nationality in all other countries which harbor within themselves large numbers of Jewish folk.[80]

He defended a Zionist state as a "triumph against great odds." It deserved the support of statesmen who cared for the world's peaceful future. Quite possibly, Dewey believed that the Zionist state would manifest social democratic cosmopolitanism and in so doing buttress a viable League of Nations. The future of world democracy was a greater goal than midwifing a number of reactionary, clerical, ethnic states in Europe.

Dewey conducted a study of the conditions among the Poles in America as a means to assist the State Department with the nationalities issue in Eastern Europe. He corresponded briefly with Colonel House regarding this matter.[81] Dewey was alarmed at the pervasive factional strife between various Polish nationalist groups. The Paderewski faction, for example, claimed the support of the Polish-American population. In fact, however, they disregarded all democratic, representative procedures by purging dissident elements from the Polish national convention.[82] Dewey feared that this small clique would successfully maneuver into a position from which it could impose an autocratic government on the emerging free Poland: the Paderewski faction was monarchical, clerical, allied with conservative business interests, and anti-Semitic. However, since they were pro-Russian, this group obtained the backing of the Allies and were even accorded semi-official status. Pan-Slavic as well as Pan-Polish, the Paderewski group proposed the creation of a Polish state, consisting of thirty-five million people, that would serve as a buffer zone between Germany and Russia. Dewey wondered how the Allies could possibly reconcile the principles of democracy with their support for Paderewski.

The other major faction among the Poles was headed by General Pilsudski. He believed that a secret treaty between the Russians and the western Allies would nullify hopes for autonomy. Historically, the Russians had been Poland's chief oppressor. In the Austro-Hungarian Empire, the Poles were at least given autonomy to preserve their culture as well as representation in the government. At that time, Pilsudski embodied the liberal social democratic element in Poland, although, initially, he supported Trialism, with Poland as the third state of Austro-Hungary. However, after the Russian Revolution, his group proposed the creation of an independent Poland. Wilson's advocacy of a free Poland prompted Poles within Austria to launch a separatist movement, their hopes being that American influence would dominate the Peace Conference. Pilsudski advocated the traditional boundaries of Poland, with independence for Estonia, Latvia, Lithuania, Ukrainia, and other Eastern European peoples. He anticipated a voluntary federation of these states.

Instead of a sovereign Poland, Dewey proposed that these federated states be allied with the western democratic powers; this would prevent any future alliance of Germany and Russia from dissecting them.[83] He insisted that unity among the Poles depended upon American mediation. Dewey's sympathies clearly favored the Pilsudski faction: he wanted to establish an American commission on Polish affairs to help the liberal element obtain a proper hearing from the government. The *New Republic* endorsed Dewey's position on the Polish issue.[84]

Dewey praised the Polish cultural contribution to America and strove to preserve their cultural identity.[85] Yet, he has been attacked for not only attempting to manipulate the Poles, but also for seeking to chain them to the American industrial machine. Did Dewey secretly collaborate with the Wilson Administration by identifying with American military and commercial interests? Dewey was concerned about efforts to return massive numbers of Poles and other ethnics in southeastern Europe to their native lands. Appealing to the State Department on the basis of its own logic, Dewey mentioned that this process could de-Americanize these ethnics; and it could also create a labor shortage after the war.[86] Actually, Dewey wanted to retain these immigrants because of their unique cultural contribution. Rather than exploit immigrant factory workers — a practice Dewey consistently opposed in several articles — he recommended that efforts be made to disperse Polish peasants throughout rural areas in order to help ease the dislocating effects of modern urban-industrial life.[87] Dewey's report was far from being an apologetic for the administration. In fact, his position was contrary to that held by Wilson. Albert Barnes, a member of Dewey's study group, was questioned by the Justice Department in connection with alleged subversive activities due to his association with the Pilsudski faction.[88] The Wilson Administration continued to support the Paderewski faction in opposition to Dewey's recommendations. The thirteenth point in Wilson's famous resolution declared an unequivocal commitment to an independent Poland, recognizing it above all other ethnic claims. Wilson endorsed Paderewski as the diplomatic head of the Polish-Americans, and Paderewski maintained close relations with Colonel House. Even in this narrow area, Dewey did not influence state policy. How could he have imagined that he was controlling political events? Ironically, by opposing a fascist Paderewski, Dewey was labeled a closet fascist.[89]

The *New Republic* endorsed Wilson's democratic leadership, but they never suspended their criticism, either before or after the declaration of war. The editors were suspicious of Allied war aims and of those forces in America who were promoting an illiberal peace. They warned that the Japanese were utilizing German tactics in the Far East.[90] The *Outlook,* stoking an anti-German vendetta by insisting that the Germans were unfit to govern any people, demanded an unconditional surrender complete with exclusion of Germany from free trade and the imposition of an occupation army.[91] The *New Republic* condemned these cries for revenge. The editors proposed a conference on war aims until the Armistice was finally declared.[92] They sensed that the chances for a reconciling peace rested almost entirely on the shoulders of Woodrow Wilson.

The war liberals were ridiculed by both conservatives and anti-war radicals. Randolph Bourne's indictment has attained the most widespread recognition. Since World War I, numerous commentatators have echoed Bourne's central themes in castigating Dewey and the *New Republic*. Portrayed by his many admirers as a prophetic voice calling out in the American cultural wilderness, Bourne largely established his reputation as a social critic through his bitter attack on Dewey. Dewey's support for American involvement in World War I epitomized the spiritual bankruptcy of pragmatic liberalism: an entire generation had been betrayed and the golden youth were to be conscripted into the muddy trenches of France. How accurate was Bourne's indictment? By connecting the Bourne legend with a realistic appraisal of the war, we are better able to make a determination as to whether Bourne or Dewey acted most responsibly in the crisis.

After studying under Dewey at Columbia, Bourne became a zealous convert to the pragmatic outlook. As a contributing editor to the *New Republic,* he praised the revolutionary edge with which Dewey's philosophy could dismantle traditions and liberate the youth. Dewey was the prophet and poet around whom the cultural nationalists could rally. According to Bourne, "he [Dewey] seems almost to feel shame that he has seen the implications of democracy more clearly than anybody else in this great would-be democracy about him. . . ."[93] Pragmatism contained a dynamic ideal that could triumph over the cultural challenge of Europe and in so doing unite the world.[94] Bourne's discipleship appeared unrestrained.

At the beginning of the Great War, Bourne reveled in the titanic clash of national cultures. He sounded like anything but a pacifist. Defending cultural particularism, he stated that "the war from this point of view may be a vast liberating movement, clearing the way for this more conscious and intense world. . . . The tendencies which they are working at are exactly those which hold the brightest promise for twentieth-century Western civilization."[95] The artistic-spiritual consciousness of the population was enhanced by the war. Traveling through Europe in 1913, Bourne was impressed with Germany. He objected to the postulation of an Anglo-Saxon standard of democracy as the good for all humanity. After his trip to England, he exclaimed that he was ready to renounce the whole of Anglo-Saxon civilization. Britain must be defeated if the world was "ever to have freedom or any life or honesty or sensitiveness of soul."[96] Germany's tenacious ideals had proven consistently superior to those of its European rivals. Its "life-enhancing" values typified a nation that lived habitually at maximum intensity. Bourne's colleague, Van Wyck Brooks, appreciated how Goethe's Faustian vision inspired the Germans to new heights of achievement. America needed a similar poet who could crystallize its cultural nationalism. Who were the leading candidates? Bourne's pro-German sympathies made his subsequent neutral posture very suspect.

Until America's full belligerency Dewey and Bourne did not confront one another publicly on the war issue. Like Dewey, Bourne spoke of the war as an incomparable opportunity for America to discover its national ideal on the foundation of a stern realism. In July 1916 he seconded Dewey's opposition to the Roosevelt-Wood plan for universal military service.[97] Though Dewey deflated pacifism, wrote a damaging critique of German culture, and suggested conditions for America's involvement, Bourne did not repudiate him or the *New Republic* before April 1917. His disillusion with Dewey may have originated from other sources than the war issue itself. Bourne considered himself to be an outcast around the *New Republic*. He disapproved of its preoccupation with political rather than cultural interests, a preoccupation that relegated his pieces to the back pages. Bourne imagined that he had enemies on the staff.[98] Later he charged that Dewey had initiated Justice Department surveillance of him. He allegedly remarked: "You don't know Dewey. He is terribly vain. He was offended by my article and would do anything to injure me."[99] Dewey and Bourne did clash over Bourne's sardonic review of T. Matthias Alexander's *Man's*

Supreme Inheritance, for which Dewey wrote an introduction. Alexander was a good friend of Dewey and Bourne ridiculed him.[100] Dewey wrote a rejoinder to the review and Bourne responded two weeks later. While some maintain that there was no evidence of personal animosity, Bourne's revolt against his teacher did assume this posture.[101] Bourne's acerbic articles on the war liberals were primarily a personal vendetta and not an effort to alter government policy.

Bourne was obsessed with fear of his own mediocrity and confessed an underlying thirst for fame. Influenced by Nietzsche, he placed his hopes for peace upon an intellectual elite who could steer the vulgar masses through the storm: a creative avant-garde could generate cultural uplift. Dewey's faith in the common man did not sit comfortably with such blatant elitism. Rather than seeking to charge the war liberals with opportunism, Bourne's rebellion seemed primarily motivated by a demonic quest for notoriety. In a letter to Van Wyck Brooks, Bourne confided his desire to supplant the stodgy intellectual leadership of the *New Republic* with his own cult of anti-war radicals.[102] The war liberals exuded "middle-aged dignity," not youthful violence. Bourne speculated that his new cult would not be judged for its concrete political results but for its ability to spin a "vital myth" capable of mesmerizing the masses. Bourne demanded an idealism that was neither muddied by compromise nor callous to creative values.

On April 14, 1917, the *New Republic* commended the role of "the intellectuals" in freeing America from its isolationist mentality. The editors praised Wilson's deliberate strategy of establishing the proper terms for involvement while educating the American people as to the nature of their international responsibilities. Those who ran the journal had no illusions about personally directing the war effort.[103] Bourne mocked this pretentious boast of leading the country into the war by a strategy of "Fabian gradualness."[104] There is no evidence that the *New Republic* sacrificed its editorial independence in order to pander to the Wilson Administration and the Anglophilic eastern ruling class. "I have found his [Lippmann's] judgment most unsound and therefore entirely unserviceable in matters of that sort," Wilson stated, "because he, in common with the men of the *New Republic,* has ideas about the war and its purposes which are highly unorthodox from my point of view."[105] Bourne accused the war liberals of harboring a craving for action that would relieve their uncertainty and critical independence. This search for a simple, unquestioning commitment ended by rationalizing the *status quo.*[106] Throughout the war, Dewey criticized the abandonment of thought. He did not slide effortlessly from education to war.

Bourne vilified pragmatism as the intellectual root of the American catastrophe. The war liberals collectively implemented Dewey's instrumental philosophy, which practiced adjustment instead of establishing ideals.[107] Young liberals accepted ends from above and had no principles except "intelligent service." Dewey was too optimistic because he naively embraced democratic idealism; he was too realistic since he gave qualified support to the Wilson Administration. To charge Dewey with subordinating value to technique fatally misunderstands his philosophy. For a lifetime he battled to overcome the means-ends dualism. Pragmatism also lacked the poetic vision necessary to nurture concern for the quality of life over the machinery of life.[108] Bourne was awed by Dewey's superb intellectual rationale for the war; however, not only the head but the heart had to apprehend, and the heart "inexorably balked." Bourne simultaneously accused Dewey of being too cold and analytical and of abdicating critical thought in favor of blind commitment. Intelligence alone was insufficient for the restless, driven Bourne.

Bourne's approach to the war is riddled with paradoxes. He actually believed that the intellectuals, commanding the power of the printed word, could have decisively altered American policy. The *New Republic* relentlessly sought to avoid direct American belligerency through a negotiated peace. Yet, Bourne accused the editors of scarcely trying to utilize America's "vast neutral power" for democratic ends. He alleged that they neither made nor suggested a solemn agreement on war aims.[109] While advocating a negotiated settlement along lines almost identical to the *New Republic,* Bourne then argued that peace without victory was a "biological contradiction."[110] With the resort to arms, war assumed an inexorable life of its own. Choices of means and ends became frozen in a desperate quest for total victory, defying any attempt at human control. All governments, whether democratic or autocratic, behaved identically during wartime. The flexibility required for pragmatic liberalism vanished; Dewey's rational approach broke down. Liberals believed in an "illusory democratic and antiseptic war." Nothing positive could transpire from war. Bourne preferred the role of a utopian pacifist who refused to compromise with evil; at least the utopian knew he was ineffectual in comparison to the realist who acknowledged evil but failed in his attempts to ameliorate it.[111] As a final source of confusion, Bourne voiced support for peoples' wars. The revolutionary armies of France were directed against autocratic governments and not people. Bourne's anarchism appeared to lead him to conclude that organized violence in uniform was bad while killing people in a uniform could be good.

Bourne formulated no concrete plan or even poetic, imaginative suggestions as to how the combatants could be deterred. He anemically proposed, "all that can be done is to try to keep your country out of situations where such expressive releases occur."[112] However, he accused Dewey of ignoring the realistic segment of the anti-war community who adopted a more positive plan to end the war. The *New Republic* sympathized with Jane Addams's effort at the Hague to create a peace conference and form relief agencies. The professional pacifists neither stopped the war nor promoted conditions for a lasting peace. Bourne scarcely bothered to analyze the consequences of a German victory. He hoped that democracy would emerge in Germany internally because the officer class would kill itself off during the war. The oppressed peoples of Central Europe would spontaneously rebel against

German control. Bourne continued to endorse an independent policy, like Norman Angell's "armed neutrality," not realizing that the context of the war had shifted. American neutrality was predicated upon Germany's restraint, which defined the conditions for involvement. Bourne insisted that the United States was being totally manipulated and exploited by the Allies. In truth, Wilson did not collapse into an endorsement of the Allies' secret treaties. He appealed independently to the Central Powers. In September 1917 he organized the Inquiry Committee in order to formulate plans for a war settlement. The Brest-Litovsk Treaty was symptomatic of a peace negotiated on German terms.

Bourne inadequately grasped both Dewey's philosophy and the facts surrounding the war. Bourne's legacy remains serviceable for those who desire a blanket ideological indictment of liberalism's "gray compromise." By 1940 many of Bourne's followers confessed that he had outlived his prophetic usefulness. Lewis Mumford blamed Bourne for instilling "romantic defeatism" and political irresponsibility among the post-war generation. This treason of the intellectuals was the worst catastrophe of the Great War.[113] To prevent the triumph of German autocracy and to hold out the prospect for democratic reform was an option worth defending. The journal's policy correlates closely with George Kennan's hindsight reflections of a prudent approach.[114] The *New Republic* policy after the Armistice could have been predicted from its earliest statements about the war. Dewey was hardly converted to pacifism by Bourne's acerbic polemics. While disappointed with the final peace terms, Dewey realized that the effects of a German peace would have been catastrophic.

NOTES

1. Randolph Bourne, "Mental Unpreparedness," *NR* (Sept. 11, 1915):45.

2. "Timid Neutrality," *NR* (Nov. 14, 1914):8.

3. Herbert Croly, "Counsel of Humility," *NR* (Dec. 15, 1917):173–76.

4. Forcey, pp. 225–27. Sidney Kaplan, "Social Engineers as Saviours," *Journal of the History of Ideas* (1956):347–69. David Noble, *The Paradox of Progressive Thought* (Minneapolis: University of Minnesota Press, 1958), pp. 23–54. John C. Farrell, "John Dewey and World War I: Armageddon Tests a Liberal's Faith," *Perspectives in American History IX* (1975):229–343.

5. Christopher Lasch, *The New Radicalism in America* (New York: Vintage Books, 1965), p. 182.

6. *NR* (Jan. 2, 1915):1. *NR* (Jan. 15, 1916):260–61.

7. "Law and Order on the Seas," *NR* (March 21, 1915):194.

8. "The Case of Canada," *NR* (July 3, 1915):220. The editors also endorsed a Pan-American League, to which American sovereignty would be subordinated. They were not Rooseveltian nationalists.

9. "Getting It Both Ways," *NR* (Feb. 27, 1915):87.

10. "Timid Neutrality," *NR* (Nov. 14, 1914):8.

11. "A League of Peace," *NR* (March 20, 1915):168.

12. "Are We Militarists?" *NR* (March 20, 1915):167.

13. "War at Any Price," *NR* (Nov. 7, 1915):85.

14. "The Difficult Peace," *NR* (May 1, 1915):316.

15. Forcey, pp. 236–37.

16. *NR* (April 3, 1915):216. *NR* (May 15, 1915):24–25.

17. *NR* (May 15, 1915):25. "Germany's Real Offense," *NR* (May 22, 1915):55.

18. "Enter Italy," *NR* (May 22, 1915):55–56.

19. *NR* (May 22, 1915):78.

20. Forcey, p. 236.

21. "Not Our War," *NR* (June 5, 1915):108–110.

22. Ibid.

23. Norman Angell, "A New Kind of War," *NR* (July 31, 1915):327–29. See Angell, *The World's Highway* (New York: Down, 1915), p. 361. "What Norman Angell Did," *NR* (Sept. 16, 1916):151. Angell desired to transfer world leadership to America.

24. "Mexico and Human Liberty," *NR* (Jan. 23, 1915):7.

25. "America to Europe, August 1916," *NR* (July 29, 1916):321. "Germany and the League of Peace," *NR* (Nov. 18, 1916):61.

26. "The Next Step," *NR* (July 31, 1915):323.

27. "Our Relation With Great Britain," *NR* (Jan. 27, 1916):292.

28. "If Germany Wins," *NR* (Sept. 11, 1915):142. Convinced of the journal's pro-British bias, Forcey could not understand this policy approach.

29. Ibid.

30. "International Security," *NR* (Nov. 11, 1916):36. *NR* (Dec. 9, 1916):136.

31. Lippmann, "The Evangelist of Middle Europe," *NR* (Jan. 27, 1917):357:59. In his review of Frederick Naumann's *Central Europe,* Lippmann sympathized with the book, contending that the Allies ought to make a liberal peace by giving "drastic concessions" to the Dual Monarchy.

32. "Peace Without Victory," *NR* (Dec. 23, 1916):201.

33. "An Appeal to the President," *NR* (April 22, 1916):304.

34. "Hypocritical Neutrality," *NR* (May 13, 1916):29.

35. *NR* (Dec. 2, 1916):106.

36. "The Note as Americanism," *NR* (Dec. 30, 1916):229. "A White Peace and Its Consequences," *NR* (Dec. 16, 1916):168–169.

37. John Dewey, "The Hughes Campaign," *NR* (Oct. 28, 1916):319–321.

38. Arthur Link, *Wilson, The Diplomatist* (Baltimore: John Hopkins Press, 1957), p. 88.

39. "A Lesson in Diplomacy," *NR* (March 10, 1917):151–53.

40. "America's Part in the War," *NR* (Feb. 10, 1917):33–34.

41. "A War Program for Liberals," *NR* (March 31, 1917):249–50.

42. "War and Revolution," *NR* (March 24, 1917):212.

43. "The Effect of America in the War," *NR* (March 17, 1917):180–1.

44. "Who Willed American Participation," *NR* (April 14, 1917):309. "The Great Decision," *NR* (April 7, 1917):279–80.

45. David Noble pounced on this statement to argue that the *New Republic* accepted the inevitability of democratic progress. Noble, *The Paradox of Progressive Thought,* p. 52.

46. *NR* (April 7, 1917):277.

47. "The Great Decision," *NR* (April 7, 1917):280.

48. John Dewey, "In a Time of National Hesitation," *Seven Arts Magazine* (May, 1917):3. See also "Background of American Hesitation," *NR* (March 3, 1917):246–48.

49. Ibid., p. 5.

50. Ibid., p. 6.

51. "American Strategy," *NR* (April 28, 1917):361. *NR* (May 19, 1917):63.

52. "The Morality of Conscription," *NR* (May 5, 1917):8.

53. "Taking Stock," *NR* (Aug. 11, 1917):31.

54. "The Center of Strategy," *NR* (Aug. 4, 1917):3–5. "The Prospect of German Democracy," *NR* (Sept. 1, 1917):128–30.

55. "Never Again," *NR* (Aug. 18, 1917):62.

56. "Ours Not to Reason Why," *NR* (Sept. 15, 1917):177-78.

57. John Dewey, "What America Will Fight For," *NR* (Aug. 18, 1917):68-69.

58. "Darkening Counsel," *NR* (Oct. 27, 1917):341-43.

59. John Dewey, *"Fiat Justitia, Ruat Coelum," NR* (Sept. 29, 1917):238.

60. John Dewey, "The Conscription of Thought," *NR* (Sept. 1, 1917):130.

61. Lasch, *The New Radicalism in America,* p. 205. John Dewey, "In Explanation of Our Lapse," *NR* (Nov. 1, 1917):18.

62. John Moreau, *Randolph Bourne: The Legend and Reality* (Washington, D.C.: Public Affairs Press, 1966): p. 133.

63. *NR* (June 22, 1918):iii. Donald Johnson, *The Challenge to American Freedoms: World War I and the Rise of the American Civil Liberties Union* (Lexington: Univ. of Kentucky Press, 1963), p. 96.

64. "War Propaganda," *NR* (Oct. 6, 1917):255-57.

65. John Dewey, "Democracy and Loyalty in Our Schools," *American Teacher* (Jan. 1918):8-10.

66. "Professional Freedom," *School and Society* (Nov. 6, 1915):673.

67. Joan Jensen, *The Price of Vigilance* (Chicago: Rand, McNally, 1969), p. 80.

68. Dykhuizen, pp. 161-168. "Beard's Resignation," *NR* (Dec. 24, 1917):249-51.

69. John Dewey, "What Are We Fighting For?" *The Independent* (June 27, 1918):474. See Walter Weyl, *The End of the War* (New York: MacMillan Co., 1918), pp. 161-77.

70. "America's Need For Haste," *NR* (Dec. 29, 1917):236.

71. John Dewey, "Internal Social Reorganization After the War," *Journal of Race Development* (April, 1918):385-400.

72. "Flanking Germany," *NR* (August 3, 1918):3-5.

73. H. N. Brailsford, "The President and Central Europe," *NR* (Feb. 16, 1918):75-77.

74. H. N. Brailsford, "On Dismembering America," *NR* (Aug. 17, 1918):135-7.

75. *NR* (August 31, 1918):138-41.

76. See Walter Weyl, *The End of the War* (New York: MacMillan Co., 1918). *The Outlook* warned that Germany wanted *mittel Afrika* as well as a *mittel Europa,* building up a colonial belt from the Indian Ocean to the South Atlantic. Its policy for world domination also included colonialism in South America in order to unite ethnic Germans. *The Outlook* (Feb. 3, 1918): 234, 238. *The Outlook* (Nov. 4, 1917):523. See Fritz Fischer, *Germany's Aims in the First World War* (New York: Norton & Co., 1967).

77. *NR* (Aug. 31, 1918):140.

78. John Dewey, "The Future of Pacifism," *NR* (July 28, 1917):359.

79. John Dewey, "What America Will Fight For," *NR* (Aug. 18, 1917):68.

80. John Dewey, "The Principle of Nationality," *Menorah Journal* (Oct., 1917):207-208.

81. Dewey-House (August 12, 1918), Colonel House Papers, Yale University Library, Yale University.

82. John Dewey, "Autocracy Under Cover," *NR* (Aug. 24, 1918):103-106.

83. John Dewey, *Conditions Among Poles in the United States* (Washington, D.C.: U.S. State Dept., 1918), p. 22.

84. *NR* (Nov. 23, 1918):83.

85. John Dewey, "Autocracy Under Cover," *NR* (Aug. 24, 1918):103.

86. John Dewey, *Conditions Among Poles in the United States,* p. 73.

87. Ibid., p. 30.

88. Albert Barnes, "The Paderewski Adventure," *NR* (Jan. 25, 1919):367-69. Irwin Edman, "The Fourth Part of Poland," *N* (Sept. 28, 1918):342-3.

89. See Clarence Karier, "Liberalism and the Quest for Orderly Change," *History of Education Quarterly* (Spring, 1972):57-80. Walter Feinberg, *Reason and Rhetoric: The Intellectual Foundations of 20th Century Liberal Educational Policy* (New York: Wiley, 1975). Charles Zerby, "John Dewey and the Immigrants," *History of Education Quarterly* (Spring, 1975): 67-86.

90. "Japan Is Menacing," *NR* (March 9, 1918):360-1. "The Need for Wilson Diplomacy," *NR* (March 9, 1918):156-8. This article called upon Wilson to substitute the politics of ideas for the politics of military power.

91. *The Outlook* (July 27, 1918):476.

92. "The Worthy Victory," *NR* (May 25, 1918):99. "Economic and Political Unity Among the Allies," *NR* (Sept. 28, 1918):272.

93. Randolph Bourne, "John Dewey's Philosophy," *NR* (March 15, 1915):154.

94. Randolph Bourne, The American Use of German Ideals," *NR* (Sept. 4, 1915):52.

95. Randolph Bourne, "Continental Cultures," *NR* (Jan. 5, 1915):5-6.

96. Christopher Lasch, *The New Radicalism in America* (New York: Vintage Books, 1965): p. 93.

97. Randolph Bourne, "A Moral Equivalent of Universal Military Service," *NR* (July 7, 1916):217-19. Louis Filler mistakenly claimed that the title, "A Moral Equivalent to Universal Military Service," was a satirical imitation of Dewey's "Universal Service and Education." Louis Filler, *Randolph Bourne* (Washington, D.C.: Council of Public Affairs, 1943): p. 148. (Hereafter Filler)

98. Jean Moreau, *Bourne: Legend and Reality* (Washington, D.C.: Public Affairs Press, 1966), p. 135.

99. Ibid., p. 193.

100. *NR* (May 4, 1918):28.

101. Filler, p. 143.

102. Lillian Schlissel, ed. *The World of Randolph Bourne* (New York: Dutton, 1965), p. 317.

103. "Who Willed American Participation," *NR* (April 14, 1917):308.

104. Randolph Bourne, *The War and The Intellectuals* (New York: Harper & Row, 1965), p. 3. (Hereafter Bourne)

105. Lasch, *The New Radicalism in America*, p. 221.

106. Bourne, p. 5.

107. Ibid., p. 59.

108. Van Wyck Brooks, *Letters and Leadership* (New York: B.W. Huebsch, 1918), pp. 112-113.

109. Bourne, p. 5.

110. Ibid., p. 24.

111. Ibid., p. 41.

112. Ibid., p. 54. See also Harold Stearns, *Liberalism in America* (New York: Boni I. Liveright, 1919), p. 182.

113. Lewis Mumford, "The Aftermath of Utopianism," *Christianity and Crisis* (Feb. 10, 1941):2. Charles Howlett claimed that Dewey was transformed by Bourne's critique. This thesis is dubious because (1) Bourne's account was distortive and impressionistic, (2) Dewey never was converted to pacifism. See Charles Howlett, *Troubled Philosopher* (Port Washington, N.Y.: Kennikat Press, 1977), p. 38.

114. George Kennan, *American Diplomacy (1900-1950)* (Chicago: University of Chicago Press, 1951), pp. 57-83. Historian Robert Osgood concluded, "The *New Republic*'s editorial policy during the neutral years was distinguished by its objectivity, its deliberate calmness, and its sense of balance. . . . In fact, throughout the war the editors of the *New Republic* seem to be consciously striving to say nothing that would look foolish in the cold light of reason after the war." Osgood, *Ideals and Self-Interest in American Foreign Policy* (Chicago: University of Chicago Press, 1953), p. 122.

5

The Retrenchment of Liberalism

When news of the Armistice arrived, the *New Republic* applauded the German acceptance of the Fourteen Points, praised Wilson's leadership, but warned that liberal efforts for a just peace were far from consummated. The future treatment of Germany, not a more complete military victory, would determine whether it would again threaten world peace or act as its guarantor.[1] Recriminations would fall primarily on the German working class, whose confidence democracy required. The editors reiterated that exclusive reliance upon force would destroy the fragile liberal coalition in Germany. The result would be either a Junker (i.e., a right-wing military coup) or a Bolshevik revolution. The war had promoted an end to autocracy, the fulfilling of national aspirations, the advance of international morality, and the creation of the League of Nations.[2] While wary of the future, the *New Republic* proclaimed that faith in the possibility of a new international order was one prerequisite for the attainment of these goals.

The editors insisted that Wilson had defined the final terms of the peace so that "no doubt" was left about it.[3] On October 19, 1918, the *New Republic* declared, "our course is in strong hands. When the time comes for the peace conference to convene, American statesmanship will stand resolutely for a peace of international justice as on the day when we entered the war."[4] What if the Allies choose to disregard Wilson's principles? The president had already secured their tacit endorsement. The Fourteen Points provided the whole moral basis for the Allied campaign. If the French, for example, seized the Saar Valley, any future appeals to international morality would be abrogated if the Germans later attempted to redress this inequity.[5] A betrayal by the Allies made their future very insecure. Instead of fighting to annihilate the enemy, Wilson had successfully conducted a liberal war. He declared beforehand his political terms and abandoned fighting as soon as the enemy agreed to those terms. War was finally subordinated to political principle.

The *New Republic* implored all Americans to close ranks behind President Wilson. It endorsed Wilson's call for democratic majorities in Congress in order to reinforce his foreign policy. The Republican Party opposition wanted to treat a demilitarized and democratic Germany identically with a Prussianized Germany. The editors backed Wilson's unprecedented trip to Europe. They encouraged him to speak directly to the peoples of Europe. The true divisions among the Allies were not between governments but between liberals and reactionaries. Wilson's foes had already mettled in the domestic politics of other nations; he was justified in practicing open diplomacy even if it meant discrediting those with whom he was negotiating.[6] Liberalism must be perceived in ruling counsels as the only alternative to the spread of Bolshevism throughout Europe. Wilson had a momentous responsibility, not just to America, but to the whole world.

A week after the Armistice, the *Dial* warned that Wilson was playing a "lone hand."[7] Editors Dewey, Veblen, and Helen Marot, were placed in charge of the journal's war reconstruction program. Dewey suspected that an influential class was manipulating war emotions for private ends. Conservatives who distrusted mob hysteria had utilized it in order to detach the war from its original goals.[8] Instead of a genuine League of Nations, a militant imperialistic nationalism was being cultivated. Centralized governmental control had also created agencies for disseminating propaganda, and the popular press was largely controlled by reactionary forces. This "new paternalism" protected the people from all knowledge that might stimulate social reform. Wilson's democratic idealism corresponded with the instinctive axioms of average Americans.[9] If the people realized how their sacrifices were being misdirected, the resentment would be overwhelming. Dewey predicted that the wartime psychology would not provide a stable basis for settling postwar problems: old conflicts would be renewed if not intensified. The sanguine millennial expectations of wartime were a "compensatory refuge" from surrounding hardships. Such emotions in lieu of trained intelligence were futile. The *New Republic* freely acknowledged the grave danger of a political defeat. By November 30, 1918, the *Dial* concluded that "the possibilities of the formation of any strong liberal public opinion in favor of a real League of Nations are slight."[10]

During the spring of 1918, a group of British and American politicians, educators, and businessmen formed the Committee on American Policy in order to formulate peace terms and to combat the militarists. This committee's approach converged with that of the League to Enforce Peace. The League to Enforce Peace had earlier stressed the prevention of war through judicial processes. They now accepted the necessity of eliminating the economic roots of war. A new organization, the League of Free Nations, was established to promote international federation and to fight for Wilson's Fourteen Points. This group included Norman Angell, Charles Beard, John Dewey, Herbert Croly, Felix Frankfurter, Hamilton Holt, and even Winston Churchill. Both the *Dial* and the *New Republic* endorsed the "victory program" of the League of Free Nations.[11] They supported Wilson but criticized him for not building popular public support for the league.

His administration was held accountable for stifling public discussion through censorship.[12] Wilson's aloof style was killing off support; he must place greater trust in the people.[13] Rather than practicing open diplomacy, the *New Republic* sought, in December 1918, to charge Wilson with not drawing the issue. It urged him to expose the forces of illiberalism. Liberals throughout the world would "bitterly resent" his evasion. Meanwhile, the *Dial* announced that liberals had lost confidence in Wilson's leadership.[14] They would assist Wilson only if he adhered to principle and to effective leadership.

The League of Free Nations' program rested upon two principles: (1) military security and (2) equality of economic opportunity. It sanctioned freedom of exchange, open diplomacy, popular representation for international government, noninterference in Russia, and a harmonious peace.[15] The league defended Wilson against efforts by Theodore Roosevelt, John Knox, and Henry Cabot Lodge to commit the United States to an entangling alliance that guaranteed American support for a peace settlement designed to divide the spoils of victory. Labeling these men the "true defeatists," the *New Republic* held that Wilson's greatest offense to Roosevelt was depriving nationalism of any "class, racial or patriotic exclusiveness."[16] In accepting international control of armaments, abandonment of national rights to military and economic coercion, and to nondiscrimination between league members, the editors believed that unrefined power politics would ultimately destroy democracy.

Both the *New Republic* and the *Dial* opposed Allied intervention in Russia. This policy supplied an additional basis for criticizing Wilson. While intervention in Germany was justified because of its autocratic regime, this Allied adventure seemed designed to starve out Russia. Economic aid and not armed intervention could overthrow the Bolsheviks.[17] These liberal journals castigated Allied propaganda stories about wholesale massacres and anarchy. The reports were not to be taken seriously or the facts were not sufficiently clear to formulate an activist policy.[18] The Allies were forcing the Russian people into the arms of the Bolsheviks by supporting political reaction. The Allies' refusal to back Kerensky's diplomatic effort to end the war in order to check the Bolsheviks was responsible for Lenin's triumph. Separating the Soviets from Bolshevism, the *New Republic* insisted that the Soviet Republic contained the seeds of a democratic experiment that would evolve into a loose federative republic. To force a centralized military bureaucracy upon Russia would imperial the whole of Europe.[19] *New Republic* editors acknowledged that the Bolsheviks were gaining popular support, though they disagreed with the tactics employed. Horace Kallen wanted to neutralize Bolshevism by cooperating with it. He upheld the right of people to choose their own form of government.[20] The *Dial* urged "sympathy and understanding" for Russia. The Russian quagmire signaled both a revolt against continued military cooperation with the Allies and a retreat from democratic internationalism. The promising end to autocracy in Russia, which helped to clarify the war issues for liberals in early 1917, was now mired in ambiguity.

Attempting to rally the citizenry behind the Fourteen Points, Dewey wrote a series of four articles in the *Dial*. Instead of advocating legalistic collective security, Dewey maintained that economic justice was the proper foundation for peace. Equality of economic opportunity did not signify merely free trade or equal access to raw materials. Free competition would perpetuate the natural advantages held by the industrialized nations and thus lead to capitalist exploitation of underdeveloped areas. Dewey proposed a "rough equalization" of economic conditions: rich nations would ultimately benefit when poor nations achieve the capacity to become steady customers.[21] A more stable economic basis for democracy would be established. Though the *New Republic* and the *Dial* stressed cooperation with the British, Dewey did not interpret this to imply a joint control over world commerce.[22] He advocated international commissions with representatives from business and labor, plus economic experts to regulate labor standards, shipping, food, raw materials, immigration, export of capital, and distribution of available credit. The old aristocratic diplomats should be supplanted by those who understood the modern forces of industry and commerce. The dividing line between domestic and foreign policies had become "wholly artificial." After all, German autocracy had brought America into the war. In reconstructing Central Europe, the civil rights of minorities, economic justice, and religious freedom must be guaranteed by an international government with executive and administrative power—otherwise, the region would remain a tinder box. Dewey concluded that "the logic of the situation demands such friendly oversight of the affairs of other states from which worldwide conflagrations might spring as will forestall wars in the future."[23] He conceded that such global planning sounded utopian, but it required no more planning than that which went into the war effort. He prescribed a general direction for policy and not specific blueprints. Dewey carried to its logical limit the implications of international democracy. For peace to be secure, democracy had to flourish world-wide.

While trumpeting Wilsonian idealism, Dewey was extremely apprehensive about the outcome of the war. Publicly, he defended Wilson against his nationalist-militarist critics; privately, by the end of 1918, Dewey conceded that the reactionaries would dictate the peace settlement though America would survive the crisis safely.[24] The more blatantly imperialistic the settlement, the better the opportunity for democratic forces to rebound later. Though some Wilsonian dressing might be expected, Dewey prophesized years of conflict and confusion before a positive peace could be established. Though the common people identified with Wilsonian ideals, the Bourbons controlled policy. The *Dial* insisted also that a small clique ran American foreign policy. It sought the release of conscientious objectors. Dewey's estrangement from the British was indicated by his personal appeal to help Hindus who faced the revocation of their American citizenship due to support for political reforms in India.[25] On January 11, 1919, Herbert Croly reaffirmed Dewey's private skepticism by terming the outlook "not hopeful."

Foreseeing a victory without peace, Croly hoped that the issue would be as unambiguous as possible.[26]

The Versailles Peace Conference convened on January 19, 1919. The *New Republic* resolutely stood by Wilson against the Republican defeatists.[27] The editors thought that the existing peace draft was not a perfect document and required some radical amendments. The settlement should be submitted for public discussion and acceptable revisions could be developed. They criticized Article X, which provided a joint guarantee of political independence and territorial integrity of the member states, not because it circumscribed national sovereignty (as Lodge thought), but because it did not create avenues for resolving the basic economic and social causes of international strife. Legislative as well as executive branches of the participating states should be represented in the league. This proposal would balance reactionary executive power, educate public opinion, and bring international unity to liberal groups. The *New Republic* was not ready to reject the whole plan even if its recommendations were not followed. Though skeptical, the editors awaited the announcement of the boundaries before committing themselves.[28] With the news from Paris, they urged that Article X be defeated. However, the editors attacked the *Nation*'s total opposition to the covenant and still remained hopeful. Despite formidable objections, the *New Republic* maintained that the good faith of the great powers was what ultimately counted. The editors pledged to support a league even if it comprised only the British Empire, France, and the United States. Predatory states, like Italy and Japan, should not be appeased. Returning from a disappointing sojourn in Paris as executive director of the Inquiry Committee, Walter Lippmann reiterated that the fabric of league power centered on Anglo-American control of the seas. Though perhaps incorporating the democratic nations only, the treaty was a foundation to build upon.[29] From Japan, Dewey urged liberals world-wide to render aid to Wilson and the league.[30]

When the final terms of the Treaty of Versailles were announced, the liberals' moment of decision had arrived. The *New Republic* was appalled by the treaty. It seemed designed to destroy the German economy at home and abroad while enhancing the imperialistic power of the victors. After losing one-tenth of its population, one-fifth of its area, and one-fourth of its natural resources, the editors wondered whether Germany could feed itself. Requiring Germany to grant most-favored-nation treatment, while denying reciprocity, rankled the editors' sense of justice. Was Britain merely trying to suppress German industrial competition? Were the French attempting to institute the continental ambitions of Richelieu and Louis XIV? H. N. Brailsford commented that the Versailles Plan rested upon exploiting Germany for a generation. It "murdered hope."[31] France's cynical occupation of the Saar, handing Shantung to Japan, the refusal to admit Germany and Russia into the league, and gross violations of the principle of nationality were completely incompatible with Wilson's Fourteen Points.[32]

Foreshadowing the revisionist conspiracy theory, Herbert Croly blamed capitalism for being the chief culprit at Versailles. Moral ends were subordinated to economic advantage. He proposed industrial democracy as an alternative to either unredeemed capitalism or Bolshevism.[33] The treaty was purely the result of a vengeful class-bound nationalism that would inevitably instigate future wars. Marx's analysis seemed vindicated: liberals would "commit suicide" by endorsing the treaty.[34] Liberalism required the avoidance of irreconcilable class conflict in order to mediate between revolution and reaction. It must synthesize democracy and nationhood. The treaty had to be defeated in order to save Western civilization. Only the radicals gained from the conflict. The seeds of revolution were planted because moral appeals were now reduced to mere propaganda. The *New Republic* called for a "fresh start" in domestic and international politics. Middle-class liberalism should be abandoned for a political party based upon the rise of labor power, like the British Labour Party. They would then possess the potential power to reshape international life. The European governments had made their hypocritical choice and American lives or interests should not be involved. Wilson had surrendered to political opportunism, not idealism. The mating of ideas with power was aborted.

Though the *New Republic* felt betrayed by Allied duplicity, it still abstained from an outright rejection of a League of Nations. However, the Treaty of Versailles was placed on the same level as the Brest-Litovsk Treaty: it could not long survive. The Shantung settlement was described as "Exhibit A" for a treaty rejection. Despite professions of national self-determination, Wilson had sold out the Chinese, an ally, in order to enforce secret treaties and save Japan's participation in the league. The editors maintained that, "Shantung, an issue divorced of all taint of pro-Germanism, has become a symbol for the whole failure at Paris."[35] Wilson should have publicly repudiated the secret treaties by June 1917. He also could have broadened his base of support by including members of both parties in his commission at Paris. Yet, the United States was obligated to assist in the economic restoration of Europe and work for a revision of the treaty. Toward that end, the *New Republic* favored "reserved acceptance" wherein the United States would participate in the league but refuse to underwrite the *status quo*.[36] In response to the debacle of Versailles, this policy was temperate and sophisticated.

Dewey confronted directly the charge that he had been gullible to idealistic cant. Visiting China at the time, Dewey felt the full force of the Chinese revulsion against the Shantung decision. He acknowledged that the defeat of idealistic aims had been "enormous." The doctrinaire pacifists might have some justification for contending that their wartime apotheosis had resulted in self-vindication.[37] However, he reminded his readers that a German victory would have been much worse. The root cause for the defeat of idealism was not the employment of force, but the failure to employ force intelligently. Sentimentally optimistic about the inevitable triumph of righteousness, Americans abandoned the utilization of force to its limit in order to compel a just peace. Wilson appealed moralistically over the heads of state without organizing the people into an effective counterweight. America's economic and financial power should have been utilized to enforce justice. Woodrow Wilson was not ultimately to blame for the disaster; rather it was the complacency and war hysteria of the American people. Though Wilson was vain and self-righteous, Dewey did not employ him as a scapegoat.

The *New Republic*'s desertion of Wilson had been considered a decisive factor in the rejection of the treaty by many historians.[38] The *New Republic* liberals should be distinguished from those of the *Nation,* however. Editor Oswald Villard opposed the war, cultivated pro-German tendencies, and remained a convinced pacifist. He gloated in the Versailles quagmire. Herbert Croly, Walter Lippmann, and John Dewey broke painfully with Wilson after realizing that he would not compromise on the treaty. Wilson had, in fact, deserted them. Throughout the war, the *New Republic* maintained an independent position: the editors' policy of reserved acceptance offered enough room for negotiation so as not to prove decisive in undermining Wilson. Dewey did not harbor utopian dreams that could provide a defense mechanism against taunting pacifist friends. When Wilson did not deliver on his visionary principles, thereby puncturing liberal idealism, Dewey did not turn on him and attempt to destroy Wilson at all costs— even by joining the reactionaries.[39] Rather than despising Wilson, the *New Republic* characterized him as a great prophet but a poor negotiator.[40]

The editors reaffirmed America's responsibilities to Europe. They pleaded for the introduction of amendments to the treaty in an effort to instigate a reassembly.[41] Yet, Senate versions of the treaty were even more stridently nationalistic. With the defeat of the treaty, the editors awaited the emergence of liberal governments in Europe. A positive basis for American entry into the league would then be established. No lasting peace could prevail without American participation. They applauded American relief operations in Europe and long-term loans to rescue Eastern and Central Europe from famine and despair. If America ignored Europe in its hour of need, no one would ever believe that America's lofty wartime ideals were anything but "humbug."[42] The *New Republic* actually boosted Herbert Hoover for president in 1920 due to his relief work. No relapse to traditional American isolationism was advocated.[43]

In July 1920 the journal detailed a foreign policy that would remove America from its directionless drift.[44] First, the Monroe Doctrine should be expanded into a Pan-American system of peace and cooperation free from outside encroachments. Second, the United States should fasten itself diplomatically, economically, and militarily to the British Empire. Instead of minimizing American entanglements, the journal proposed to merge the British and American fleet into a joint world maritime trusteeship. The Versailles treaty could then be reopened for negotiation. (Only the French completely opposed any revision.) Third, the United States should pursue friendship with China, even at the expense of Japan. China's massive population would eventually assert itself as a great power. Fourth, the United States should welcome Russia back into the family of nations. Once relieved of the fear of foreign attack, the Bolsheviks would lose popular support. Peace and trade would revive factionalism in Russia thereby forcing the Bolsheviks to surrender autocratic power and enlist democratic support.[45]

Dewey was in partial agreement with the *New Republic*'s approach. While criticizing Bolshevist absolutism, he argued that if democracy was to have any meaning, the Russian people should be left alone to conduct their own social experiment. Bolshevism would ultimately fail, but much could be learned from the effort. The worst policy would be to construct a rival, capitalist absolutism that would mimic Leninist tactics while either declaring war on Russia or adopting a policy of nonintercourse.[46] Opening up relations with Russia would relieve its suspicions and stimulate gradual liberalization. The nondemocratic policies of France and Britain were not an anomaly but a tradition. After learning of the proposed Anglo-American naval alliance in the *New Republic,* Dewey speculated about its tacit purposes. Would this not strengthen Britain's hold on its Asian colonies, particularly India? Would not the United States be persuaded to block Philippine independence? Should America engage in a special alliance with an imperialist power, when democratic control of its own foreign policy was highly suspect? After witnessing British activities in China first-hand, Dewey opposed any rapprochement. He advised that "in the meantime we should avoid all general commitments, and confine ourselves to the irreducible minimum, and that most specifically stated."[47] America should wary of contamination through contact that could deteriorate the quality of domestic democracy.

Dewey recognized that the United States had to have a foreign policy because domestic and international life had become largely indivisible. Even in the freest of nations, foreign policy was insulated from democratic control. Diplomacy still retained the aura of secrecy, exclusiveness, power madness, and, not the least, stupidity. Americans had to become more knowledgeable about international affairs. Along with the grassroots "Outlawry of War" movement, Dewey sought a level of popular educational enlightenment that could replace elitism with democratic control. The nakedness of imperialist ambitions made public at Versailles had turned out to be an indirect blessing. Americans were revulsed by the subterfuge. Besides national exclusivism, America's basic preference for democracy was largely responsible for the rejection of the league. America did not possess any transcendent virtue among nations; but its nineteenth-century isolation, due to British supremacy on the high seas, had preserved a relative innocence from militarism. European cooperation was premised upon the rise of democratic labor parties. Until popular control emerged, caution and inactivity was the most prudent course.[48]

On January 14, 1920, the *New Republic* began a serialization of John Maynard Keynes's *The Economic Consequences of the Peace.* The editors endorsed Keynes's program for a magnanimous peace, including drastic indemnity reductions plus the cancellation of Allied debts.[49] Keynes's book provided anti-league liberals with compelling arguments against the Versailles Treaty. Throughout the 1920s, Keynes contributed regularly to the *New Republic,* dealing with the politico-economic conditions of Europe. Rather than German writers influencing the American intelligentsia against the league, British liberals were the most effective polemicists.[50] J. A. Hobson, Norman Angell, H. N. Brailsford, and R. H. Tawney maintained intimate ties to the *New Republic* and wrote prolifically in opposition to the treaty. Aligned with the British Labour Party, their suggestions included a substitute for the league through a new international labor organization. Calling for a "year of appeasement," the *New Republic* declared that admission of Germany and Russia into the league was a prerequisite for peace.[51]

After the 1920 elections, the journal formally divorced itself from the league irreconcilables who were attempting to secure an independent privileged position for the United States outside of the family of nations. It endorsed Elihu Root's reservationist proposal to negotiate with the league and allow American participation without becoming a guarantor of the treaty.[52] Not abandoning hopes for league participation, its policy differed radically from Villard's in the *Nation.* Commenting upon Croly's confession that liberalism had been eclipsed, the *Nation* chortled that the death knell of liberalism was sounded when Wilson put America into the war. The *New Republic* boasted about its role in leading the country into war; and for so doing, its discredited reputation was fully deserved.[53] Croly reacted sharply to the *Nation*'s editorial. He charged that no absolute incompatibility existed between liberalism and war; each confrontation had to be judged separately. Though America was not psychologically prepared for war, any position it might settle upon would eventually effect the outcome of the conflict; even neutrality would have proved to be decisive. He reiterated that the *New Republic* had urged intervention but predicated its involvement upon Allied acceptance of American peace plans.[54] Intervention was not a total failure, because there still lingered the possibility of discovering a substitute for war. The permanent historical justification for American entrance would depend upon its open encouragement of international conciliation. Intervention acknowledged the mutual destiny of America and Europe and their joint responsibility for human welfare.

Two years later, the *New Republic* reaffirmed that the United States had an obligation to all of Europe since it bore at least some of the responsibility for Versailles. Great Britain was judged sympathetically, while the editors' attitude toward France darkened to such a point that demonic images of Napoleonism emerged from their prose. French enforcement of the Versailles treaty was compared to the penalty exacted upon Carthage by Rome. The journal proposed that Germany repudiate the treaty in order to bring the conflict to a head.[55] Outside of extermination, their plight could not worsen. With the occupation of the Ruhr, French plans for European

domination became more than figurative: they were engaged in actual warfare against Germany, planning to occupy and dismember it.[56] The editors
contended that, "France does not want to be paid. She knows the value of
gold. But she has a higher value apparently within her reach. It is a pound
of flesh, cut off nearest to the heart."[57] The *New Republic* urged that America and Britain evolve a joint policy to counteract the French. Since France
offered the alternative of either war or collusion, the United States should
withdraw temporarily from Europe. America could force France to abandon its policy by providing moral and financial pressure to allow Europe to
throw off French hegemony. Britain should break immediately with France
by repudiating the treaty.[58] Would moral pressure and the withholding of
credits deter France?

The roles of the participants in World War I had been completely reversed:
Germany was the new Belgium and its helpless moral appeal for the basic
human right of self-determination deserved the support of liberals everywhere. "It is a disarmed Germany which is now carrying on the war to end
war by her foes," exclaimed the *New Republic*. Germany was referred to as
a "European colony." The editors rebuked pacifists for their silence at a
time when one European nation sought to subjugate another. American
aloofness could not guarantee its safety in the next war. While the journal
generally favored disarmament, it looked with horror at what had happened
to such defenseless states as Armenia, Egypt, Morocco, Bulgaria, Austria,
and Germany. It was advisable to keep arms ready-at-hand.[60] Dewey wrote
an appeal for the Emergency Society for German Science and Arts, designed
to enable scholars to carry on their studies amidst the political turmoil.[61]

Throughout the 1920s, pro-leaguists gradually revived their standing
through the dedicated efforts of an influential minority of Wilsonian inter-
nationalists. At the behest of Lloyd George, Lord Robert Cecil traveled to
America in 1923 for the purpose of enlisting America into the league. Despite
the French invasion of the Ruhr, Dewey was alarmed at the rising propaganda for league entrance. According to Selig Adler, in an era when no
issue was firmly resolved for liberals till John Dewey had spoken his mind,
Dewey wrote two articles expressing his opposition to American participation in the League of Nations.[62] He argued that the crucial post-war issues
were not discussed by the league, which was composed of the very governments who had played a part in bringing on the war. With this Dewey indicated that he had accepted the mild revisionist thesis concerning war guilt.
The exclusion of Germany and Russia destroyed any pretense of universal-
ity, transforming the league into a defensive alliance of *status quo* powers.
Europeans, particularly the British and French, were badly split on the
issues; American participation would instigate further divisiveness. Dewey
neglected the possibility that American entrance, along with British cooperation, could apply additional pressure on France to revise the treaty. He
insisted that America had no defined policy. Until specific proposals were
formulated and then accepted by the league as a condition for American

entrance, the United States should not plunge again into the snake-pit of European diplomacy. Confused and disillusioned at home, America had not attained the public sophistication to mold a workable policy. Dewey conceded that Americans were "ignorant, inexperienced, governed by emotion rather than information and insight."[63] Europe would only accept America on its terms. Dewey rejected political cooperation with the old diplomacy, even with the British. He sought a judicial approach through the outlawing of war. Until the people were educated, no policy was preferable to one conceived by a foreign policy elite.

The *New Republic* endorsed Lord Cecil's revisions of the treaty, which sought to remove obstacles to American entrance. Cecil proposed a defensive alliance among European states that would outlaw military operations.[64] The journal presented an international program that could initiate the appeasement of Europe. Neither unconditional adherence to the league nor remaining aloof amidst the crisis were acceptable alternatives. The editors' plan included the abolition of warfare as a legal institution, the creation of an international court, the convening of a conference for settling reparations, the admission of Germany and Russia into the League of Nations, and the creation of a European nonaggression pact that would preclude American military involvement.[65] While Dewey undoubtably agreed with this platform, he was hesitant to enter any compact without popular participation or understanding.

Arthur Lovejoy, both a philosophical and political critic of Dewey, bemoaned the fact that Dewey added his "great name and influence" against the league.[66] Lovejoy contended that all human institutions were imperfect and that the American public was no less mature than other peoples. The crucial question was whether American participation in the league would reduce the chances of war in the future. Dewey replied by insisting that "no thoughtful person" could fail to recognize that the idealistic reasons given for American entrance into the war were not held by the masses of the people either before or after the war nor by our supposed Allies. Hence, the peace was lost and this error should not be repeated. Previously, Dewey was convinced that Americans instinctively identified with Wilsonian international democracy. The motives of groups urging American entrance were suspect. Was it merely to reinforce *status quo* policies? European propagandists who decried American moral indifference should tend to their own garden. Conceding that the league might have some stabilizing effect, Dewey was unable to discover a sufficient reason for joining. Bound to the inequities of Versailles, incapable of coping with major issues that could breed future wars (reparations, the Ruhr, and the Near East), and dominated by predatory Napoleonic French diplomacy, the League of Nations offered America only the opportunity to be a partner-in-crime.

Another consequence of the war was disillusion regarding popular democracy itself. It was an era of Sacco-Vanzetti, the Scopes Trial, H. L. Mencken and Prohibition. Underlying the liberal, middle-class revolt against privilege, an intellectual ultra-conservatism presided, which was founded upon an evangelical quest for doctrinal security. William Jennings Bryan epitomized this condition in his Scopes Trial revolt against science. Dewey hoped to transform this sentimental moralism of the middle class into critical intelligence. This American mediocrity of mind was the fundamental cause of the eclipse of political liberalism and reformism.[67] Liberal faith in the good reason of public opinion had been shaken severely by the war hysteria with its accompanying bigotry and persecution. Propagandists seemed capable of manipulating the gullible masses with relative ease. What should be the relation between public opinion and public policy? When democracy moved from the local to the national level, the sphere of intellectual awareness failed to accommodate the shift. The democratic myth about the omnicompetent citizen and the beneficence of public opinion had broken down. Human perception had become selective and extremely limited: in foreign policy it was ignorant to the point of undermining the dignity of human nature.

Dewey acknowledged that the people lacked an adequate educational background to examine intelligently the outstanding issues of foreign policy. The *New Republic* declared that it was "utopian" to expect an informed public opinion on sophisticated issues confronting the world.[68] Instead, the editors proposed an organization of scholars to assemble facts and present dispassionate recommendations. John Dewey, much more than either Herbert Croly or Walter Lippmann, preferred isolation to sacrificing democratic control.

Walter Lippmann's *Public Opinion* (1922) relentlessly criticized pure democracy. Exploding notions of backwoods intelligence, the book revealed that the people had no idea of their economic self-interest, were entrapped by stereotypes that captured their emotions, and were generally unable to grasp public issues. Lippmann suggested that a trained elite must be constituted for effective government rather than reliance upon spontaneous public opinion. To alleviate mass prejudices, a censorship board could implant scientific conceptions into the public educational program.[69] After offering Lippmann full credit for revealing the fundamental difficulty of democracy, Dewey maintained that public enlightenment should be given preference over the specialized training of officials. Lippmann had exaggerated the importance of political management over the retarded masses. How experts could be held in check was an issue that Lippmann left unanswered.

Lippmann's assault was a challenge to educators to effect more successful means of public education and not a rejection of democracy. The debate over intelligence quotients (I.Q.) also jeopardized certain democratic precepts. George Cutter, president of Colgate University, declared that a low level of intelligence, a median of thirteen years, would not permit democracy. He prescribed a class stratification based upon exhaustive mental testing. No matter what these statistics proved about the intelligence of the average citizen, Dewey claimed that little knowledge could be obtained about the limits of innate intelligence until an educational practice evolves to such an extent that the mental capacities of the students are liberated.[70]

Lippmann's *The Phantom Public* (1925) crystallized the elitist strain in his approach to government. He systematically constricted the means by which the public could involve itself. A few insiders would manage the government and compete for power periodically with another elite group. Dewey projected into Lippmann's approach an effort to decentralize government, since it would be operated by nonelective bureaucratic agencies. Guided by experts possessing the same facts, these autonomous agencies would have synchronizing policies. Lippmann's proposals could be adapted to guild socialism. By reorganizing society along occupational lines, the public could deliberate democratically in matters affecting their daily lives. Dewey charged that Lippmann's debunking of pure democracy was a strawman attack. Utilizing the prohibitionist and Scopes Trial controversies as proof of the dangers of crude, populist democracy, Lippmann actually attacked the beliefs that had their grounding in religion rather than in a theory of democracy. Ignorance, not democracy, was responsible for contemporary attitudes.[71] Dewey's *The Public and Its Problems* (1927) offered an extended defense of democracy against its formidable critics, like Lippmann. Despite the uninformed nature of public opinion, its supremacy was a greater safeguard to democracy than any law, constitution, or rule by experts.

The reaction against various ethnic populations in the United States during and after World War I reached fruition with the passage of the Immigration Act of 1924. The bill severely restricted the immigration of populations who were not northern European. Though admitting that it was illiberal to engage in exclusionary policies, the *New Republic* reasoned that America had a greater obligation to provide the world with a democratic example and cure the domestic problems of poverty and unemployment. A flood of immigrants would merely exacerbate these difficulties.[72] Decrying racism as a "moral prejudice," Dewey held that the most rational factor leading to racial animosity — notwithstanding deep physical, religious, and national differences — was economic.[73] Economic distress was the chief cause of the massive immigration during the nineteenth century. The new immigrants provided a cheap source of labor that threatened the living standards of the rest of the population. Until political nationalism is subdued and the standards of living come roughly into balance, physical contacts between peoples should be strictly limited. Like the necessary restrictions Chinese placed on foreigners, unrestricted immigration only multiplies the effects of racial friction. Only through the slow process of education could these racial fears be minimized. Autocratic and democratic societies existed and their aims, which not only differed but conflicted, fostered a world that could not forever remain "half-slave and half-free" amidst such rival political cultures. However, Dewey adjusted his time-scale for reconciliation so that it covered several generations. Earlier he had hoped that the cataclysmic events of World War I would usher in radical change in just a single generation. Democratic internationalism was clearly on the defensive.

The Sacco-Vanzetti Trial encapsulated the antipathy intellectuals felt toward native American extremism in the twenties. Their suspicions about power in high places were also reinforced. As a member of the Sacco-Vanzetti Defense Committee, Dewey was outraged by the apparent miscarriage of justice perpetrated against these two Italian anarchists. Analyzing the Fuller Advisory Committee Report, he concluded that a retrial was justified. Dewey was convinced that the defendants were persecuted for being foreigners and radicals.[74]

Cynicism about the Versailles treaty was channeled in the direction of debunking idealistic war aims and critically examining the causes of the war. Rebounding from the flag-waving partisanship of the war period, scholars like Charles Beard, Carl Becker, and Harry Elmer Barnes, condemned ultra-nationalist historical literature for contributing to the hostility among nations. Dewey remarked that "the acute nationalism of the present era cannot be accounted for without reckoning with historical writing." Barnes likened his opponents with "know-nothing," patriotic boobs.[75] Sidney Fay's erudite article on the origins of the war, written in 1920 after the Central Powers and Russia had released their diplomatic records, appealed to reform liberals who linked the guilt clause of the Versailles treaty with the reparations issue.[76] When Barnes reviewed a series of war books in the *New Republic,* he specifically intended to move the issue out of the realm of scholarly discourse and into the public forum.[77] Given impetus by Beard's *Economic Origins of the Constitution* (1914), the intellectual temper of the twenties popularized denunciations of existing mores and institutions. The revisionist thesis met with a receptive audience. Many scholars forsook their academic refuges and became public celebrities, including John Dewey.

Both Charles Beard and Harry Elmer Barnes were associates of Dewey during this period. They exemplified the pragmatic technique of focusing scholarly research upon current issues. History is constantly being examined from new perspectives and no issue was finally settled. Barnes published a series of articles in the *Christian Century* focusing on the war issue. He utilized his findings to liquidate the reparations clause.[78] Oswald Villard, H. L. Mencken, and Charles Beard encouraged Barnes's polemical activities. While agreeing that the notion of sole war guilt was a "Sunday school" thesis, Beard was still convinced that American participation had been necessary. Though not categorically precluding intervention, Beard called for a policy based upon the national interest rather than ethnic sentiments. Though not participating directly in the war guilt debate, Dewey endorsed the conclusions of the revisionists. Reviewing Barnes's *World Politics and Modern Civilization* (1930), Dewey concluded, "I know of no better way for an intelligent reader to understand the moving forces in modern international life, and their fundamental bearing upon the significant problems of human destiny, than by becoming acquainted with this book."[79] Barnes attributed the outbreak of the war to four causes: (1) industrial rivalry among capitalists, (2) an imperialist struggle for territory and markets, (3) munitions manufacturers and the arms race, (4) secret alliances and diplomacy. Germany had no special reason to disturb world order, because it was outstripped in armaments but gaining in trade. Dewey accepted all of these explanations except the exoneration of Germany. He deemed Barnes's polemics refreshing and agreed that the "war myth" should be laid to rest.

Selig Adler charged that Dewey became the fountainhead of leftist isolationist thought in the post-war period. Influenced by the tragedy of Versailles, his experience in China, revisionist historians, and his activities on behalf of the "Outlawry of War" movement, Dewey did adopt a skeptical position toward international politics. He stressed nonmilitary, domestic cultural reform through the gradual evolution of public opinion as a vehicle for eventually reordering international life. He sought a reconciliation of peoples, not governments. Though he did not preclude utilizing the existing system as a tool for reform, Dewey was extremely suspicious of any contact. He could hardly be accused of sanctifying gray compromise.

The intellectuals' estrangement from democracy was accompanied by an indictment of America's philistine culture. Though a persistent critic of American society himself, Dewey was accused of acquiescing in the crude materialism and commercialism of American life. His pragmatism was the philosophical expression of this life and replicated all of its deficiencies. Such charges were lodged by native literary critics and harried Europeans who feared that an American invasion of mass standardization would pollute the higher spiritual life. They condemned the bourgeois values of material utility, comfort, and cultural disinterest. This superfluous pursuit of pleasure could not fathom destiny, eternal values, or cultural greatness. Count Keyserling believed that Bolshevist Russia and America were essentially identical since both considered man nothing but an animal. The standard of living was regarded as the highest ideal.[80] Charles Beard wrote satirically:

> The America which Europe's ethereal mortals appear to fear, if not despise, is a land of mass production, mob uniformity, artistic and intellectual passivity, a people dedicated to the pursuit of materialistic ends, such as comfort and luxury, indifferent to morals and values, cold to culture and Kultur, hard and selfish, utilizing religion for practical ends, without capacity for disinterested exaltation, trampling rights under collectivist tyranny, insensible to mystic thought and spiritual joys. Prose against poetry, dollars against sacrifice, calculation against artistic abandon.[81]

While not apologists for American cultural life, Dewey and Beard saw positive potential in the industrial age and the American experiment with democracy.

Lewis Mumford's book, *The Golden Day* (1926), launched a vitriolic attack on Dewey's pragmatism. Since, at bottom, Dewey championed democracy, he was also constrained to accept the mindless mass values of his time. Dewey had embraced technology and the machine age with "the same esthetic faith as Henry Ford." Technology and science became ends in themselves, resulting in the "desiccation and sterilization of the imaginative."[82] Idealizing practical contrivances, gadgets, and creature comforts, Dewey's instrumentalism subordinated technique to value. It assumed that high culture would flourish automatically once all of the material means were provided. Pragmatism lacked vision, a sense of beauty, and a compelling world-view capable of supplying meaning and direction to men's lives. History had proved the insufficiency of pragmatism. It was no longer fashionable among insiders. A new generation searched and explored alternative thinkers who did not neglect the esthetic dimensions of life. Under the inspiration of Randolph Bourne, seminal thinkers like Lewis Mumford, Van Wyck Brooks, and Waldo Frank had broken with Deweyan pragmatism.[83]

Dewey answered Mumford by accusing him of fatuous sloganizing. Mumford attributed to Dewey ideas that the latter had not only never accepted but vigorously rejected.[84] Economic security did provide the necessary foundation for the emergence of a dynamic civilization. However, the economic should not be degraded by exponents of high-brow culture. Dewey insisted that the highest ends of human activity were esthetic and artistic. This spiritual sense of striving toward beauty and truth was universal. Good art at once expresses the highest degree of individuality and mirrors the entire culture. Fixation on the material was truly corruptive. According to Dewey:

> . . . if the economic dominates life, and if the economic order relies chiefly upon the profit motive as distinguished from the motive of professional excellence, i.e. craftsmanship, and from the functional motive of giving a fair return for what is received . . . there is a danger that a part of life which should be subordinate or at least coordinate with other interests may be supreme . . . and when wealth is made the chief, if not sole interest, some of the precious and finer things of life—love, justice, knowledge, beauty—are liable to be displaced.[85]

He sought simultaneously to humanize the industrial process for workers and remove the vicarious pleasure of profit-making by reducing most economic activity to the mere mechanical. Attention could be redirected to artistic-cultural pursuits. With proper planning, modern science could produce material abundance. Fear of privation need not motivate the economic system. Service and use rather than profit-making should be the legitimate ends of business. Dewey consistently pointed out the shortcomings of the capitalist system.

Henry Seidel Canby, editor of the *Saturday Review of Literature,* promoted a feverish debate between the New Mechanists and the New Humanists.[86] Charles Beard insisted that Western civilization rested upon science and invention. He predicted that the Machine Age would expand indefinitely. The failures of the modern era were not due to technology but rather to a reluctance to apply scientific planning systematically. He chastised those who prepared, amidst a depression, to sacrifice the standard of living of the population in order to promote circumstances favorable to the creative arts. Artistic genius certainly could not be mass produced. However, encouraging social mutants and deviants would not guarantee high culture either.[87] Beard reasoned that, "esthetes writing under soft lamps in steamheated studios about the necessity of recovering humanism and religion would be sent scurrying to the nearest forest to gather twigs with which to warm their blue hands."[88] What value did the esthetes cherish that scientists and engineers do not also recommend?

Lewis Mumford responded by accusing the New Mechanists of disintegrating the human spirit through their emphasis upon material progress, behaviorism, and the superiority of activity to contemplation. Science and technology had expanded their domains and threatened to eradicate philosophy, esthetics, and human refinement.[89] Mumford demanded a new ideology that could mold facts according to human wishes. This new religion could transcend naturalism and incorporate the ultimate values of mankind. Irving Babbitt also insisted that Dewey ignored the religious and humanistic dimensions of experience. Babbitt claimed that Dewey would blandly sweep away all of what had passed for civilization, impoverishing the human condition. He concluded, "it is not surprising that he [Dewey] is held in high esteem in the Soviet Union."[90] The New Humanists located in Dewey's philosophy all of the pernicious aspects of modern life that they despised.

The challenge of the New Humanists did not go unanswered. James T. Farrell and Joseph Ratner, two of Dewey's disciples, wrote extended letters to the *Saturday Review of Literature*. Ratner delineated the doctrines that Mumford ascribed to the New Mechanists. They were as follows:

> (1) That our mechanical and industrial world is an independent realm like that of Nature: human needs, human desires and wishes, human standards are secondary and subordinate. (2) The Machine and the world conceived as machine are 'real': the human personality and the products of personality are, for the mechanist, dead, unreal, empty, impotent. (3) Since the New Mechanists by a deep, persistent bias look upon the external physical fact as the abiding reality, . . . the main problem of life, as they see it, consists in the adjustment of human ideas and needs to these moral obdurate externals . . . in adjustment to the dominant physical environment.[91]

Ratner claimed that Dewey never supported any of these positions. He challenged Mumford to supply documentary evidence. It was a challenge Mumford never accepted. After this incident, Mumford would refer vaguely to "pragmatic liberalism" instead of Dewey specifically. Ratner reiterated that Dewey afforded the qualities of human experience a higher metaphysical significance than the empiricist understanding of Nature. Reflection meant for Dewey a remolding of the environment in order to meet human desires, not acquiescence. Dewey termed "a childish animism" the belief that the machine itself was the source of our troubles. These literary critics prided themselves on superior taste, while dreaming of a romantic return to the Middle Ages.[92] Dewey simply could not understand those who objected to an intelligently controlled approach to human problems. Reviewing Mumford's epithet against Dewey, John Childs openly wondered how any "sincere mind" could have so badly mistaken Dewey's position.[93] The publication of Dewey's *Art as Experience* (1934) must have stunned his literary adversaries.

Individualism Old and New (1930) responded specifically to those genteel critics of American civilization who sought escape in the past or in Europe. Instead of individuals regaining their bearings by internal conversion, Dewey emphasized the reconstruction of social and economic life. The industrial revolution should not be reversed. Affluence and mass social organization were compatible with a dynamic culture. During the 1930s, many of pragmatism's critics searched for an unfailing ideological commitment. They were oriented first toward Marxism and then to a zealous crusade for war. At the end of this decade, democracy still confronted a severe challenge. However, Dewey did not retreat in despair. He rejected the Spenglerian dualism between culture and civilization adopted uncritically by so many. Spengler held that the growth of industry, technology, and urban life had torn people from their roots in local folk communities. Technology enforced standardization and mediocrity, slowly draining the spiritual vitality out of human life. Dewey affirmed that technology had the power to relieve man's estate as well as potentially to enslave him. If men examined technique with interest and sympathy, a genuinely humanized democracy could emerge out of industrial civilization. Along with Charles Beard, Dewey endeavored to preserve and extend the unique emancipating values of American civilization.

NOTES

1. "The Surrender of Prussia," *NR* (Oct. 12, 1918):300.
2. "Empires at the Bar of Judgment," *NR* (Oct. 19, 1918):331–32.
3. *NR* (Oct. 26, 1918):356.
4. "Empires at the Bar of Judgment," *NR* (Oct. 19, 1918):331.
5. *NR* (Jan. 18, 1919):324
6. *NR* (Dec. 14, 1918):175.
7. *The Dial* (Oct. 19, 1918):311. The editorial also maligned the fact that liberal opinion was too often associated with anti-war sentiment.
8. John Dewey, "The Cult of the Irrational," *NR* (Nov. 9, 1918):34.
9. John Dewey, "The Post-War Mind," *NR* (Dec. 7, 1918):157–59.
10. *The Dial* (Nov. 30, 1918):497. "America and the League of Free Nations," *NR* (Nov. 30, 1918):116.
11. "League of Free Nations Statement," *NR* (Nov. 30, 1918):116–118. "League of Free Nations Association," *The Dial* (Nov. 30, 1918):493–96. See Ruhl Bartlett, *The League to Enforce Peace* (Chapel Hill: University of North Carolina Press, 1944), pp. 111–112. In 1919 the League to Enforce Peace and the League of Free Nations evolved into the Foreign Policy Association. Dewey was a member of this new group.

12. "Censorship and the Peace Conference," *NR* (Nov. 30, 1918):113–14.

13. "The Lone Hand," *NR* (Jan. 4, 1919):264–7.

14. "The President Relapses," *NR* (Dec. 14, 1918):185. *The Dial* (Dec. 14, 1918):361.

15. "The Issue," *NR* (Dec. 14, 1918):179.

16. "Foes of American Unity," *NR* (Nov. 9, 1918):30. "Exit Royalty," *NR* (Nov. 23, 1918): 87.

17. "Intervention vs. Economic Help to Russia," *NR* (Nov. 9, 1918):312–313. "Withdraw from Russia!" *The Dial* (Dec. 14, 1918):562.

18. *The Dial* (Dec. 14, 1918):527.

19. "Revolution-Reaction in Russia," *NR* (Jan. 4, 1919):267. *The Dial* (Nov. 16, 1918): 387–8.

20. Horace Kallen, "The Crisis Among the Allies," *NR* (Dec. 7, 1918):168.

21. John Dewey, "A League of Nations and Economic Freedom," *The Dial* (Dec. 14, 1918):538.

22. *NR* (Dec. 14, 1918):175. *The Dial* (Dec. 28, 1918):230.

23. John Dewey, "The Fourteen Points and the League of Nations," *The Dial* (Nov. 30, 1918):467.

24. John Dewey to Salmon Levinson (Dec. 30, 1918), Levinson Collection, Joseph Regenstein Library, University of Chicago.

25. John Dewey, "An Appeal to Americans," *The Dial* (Feb. 27, 1919):207.

26. Herbert Croly, "Victory Without Peace," *NR* (Jan. 11, 1919):301–3.

27. "Borah the Fable Maker," *NR* (March 1, 1919):129–32.

28. "Agitation for a League of Nations Without Criticism," *NR* (March 15, 1919):201. *NR* (March 22, 1919):231.

29. "The Treaty Is Ready," *NR* (May 10, 1919):35

30. John Dewey, "Japan and America," *The Dial* (May 17, 1919):501–503.

31. H. N. Brailsford, "An Impression of Germany," *NR* (June 6, 1919):249.

32. "Europe Proposes," *NR* (May 17, 1919):67–71. The *Dial* simultaneously rejected the treaty. *The Dial* (May 17, 1919):511–13.

33. Herbert Croly, "An Obstacle to Peace," *NR* (April 26, 1919):405.

34. "Peace at Any Price," *NR* (May 24, 1919):102. "A Panic Peace," *NR* (May 17, 1919): 72. Walter Weyl, "Prophet and Politician," *NR* (June 7, 1919):173–76.

35. "Exhibit A: Shantung," *NR* (July 30, 1919):407.

36. "A Protest and Some Comments," *NR* (July 1, 1919):327.

37. John Dewey, "The Discrediting of Idealism," *NR* (Oct. 8, 1919):285–87.

38. Selig Adler, *The Isolationist Impulse* (New York: Free Press, 1966), p. 55. Eric Bentley, *Rendezvous with Destiny*, p. 203.

39. Selig Adler, *The Isolationist Impulse*, p. 57.

40. "The Living Ideas of Woodrow Wilson," *NR* (March 17, 1920):73.

41. "The Shirking of Responsibilities," *NR* (Nov. 12, 1919):306.

42. *NR* (Dec. 31, 1919):131.

43. Walter Lippmann, "Assuming We Join," *NR* (Sept. 3, 1919):145.

44. "The Essentials of Anglo-American Understanding," *NR* (Dec. 17, 1920):66.

45. *NR* (Sept. 1, 1920):7.

46. John Dewey, "Social Absolutism," *NR* (Feb. 9, 1921):315–318.

47. John Dewey, "Our National Dilemma," *NR* (March 24, 1920):117–118.

48. Selig Adler, *The Isolationist Impulse*, p. 51.

49. "Europe on the Rack," *NR* (Jan. 21, 1920):213.

50. Both Warren Cohen and Selig Adler agree with this appraisal. Warren Cohen, *The American Revisionists* (Chicago: University of Chicago Press, 1970), p. 40.

51. *NR* (Sept. 24, 1920):111.

52. *NR* (Nov. 3, 1920):229.

53. *N* (Nov. 3, 1920):489.

54. Herbert Croly, "Liberalism vs. War," *NR* (Dec. 8, 1920):37.

55. *NR* (Nov. 8, 1922):267. "Back to Europe," *NR* (Sept. 20, 1922):85. "America's Responsibility," *NR* (July 8, 1926):270-71.

56. "The Nemesis of France," (Sept. 29, 1923):5. *N* (Jan. 1, 1924):184.

57. "France's Pound of Flesh," *NR* (May 16, 1923):309. "Doing Justice to France," *NR* (Feb. 28, 1923):4-5.

58. *NR* (Nov. 21, 1923):321. The editors even suggested a closed security system of English-speaking nations of the British Empire. With one-half of the wealth and one-third of the white population, this collectivity could live unto themselves if necessary. "British Protectionism and Empire," *NR* (Nov. 7, 1923):272.

59. *NR* (March 21, 1923):82.

60. *NR* (May 16, 1923):311. "America and the Next War," *NR* (August 8, 1923):275. Meanwhile, Germans were secretly dodging the provisions of the Versailles treaty by building armaments factories in Russia and establishing tank and flying schools for German and Russian officers. Buying into the Bofors Arms factory in Sweden, Krupps manufactured and designed artillery pieces, anti-aircraft guns, and tanks. Carl von Ossietzsky was later convicted of high treason for exposing this rearmament. At Cooper's Union, Dewey spoke to a mass rally honoring Ossietzsky as a Nobel Prize winner. Sponsored by the International Relief Committee (Dewey being a member), other speakers included Mayor La Guardia and Reinhold Niebuhr. Dewey was a member of the International League of Academic Freedom, which recommended Ossietzsky for the Nobel Prize. *NR* (Dec. 16, 1936):iv.

61. John Dewey, "In Behalf of Culture," *The Freeman* (March 21, 1923):33-34.

62. Selig Adler, *The Isolationist Impulse*, p. 157.

63. Dewey, "Shall We Join the League," *NR* (March 7, 1923):36-37.

64. "Lord Cecil's Visit," *NR* (March 28, 1923):121-3.

65. "An International Program for the American People," *NR* (April 18, 1923):200-201.

66. "Dewey and Lovejoy Letters," *NR* (March 28, 1923):138-40.

67. John Dewey, "The American Intellectual Frontier," *NR* (May 10, 1922):303-305.

68. "Democratic Control of the League," *NR* (Dec. 1, 1920):6-7. Croly, "American Withdrawal from Europe," *NR* (Sept. 12, 1923):67-68.

69. John Dewey, "Review of Lippmann's *Public Opinion*," *NR* (May 5, 1922):286-88.

70. John Dewey, "Mediocrity and Individuality," *NR* (Dec. 6, 1922):35-37. Dewey, "Individuality, Equality and Superiority," *NR* (Dec. 13, 1922):61-63.

71. John Dewey, "Practical Democracy," *NR* (Dec. 2, 1925):52-54.

72. "The Immigrant Flood," *NR* (Dec. 12, 1922):59.

73. John Dewey, "Racial Prejudice and Friction," *The Chinese Social and Political Science Review* (1922):14.

74. John Dewey, "Psychology and Justice," *NR* (Nov. 23, 1927):9-12. Evidence today points toward the guilt of Sacco and Vanzetti. One suspects that the issue, like the Hiss case, will never be satisfactorily resolved for some partisans. See David Felix, *Protest: Sacco-Vanzetti and the Intellectuals* (Bloomington: Indiana University Press, 1965), p. 166. Robert K. Montgomery, *Sacco-Vanzetti: The Murder and the Myth* (New York: Devin-Adair Co., 1961).

75. John Dewey, *Logic: The Theory of Inquiry* (New York: Henry Holt & Co., 1938), p. 236. Harry Elmer Barnes, "History and International Good-Will," *N* (March 1, 1922):251-54.

76. Sidney Fay, "New Light on the Origins of the World War," *American Historical Review* (1920):619-639. *NR* (March 22, 1921):322.

77. Harry Elmer Barnes, "Seven Books of History Against the Germans," *NR* (March 19, 1924):10-15. Barnes, "Assuming the Blame for the War," *Current History* (1924):171-195," Barnes, "The New History," *American Mercury* (May, 1925):68-76. Oswald Villard, "Historians and Truth," *N* (May 21, 1924):576.

78. "Professor Barnes on War Origins," *Christian Century* (Oct. 8, 1925):231. (Hereafter *CC*) Charles Beard, "Heroes and Villains of the World War," *Current History* (1926):735.

79. John Dewey, "The Course of Modern History," *World Tomorrow* (Dec., 1930):522-23. (Hereafter *WT*)

80. Count Keyserling, "The Animal Ideal in America," *Harpers* (August, 1929):265-76.

81. Charles Beard, *Harpers* (Dec. 1928–May, 1929):470.

82. Lewis Mumford, "The Pragmatic Acquiescence," *NR* (Jan. 5, 1927):182.

83. In a letter to Van Wyck Brooks, Mumford expressed personal delight in how he had punctured those "smug and obtuse" pragmatists. George Spiller, ed., *The Van Wyck Brooks— Lewis Mumford Letters, 1921–1963* (New York: Dutton, 1970), p. 45. Max Otto wrote Dewey that he was depressed for days after reading Mumford's conscious distortion of Dewey's ideas. Max Otto—John Dewey (Oct. 22, 1928), Max Otto Papers, The State Historical Society of Wisconsin, Madison, Wisconsin.

84. John Dewey, "The Pragmatist Acquiescence," *NR* (Jan. 5, 1927):186–89.

85. John Dewey and James Tufts, *Ethics* (revised edition) (New York: Holt, 1932), pp. 487– 88. John Dewey, "Industry and Motives," *WT* (Dec., 1922):357–8.

86. Walter Lippmann, "Humanism as Dogma," *NR* (March 15, 1930):817–818. Kenneth Saunders, "Analyzing Mr. Lippmann," *Saturday Review of Literature* (March 22, 1930):854. (Hereafter *SRL*)

87. Charles Beard, *Whither Mankind* (New York: Longmans, Gran & Co., 1928), p. 21.

88. Charles Beard, "Toward Civilization," *SRL* (April 5, 1930):844–45.

89. Lewis Mumford, "A Modern Synthesis," *SRL* (April 12, 1930):920.

90. Irving Babbitt, "Experience as Dogma," *SRL* (Nov. 1, 1930):281.

91. Joseph Ratner, "John Dewey's Philosophy," *SRL* (July 12, 1930):1194.

92. *ION,* p. 97.

93. John Childs, *Education and the Philosophy of Experimentalism* (New York: Century Co., 1931), p. 240. See Sidney Hook, "John Dewey and His Critics," (June 2, 1931): 73–74.

6

John Dewey and the Far East

Dewey departed the United States on January 22, 1919, to begin a venture in the Far East that would last more than two years. As an unofficial ambassador of American democracy, his attention was focused primarily upon the difficulties of political transformation in third world countries. For the rest of his life, he was to retain an active interest in Chinese affairs. Indeed, Dewey's visit attracted considerable notice among Chinese students and teachers. Led by disciples like Hu Shih, a movement for liberalism was energized both by Dewey's presence and by the views he expressed. In the midst of a crisis-riddled China ruled by warlords, the adequacy of pragmatic liberalism was to be severely tested.

Upon his arrival in Japan, Dewey began a lecture tour sponsored by Baron Eiichi, a Japanese philanthropist and industrialist. The lectures were later organized into a book entitled *Reconstruction in Philosophy* (1920). Dewey never revealed the source of his curiosity about the Orient, although he did mention that this would probably be his last opportunity to travel in this part of the world.[1] Herbert Croly and Walter Lippmann, as well as the *New Republic*'s owner, Willard Straight, stressed the crucial role of China in the future of the world. Dewey believed that the conditions for another cataclysmic war were embedded in the Chinese political crisis.[2] What were the possibilities for democracy and a peaceful settlement of the conflict? What should be the American role in the Far East? Such questions must have concerned Dewey as he announced his intention to confer with Japanese leaders and to relay his impressions back to the *New Republic* and the *Dial*.

Dewey observed that the victory of democracy in World War I had temporarily discredited Japan's militaristic clique, which had idealized Germany's style of government. Liberalism and democracy were in the air, particularly on university campuses. These liberal Japanese groups must triumph if peace was to be attained in the region. In his lectures, Dewey reiterated that German statism had been eclipsed by the war. He anticipated the emergence of a transnational mind that could comprehend the movement of modern scientific and economic forces. The destiny of any one state was indissolubly linked to the rest of the world. According to Dewey: "weakness, disorder, false principles on the part of any state are not confined within its boundaries. They spread and affect other states."[3] He still espoused an activist-interventionist internationalism. Japan's progress toward democracy depended upon the behavior of other nations, particularly the United States. Through April 1919, Dewey pledged support for a genuine League of Nations. Every cynical attack upon Wilsonian ideals and every outburst of racial prejudice reinforced the "waning cause" of bureaucratic-militarism in Japan. The Japanese were wary of Anglo-American economic domination; Americans had to maintain a purity of purpose. Dewey expressed sympathy for the Japanese people, separating their customs from the regime itself. After arriving in China, his feelings about Japan darkened.

What were the prospects for political liberalism in Japan? Dewey detected an impossible dualism between a westernized technology and an essentially feudal social structure upon which it was grafted. The strains of industrialism served to dislocate Japanese traditions and for that reason could conceivably promote political liberalism. Like Imperial Germany, modernization offered no guarantee of democratic evolution. The government stifled open political discussion, the press disseminated nativistic propaganda, and the Shintoist emperor cult clothed the politics of industrial-military clique with a theological sanction. Criticism easily became associated with disloyalty. Liberal influences were further stymied by the Versailles treaty, which Dewey depicted by November 1919 as an "imperialistic settlement." The refusal of the Western nations to endorse the principle of national equality opened deep wounds, which Japanese propagandists cleverly exploited. Even Japanese liberals believed that military might alone saved Japan from colonial status. Irresistibly, a Pan-Asian doctrine emerged with Japan cast as a redeemer, protecting Korea and China from European imperialism. Despite Dewey's recognition of the reactionary power in Japan, he seemed confident that the nation would evolve peacefully toward democracy.[4] Circulating among liberal academics, Dewey undoubtably exaggerated liberalism's actual strength. This contributed to his approach being misdirected within the context of the Far Eastern crisis.

Three days after his ship docked in China, the May Fourth Movement shook the country's political foundations. During World War I, Japan utilized its free hand in the Far East to encroach upon a China that had been torn by civil war. This aggression was climaxed by the infamous Twenty-One Demands. In a series of treaties with the Allies, Japan stabilized its control over Manchuria and obtained rights to the German concession at Shantung. The Japanese sought formal recognition of their advances at Versailles. The American ambassador to China, Paul Reinsch, committed the United States to returning Shantung to China after the war. Despite Wilson's professions about self-determination, he finally capitulated. An ally was abandoned in order to obtain Japanese participation in the League of Nations. Reinsch resigned in agony. The Shantung settlement crystallized liberal opposition to Wilson in the United States. Receiving the news from Paris, Chinese students took to the streets by the thousands in an appeal to the Chinese delegation not to ratify the treaty. Their faith in American support and Wilsonian idealism had been strained irreparably. The Chinese interpreted this outcome as proof that force still ruled in foreign affairs.[5] Dewey derided America's "completely futile" policy. If the Senate failed to reject the Versailles treaty, China would be abandoned to Japan.

During the May Fourth uprising, students organized a general strike and, with the aid of local merchants, they boycotted Japanese goods. A number of students were arrested but they were released shortly thereafter due to overwhelming public pressure. The Chinese delegation did refuse to ratify the treaty. These events illustrate how the moral force of public opinion ultimately deposed the corrupt Anfu government, which had initially favored signing the treaty. Dewey credited the student movement with awakening China from its passivity. The popular belief that China could be saved only by outside intervention was undermined. Inverting the politics of World War I, Dewey witnessed how the general strike, the boycott, and other nonmilitary tactics could institute change from outside the political system.

Though the student revolt had specifically targeted the militant clique in Peking, it also reflected a more pervasive discontent with the antiquated traditions of Confucianism. The May Fourth protest inaugurated the New Culture Movement, which endeavored to regenerate and modernize China. Identifying himself with this cause, Dewey's lectures prompted spirited discussions on the merits of science and democracy. Hu Shih revolted against Confucianism by initiating a large outpouring of literature in the people's vernacular. Young China professed education as the exclusive device for social reconstruction.[6] They recognized that the West's supremacy rested on a method of investigation and not on specific institutions. The scientific method offered an instrument for debunking antiquated Chinese traditions. Young China was resolutely dedicated to the nonpolitical approach. Democratic transformations would transpire in education and industry first. Basic cultural habits could be reoriented, while the people observed a policy of strict nonintercourse with the corrupt warlords.

The New Culture Movement, representing a synthesis of East and West, was China's finest hope for the future, according to Dewey. While Japan modernized through centralized political control, China's slow assimilation of Western influence permitted a structure of reform built upon voluntary persuasion. In an effort to reconcile Chinese customs with empirical scientific methodology, Dewey's followers wrote lengthy theses designed to provide philosophical bridges to the past. In this way, the Chinese sense of inferiority would be eased. Dewey insisted that there was something permanently valuable in Chinese civilization, something that ought to be preserved even if it required continued chaos. He admired the patience of the Chinese, their aversion to the struggle for political might, and their belief in the continuity between man and nature. China embodied more of a civilization than a nation. Its patriotism centered on the soil rather than the state. Dewey proclaimed that China possessed a nonparliamentary "democratic spirit" that could eventually transcend the militaristic nation-state system of the West and offer an advanced model of the democratic way of life for the entire world. He clearly overstated the appetite of Chinese students for an incremental approach in the midst of political chaos.

Dewey granted that the Chinese liberals were only a vanguard. Their legitimacy was secured because they manifested the unconscious sentiments of the Chinese people. However, the liberals were advised not to assume a leadership role as a disciplined political cadre. Dewey resolved that only in a crisis could a small minority possess the capacity to dominate.[7] Was China not already enmeshed in just such a crisis? Dewey voiced faith that each new upheaval would bring the country closer to civilian supremacy. Disgust with military despotism was firmly rooted in the Chinese character. Trusting in the prospective blossoming of the newly educated generation, Dewey consoled his supporters that they could hardly expect an early victory. Emphasis should be directed to educating the Chinese people in the "meaning of democracy."[8] He conceded that democracy necessitated a basic consensus of values and that this consensus, unconscious sentiments notwithstanding, did not exist in China. Dewey stated clearly the dilemma that "although gradual political reform was possible only through cultural reform, cultural reform could not progress until there was political reform."[9] His educational-missionary approach to social progress demanded political stability to ensure continuity.

He was horrified by the chaotic conditions of a China ruled by warlords. Over sixty percent of that nation's income was being consumed by the military. For example, Dewey related the story of one warlord who shut down the schools in his region for a year in order to supply weapons for his troops. These military leaders would accept bribes from any country, including Japan, if by doing so they could widen their individual spheres of oppression. Collusion with foreign powers seemed more acceptable than cooperation with their countrymen. Disillusioned by the passivity of the Chinese people toward such graft, Dewey confessed that the Japanese could hardly be blamed for desiring to run a country that refused to rule itself. China was not a republic; it was a decadent remnant of the old Manchu bureaucracy. In the midst of this stagnation, even well-informed Chinese were waiting for a war between Japan and America to extricate them. The mind of China was being militarized: military training in the colleges was enthusiastically supported by students as relevant education. As a final blow, the Boy Scouts of Shanghai sought formal enlistment as a military unit. Students often asked Dewey why China should not adopt militarism as part of its educational curriculum, especially since events had clearly demonstrated that strong countries often enforce their will upon the weak.

Dewey advised that there could be no compromise with militarism. Yet, brute physical security is the first priority of any social system. How could liberalism triumph without political leverage?

Dewey proposed a federalist model for China. Nonpolitical reform could begin at the grassroots level with the village people and then expand outward. The local guilds might function as the central political unit. Arbitration by village discussion and the activity of local guilds corresponded closely with Dewey's idealistic guild socialism. The country could be unified gradually and noncoercively by the people themselves. From 1920 to 1923 the federalist movement obtained substantial backing, including important social figures like Hu Shih and Sun Yat-sen. Relying upon strong provincial particularism, Western-oriented federalists supported decentralization in order to place more control in the hands of the people, to undermine the power of the warlords, and to facilitate economic development. However, democratic proposals on paper merely reinforced the reactionary warlords; they manipulated the parliaments and used the rhetoric of federalism to legitimatize their independence from Peking. Dewey recognized this danger but offered no political remedy. By proposing a divided China, Dewey tacitly defended the "republican" regime of south China. The United States should reject any diplomatic move toward restoration of a monarchy in the Peking government. Furthermore, a harsh policy of insisting upon the payment of loans and interest would force Peking to disband its army and to engage in a general retrenchment. Threatening to withdraw recognition unless these demands were met would render impossible any new military expedition to reconquer the south.

By 1923 the federalist movement was in both disarray and disrepute.[10] While Hu Shih and Dewey argued that federalism was the best weapon against the warlords, these military leaders were the very individuals who controlled the federalist provinces. This contradiction prompted Ch'en Tu-hsiu, a Marxist-Leninist, to attack Hu Shih and the entire federalist approach. Sun Yat-sen also discarded federalism, which was never more than an expedient for him anyway. Sun turned Dewey's political program completely on its head. He advocated political centralism and elite control of the revolution. Unification could not come about through utopian, voluntary association; only armed might would assure it. China was obliged to undergo a period of political tutelage. With the friendly encouragement of Soviet advisors, Sun reorganized the Kuomintang Party as a mass movement utilizing both ideology and power. Hu Shih rejected all "isms," branding appeals to ideology as utopian delusions. Yet, the school that actually trained the future leaders of Asia was none other than the Whampoa Military Academy. Chiang Kai-shek, Chou En-lai, Mao Tse-tung, and Ho Chi-minh congregated at this Soviet sponsored school during the 1920s.

Dewey had initially warned that the chances for a Bolshevized China were "fifty-fifty," with Japanese domination as the other possible outcome. By December 1920, however, he downplayed the threat of a Red menace in a State Department report.[11] In a report to Walter Drysdale, military attache in Peking, Dewey held that no signs of Bolshevik intrigue existed. This shift was indicative of his "hands-off" isolationist policy. Dewey consistently opposed Marxist doctrine in his lectures. Marxism was inappropriate for Chinese peasant society and contained an inflexible dogma. Opposing Japanese claims that Bolsheviks controlled the student movement, he defended the students as "democratic socialists." In March 1920 the Soviet Union's "Karahkar Manifesto" announced its intention to return to the Chinese the Eastern Railway and other concessions without requiring any compensation. This action advanced the Soviet's anti-imperialist image in China. During the 1920s, a central academic debate focused on the alternative paths of Marxism and pragmatism. Marxism-Leninism provided some Chinese radicals with ideological fervor, revolutionary discipline, and a concrete program of action.

In addition to a federalist approach to China's internal development, Dewey's foreign policy proposals shifted from a recognition of international supervision to a noninterference policy. Had a genuine League of Nations existed, it might have provided an ideal instrument for removing Japan and overthrowing the military clique in Peking.[12] In 1919, Dewey warned Americans not to forget Japan's deceit over Shantung. What decisive action could the United States adopt? Dewey proposed the following set of alternatives:

> I didn't ever expect to be a jingo, but either the United States ought to wash its hands entirely of the Far Eastern question and say it's none of our business, fix it up any way you like, or else it ought to be as positive and aggressive in calling Japan to account for every aggressive move she makes, as Japan is in doing them. . . . Met by force, she would back down. I don't mean military force, but definitely positive statements about what she couldn't do . . . that she knew we meant business.[13]

Would harshly worded statements deter the Japanese any more than they had thwarted the Germans in Belgium?

Dewey admitted that Japan's political growth had been the product of war. He spoke of Japanese torture in China, her corrupt bargaining with Chinese traitors, and collusion between the Japanese military and its industry. He also conceded that Japan and Russia would have partitioned northern China long ago had it not been for the British fleet. Japan's actions were carefully calculated to absorb as much as possible without instigating a war among the Great Powers. Yet, Dewey reasoned that if Japan was to advance in Asia it "needed the moral support" of the United States.[14] Likewise, the *New Republic* explained that, more than anything else, the Japanese dreaded losing the friendship and esteem of the Americans and the Europeans. A nonrecognition policy would drain their spirit.[15] In order for Japan to return to the good graces of America, Dewey suggested that it unilaterally withdraw from Shantung and support a genuine, not a Manchurian, Open Door policy. After World War I, the advocacy of military force among liberals became nearly an absolute taboo. Dewey tended to couple injunctions of moral pressure with a discomforting recognition that such appeals were impotent.

At Versailles it became apparent that no great power demonstrated vital concern about saving China. Not one would fight to defend China's integrity. The *New Republic* editors called for Japan to forsake its aggressive policy and unite with other powers to build Chinese nationhood. They condemned any effort to coerce Japan by threatening her with rearmament. That policy would breed Japanese resentment since veiled threats intensified all of the psychological and moral causes of war. The real strength of American policy was rooted in its "decency, order, and peacefulness."[16] The source of the Asian conflict was economic: Japan needed access to raw materials, and Dewey presumed that the Japanese could be pacified by an international guarantee of coal and iron supplies for its burgeoning population. In 1936, Japan actually adopted a pro-natalist policy to augment its war potential. Dewey sought to temper the war hysteria by claiming that a deliberate Japanese war against the United States was "unthinkable." Individuals might commit *hari kari* but no nation would undertake a military posture that could result in its total destruction.[17] Japan's program of divide and conquer was "immeasurably stupid"; these tactics could not last for more than fifty years before Japan would be driven out. Dewey neglected to realize that politics rarely involves such distant calculations. Japan might consider fifty years of dominance well worth the price it would have to pay in blood and treasure.

Initially, Dewey maintained that a withdrawal of active American interest would merely serve up China to the aggressive powers.[18] Enlightened American investment could help place China back on its feet. In December 1919, Dewey stated that "clearly, an international consortium which should loan money to China in bulk without assigning the return of spectacular concessions and spheres of influence is the obvious solution."[19] This arrangement was not inspired by bankers but by the United States government in order to maintain the Open Door policy, to stunt political corruption, and to secure the eventual political integrity of China. No intelligent person, Dewey remarked, could realistically expect financial reform to emerge from within the country. China was a "rotten carcass" jeopardizing the peace of the world. Hu Shih also sanctioned the consortium because it sought to assist Chinese development by breaking the futile cycle of warlord factionalism and foreign intrigue. Since the United States was relatively innocent of aggression against China, it could act as mediator and thereby protect China against foreign exploitation.

Dewey returned from China in July 1921, but his attention continued to be focused on the Far East as the Washington Conference convened. He drafted a series of articles about the conference which were published in both the *New Republic* and the *Baltimore Sun*. Dewey believed that the United States ought to be the spokesman for China in relation to the Great

Powers. America must tailor a settlement not only to prevent entanglements with European imperialism but also to avoid the risk of an anti-American alliance developing in the Far East. Dewey specifically rejected any suggestion that America should engage in active military intervention. "Apart from the question of how far war can now settle any fundamental issues without begetting others as dangerous," he cautioned, "China of all countries is the one where settlement by force, especially outside force, is least applicable, and most likely to be enormously disserviceable."[20] A successful war would leave untouched the basic problems of education, industrial backwardness, and political immaturity. Again, Dewey ranked cultural change over political order; moral suasion enjoyed more compulsive power than physical coercion.

Having previously contended that an international consortium had assisted China's movement toward democracy, Dewey now worried that it could become excessively paternalistic. The consortium's role should be sharply restricted. On a temporary basis outside aid might be advisable, but in the long run China had to save herself. The United States should be patient and persistent in offering China a chance to obtain the needed time for gradual internal development. Dewey rejected H. N. Brailsford's proposal of an international syndicate, comprised of the United States and Britain, to manage China's economy.[21] This syndicate could also ration raw materials to Japan in return for her good behavior. Brailsford defended this frankly capitalistic collusion as the "lesser of evils." Dewey, on the other hand, was skeptical of its benevolence: (1) China was treated too much as a helpless patient; (2) Russia was left out entirely; and (3) it endeavored to conduct state-to-state relations without accommodating the volatile factional feuding within China. He discarded the radicals' allegation that the Washington Conference was actually convened in order to unify American and British high finance. However, he suspected that this collective action might throw China into the arms of Japan or Russia. The educated Chinese feared uncontrolled industrial expansion. A centralized state, a socially obligatory component of industrialization, would trample local autonomy and self-government. Dewey did not want to set Western industrialism loose in China before the Chinese had attained the maturity to deal with the forces that would be released. Implementation of an incremental cooperative plan could circumvent the dislocations of nineteenth-century European capitalism.[22] Unfortunately, other nations concocted ambitious plans for the modernization of China.

The Washington Conference symbolized for many an idealistic alternative to the avaricious diplomacy of Versailles. Dewey sensed the emergence of a worldwide liberal social consciousness activated by this event. The educative effect of the conference, rather than its military aspect, might be its most durable significance. Elihu Root proclaimed Four Principles for China to which all parties eventually agreed.[23] The crucial issue for Dewey was whether these principles merely acceded in the status quo or were they intended to provide the foundation for a just future settlement. Indeed, the provisions for China's administrative integrity and its equality of trade opportunity (Open Door) were difficult to reconcile with the status quo. However, did Root's principles create the conditions for enforcing all treaties and commitments against China? Dewey proposed that a permanent commission with popular representation and open publicity be created to arbitrate these conflicts. Nations could then cooperate intelligently without military alliances.[24] The Great Powers should regulate themselves first. Dewey advocated that all monopolistic contracts be declared null and void, that loans for military purposes be outlawed, that a temporary government subsidy be created for the consortium, and that the power of tariff control be returned to China. In fact, he entertained the idea of a total embargo on foreign loans as a means to force China to rely on its own resources.

After the Four Power Pact was signed, Dewey noted its accomplishments: the pact set a precedent for consultation, ended the Anglo-Japanese alliance, rendered war less likely between the United States and Japan, and indirectly offered hope to China by not officially acquiescing in the status quo on the Asian mainland. Japan had been spending one-half of its total revenues on military provisions. By limiting the naval arms race, the treaty enabled Japan to maintain its relative strength at less cost. Dewey contended that if the United States had unilaterally reduced its naval program, public pressure and economic necessity would have constrained Japan to follow suit. The *New Republic* viewed the treaty as having removed national defense as an excuse for Japanese militarism.[25] Could world opinion actually harness Japan? Dewey had apparently become victimized by the American sentimental belief in the inevitable triumph of righteousness. The central motive behind Dewey's policy was to reinforce liberalism in Japan in the hope that Sino-Japanese friendship could blossom. The United States must not compromise principle with Japan in order to secure a part of China.[26]

Dewey warned against expecting too much as a result of the Washington Conference. The Four Power Pact left both China and Russia out of account; the treaty should be amended to afford Russia equal representation in the Far East committee. Dewey sympathized with Senator Borah's contention that the treaty would require a collective security arrangement with Japan. The Four Power Pact did entail a pledge not to use force against Japan, or to intervene on the mainland; however, this clause served to restrict America's ability to guard against Japanese encroachments. The Japanese army was bolstered because it was not limited in any way by disarmament proposals. Japan was to be restrained only by the moral pressure of the Western powers. Was peace at Washington purchased by jettisoning the Open Door policy?[27] The *New Republic* recognized that the British would not aid the United States in China. American concern might also fade into disinterest. Pressure for revisions must come primarily from the Chinese themselves. Through the use of the boycott and noncooperation with Japan, China was left with no alternative but to make a sufficient nuisance of itself that Japan would abandon its imperial adventure.[28] Was this what Dewey meant by leaving China to its own resources?

Dewey's skepticism about the prospects for international cooperation intensified during the 1920s. The sources of conflict between East and West emanated from deep-seated cultural and philosophical misunderstandings. A lasting union of nations could not be grounded on economics alone; it required a moral and intellectual foundation as well. Dewey acknowledged that "the simple fact of the case is that at present the world is not sufficiently civilized to permit close contact of peoples from widely different cultures without deplorable consequences."[29] The advance of technology had enforced a physical contact for which people were unprepared, producing another cultural lag. Though he loathed the hostility fomented by the Immigration Act of 1924, Dewey supported restrictions on immigration. A truly international mind must be nurtured very slowly. The world required "rest and recuperation." By 1922, Dewey advised economic and political disengagement from China, although cultural and educational contacts should be continued and strengthened. China must be left alone to solve her own problems.

After the Washington Conference, the feuding among anarchic warlords continued unabated. Wu Pei-fu (an alcoholic), favored by Dewey and the *New Republic,* assumed control over Peking and announced plans for Chinese reunification with a constitutional convention. The editors endorsed Wu, reasoning that his regime might liberalize China. China was roughly divided into three geopolitical sections: the north, led by Chiang Tso-lin, who the editors labeled as a reactionary, a terrorist, and pro-Japanese; the center, held by Wu; and the south, nominally ruled by Sun Yat-sen.[30] The crafty Sun had previously allied himself with the despised Anfu Club in his obsession to regain the presidency. Dewey accused Sun of being aided by Japan and deemed him a "ridiculous figure" who exemplified a desire for vengeful militarism rather than democratic self-determination. Sun seemed more concerned with removing foreigners than tackling concrete problems. The *New Republic* concluded that he could not become a serious factor in Chinese politics. He was a historical anachronism. His obstructionist tactics and outmoded parliamentarianism had pulled the weight of Chinese opinion (liberal opinion) solidly against him.[31]

Nationalism was a primitive impulse. But how could a nation be built without it? Acknowledging that Sun had gained the sympathy of many Americans, the *New Republic* maintained that the transformation of China into a Western-style democracy was unpopular with both Chinese leaders and the masses.[32] The cost of any American intervention would be prohibitive. The United States should back the Young China Movement, supplying books not guns. Influenced by social democratic ideas of reform without class struggle, Sun received little more than sentimental sympathy from the West. The *New Republic* defended British efforts to force Sun to send customs revenue to the Peking government even though a civil war raged. The money would be utilized to conduct a military campaign against the Kuomintang.[33]

Sun Yat-sen found a willing partner in the Soviet Union in January 1923. The Soviets approved a popular front alliance with bourgeois republican elements as a means to overthrow feudalism and colonialist imperialism. The Russians sent Michael Borodin, a skilled communist agent, to reorganize the Kuomintang on a Leninist model and deliver economic and military aid. Gaining support from labor and peasant groups through its disciplined propaganda efforts, the Kuomintang consolidated its following in south China. While Russia advanced, the *New Republic* claimed that if American troops intervened, a civil war would evolve into an anti-foreign war. The party accepting American aid would commit suicide. What about covert aid? The editors admitted despairingly that a dictated peace was the only possibility until a strong civilian regime emerged. The United States should stand aside and let China go her own way no matter how politically inadequate she appeared.[34] Meanwhile, with shiploads of Russian arms and with Soviet advisors to train them, the Kuomintang had risen from the political depths. It was offered membership in a coalition government by the warlords who deposed Wu in October 1924, but this arrangement failed to materialize. When Sun died on March 12, 1925, the *New Republic* anticipated that his death would disintegrate the Kuomintang since Sun's personality rather than any one idea had been its unifying force.[35] Events would again overtake the journal.

On May 30, 1925, an anti-foreign demonstration began in Shanghai. It effectively transformed into a general strike, a boycott, and eventually culminated in violent clashes with foreign troops. As the cries for militancy rose, pro-Western reformers were estranged from the nativistic emotional current running throughout China. The communist left-wing of the Kuomintang, downplaying Bolshevism but emphasizing anti-imperialism, gained appreciable power within the party and in the entire country. The *New Republic* conceded that Moscow planned a concerted campaign to spread communism in China but termed the Red scare "a bogeyman." A "miracle" was necessary for an agrarian country like China to find abstract Marxist doctrine useful.[36] Similarly, Dewey was disgusted by a climate of fear and suspicion in which "silly stories" about Bolshevizing China and a conflict between colored and white races circulated in the shadows. Writing in the pacifist *World Tomorrow,* Dewey expressed alarm over wild propaganda about a war with Japan. Earlier, this journal of the Fellowship of Reconciliation printed an article entitled "Our Friends the Japanese." Pro-Chinese sympathy could easily be translated into demands for American military pressure on Japan.

Even though Dewey commended American paternalism and the Open Door policy, the rise of Chinese nationalism convinced him that such a parental role had clearly outlived its efficacy.[37] America's relations with China were primarily cultural, offering a democratic example to be emulated. In its place, he proposed a "hands-off" policy in which China would be treated as an equal among nations. As a symbol of good faith, the United States should immediately abrogate all special treaties, like extraterritoriality and tariff autonomy. The Chinese must be given no more reason to continue their habitual tactic of blaming foreigners for all of their problems. Instead of maintaining its position as one of the Great Powers pursuing a joint policy in China, the United States ought to remain independent and thereby avoid collusion. The Chinese sought a radical break with the past. The pecuniary interests of manufacturers and merchants should not be promoted by American policy. A policy of nonintervention might not be benevolent, but Dewey maintained that no nation was "at present wise enough or good enough to act upon the assumption of altruism and benevolence toward other nations."[38] Amidst a gross misunderstanding and hostility, mutual cooperation could only proceed very deliberately.

During the spring of 1926, the Kuomintang, under Chiang Kai-shek's leadership, started its northern march to unify China. Though bitter feuding between communists and traditionalists plagued its ranks, the Kuomintang entered Peking in 1928. Chiang Kai-shek was enthroned as temporary dictator. The nation underwent a period of political tutelage before democracy could be established. The United States adopted a conciliatory policy regarding assaults on foreigners, and China's tariff autonomy was recognized. The Coolidge Administration did not follow other great powers in seeking retribution. Dewey agreed and advised Americans to avoid provocation. The destruction of American property and lives did not constitute a sufficient pretext for imperialist intervention.[39] Americans who invested in backward countries should do so at their own risk. These developing nations were merely fighting to control their own integrity. China's transformation into a modern nation would necessarily involve some antiforeign outbursts.

Like Dewey, the *New Republic* considered Western interference to be the worst possible course of action.[40] If Chiang accepted foreign military aid, he would write his political obituary. Despite its passive noninterventionist policy, the *New Republic* exclaimed that the outcome of the Chinese Revolution would alter the balance of power in the entire world, even more than World War I.[41] Dewey publicly opposed General Crozier's plan to intervene beneficently in China's hour of agony in an effort to stop the blood-letting. China's "noncooperative" passive resistance would weld it into a solid unit if Crozier's approach were adopted. The Chinese had clearly scrapped this passive approach by 1928.[42] American aid should rely on "patience, sympathy, and educative effort" and not military policing.

Though the *New Republic* had originally hailed the new Kuomintang regime as the best hope for peace and progress, its disaffection with Chiang Kai-shek soon began to surface. The editors supported nonmilitary aid to the Nationalists, who had the unified backing of nearly all the nonpolitical educated classes.[43] Regretting China's political disintegration, by October 1929 the editors had remarked that the outcome of the civil war would make little difference to foreign powers. Nationalism would prevail regardless of who eventually ruled.[44] The establishment of order and security was the primary objective. The journal reinforced its sense of neutrality by insisting that even famine relief was virtually impossible. Yet, when Nathaniel Peffer, a regular Far East contributor to the *New Republic,* implied that Americans should not be aroused by "distant evils," the editors reacted. Human suffering was universal. To argue that Western standards should not be applied to the Orient would only serve to legitimatize the immorality of the imperialists. However, the editors failed to recommend any specific action to ameliorate China's torment.[45] The *New Republic* coupled its neutrality with the observation that the Chinese communists had accomplished extraordinary progress in winning the support of peasants.[46]

On September 18, 1931, Japan's Kwantung Army finally decided to resolve the Manchurian issue. This crisis tested both the Kellogg-Briand Pact (which endeavored to outlaw war altogether) and the League of Nations. When the league responded timidly by merely sending a commission to investigate, Japan confidently consolidated its position, controlling all of Manchuria by 1932. The Chinese boycotted Japanese goods. Japan deemed this tantamount to an act of war and attacked Shanghai. American Secretary of State Stimson invoked the doctrine of nonrecognition. In addition, he contemplated the imposition of sanctions against Japan and considered increasing the American military presence in the Far East.

John Dewey's League for Independent Political Action sent a letter to President Hoover urging him to withdraw the American ambassador from Tokyo unless Japan removed its troops from nontreaty zones in Manchuria.[47] This action would apply moral pressure by threatening Japanese diplomats with humiliation. Yet, the existing treaty already violated Chinese sovereignty. The letter appealed for an American embargo of arms shipments to both China and Japan. It disapproved of any loans to either country until the fighting ceased. The letter characterized this proposal as "drastic action in order to prevent war." In denying arms and loans to both China and Japan, LIPA treated both the aggressor and victim equally. The league's policy was designed not so much to prevent war but to define a legal state of war out of existence and avoid direct or indirect American participation in the conflict.

The reaction of the *New Republic* and the *Nation* was still more tremulous. These journals muddied the issue by indicating that none of the nations involved were free of blame in the China crisis. They had all been imperialistic; Japan was merely behaving like the United States in the Caribbean, and China must also assume some of the responsibility.[48] The editors adopted a passive policy of simply waiting until militarism and war would collapse the Japanese economy and redirect that nation from its insane course. The Japanese people would eventually rise up in revolt. The editors ignored Charles Beard's contention that the civilian government and public opinion had no power over the Japanese military, whose ambitions were "overwhelming." The *New Republic* pontificated about the inevitable destruction of tyrannical governments that maintained control without the consent of the population.[49] Admitting that American rights had been violated by Japan, the *Nation* explained: "We must not by our presence in China tempt them [the Japanese] to turn upon us. We have only one course — withdraw now, and have American rights left to some future conference."[50] Confessing that Japan was guilty of an aggression more blatant than the German invasion of Belgium, the editors argued that China, America, and Britain had "everything to gain by a pacifist waiting policy."[51]

The *New Republic* officially regretted its "naive" support of one war to end wars. According to the editors: "Peace could not be kept by force or the fear of force. Force intensified and widened conflicts. It solved nothing. . . . To advocate its use in the belief that one is thereby furthering international amity is the most terrible of mistakes and is founded on a complete delusion."[52] America should not cooperate with the League of Nations to discipline Japan by an economic boycott short of war. The *New Republic* was outraged at Stimson's hint of building battleships and new defenses in order to protect American trade. The China trade was not worth "one drop of American blood." Arming to fight for Chinese self-government was the most "recklessly quixotic" foreign policy ever adopted.[53] Even if such sabre rattling actually prevented a war, it was still foolhardy because America must consistently employ the methods of peace. An American economic boycott was a different form of war — one that also required a war psychology. The editors even opposed a voluntary American boycott, insisting that it would arouse uncontrollable hatred of the Japanese. The path to peace consisted not of punishing guilty nations but of removing the root causes of war.

Within this climate of appeasement, Joseph Ratner persuaded Dewey to prepare an article on the Manchurian crisis. The Stimson Doctrine of nonrecognition appeared to reopen possibilities for a revival of the Outlawry of War Movement. Dewey campaigned tirelessly to outlaw war but he felt that, with world opinion not fully re-educated, the Kellogg-Briand Pact was somewhat premature. The treaty's power depended exclusively on the moral force of the peoples who were defending it. Dewey sought to clarify the future path to be taken for those, like himself, who desired to outlaw war and to rid international diplomacy of the threat of physical coercion. He fastened upon the principle of Outlawry as the fountainhead of American foreign policy. By removing the juridical status of the war system, Japan did not have to declare war. Therefore, other nations were not obliged to recognize a state of war that would eventually prompt intervention. In resorting to force regardless of the provocation, Japan violated its word under the Kellogg-Briand Pact. It should be chastised by world opinion. However, Dewey scolded Stimson for his veiled threat of force. Dewey warned that "lovers of peace should concentrate attention upon the Peace Pact; they should deny themselves the use of all methods of agitation and appeal which are contrary to its spirit and letter."[54] Concentrating upon

Japan's murder and pillaging merely distracted the movement's attention from its basic cause, the war system itself. Would this console the Chinese? With the *New Republic,* Dewey urged that the force clauses in the League of Nations covenant (Articles X, XV, XVI) be abrogated to bring international law in concert with the Kellogg-Briand Pact. Pristine moral force should be the ultimate basis for government policy.

In a debate published by the Foreign Policy Association, Dewey opposed Raymond Buell's call for economic sanctions against Japan. Buell asserted that significant differences existed between an economic boycott and war. Gandhi's boycott of British goods in India and the right of labor unions to strike were viable examples analogous to an economic boycott of Japan. A "business as usual" policy would merely strengthen Japanese militarism.[55] Dewey replied that sanctions would not only force Japan to cut deeper into Asia, they would also increase resentment among the Japanese people. On the other hand, he approved a voluntary boycott as a "nonpolitical" expression of popular moral disapproval. Official sanctions were a pretext for war that would only serve to reinforce the prestige of the military party in Japan.[56] Economic loss would not deter Japan. Dewey conceded that, thus far, pacific means had not been highly successful. However, community consensus rather than coercive force had built America; and a similar growth of public opinion was needed internationally. The *New Republic* regarded sanctions as a ploy created by the status quo nations in the league to reinforce their power and advantage.[57] Felix Cohen responded by mocking those energetic peace societies that had passed resolutions "designed to delude the Japanese into the absurd belief that international respectability is worth more than Manchuria."[58] Nevertheless, Dewey argued that by not employing sanctions against Japan, the United States had succeeded in inflicting a grave moral defeat. He doubted whether any other nation had the desire to imitate its tragic course. International law should enforce the principle that any dispute not settled by negotiation should remain null and void. Although it might appear unrealistic to rely solely on moral agencies, Dewey was convinced that the history of war had proven that alternative methods were doomed to failure. Bewitched by the spectre of World War I, Dewey asked whether the employment of force would ever serve as its own deterrent.

Shortly after the Manchurian Crisis, the *New Republic* assumed a procommunist posture toward China. It condemned the "disastrous" effort by nationalists to suppress the communists. Without external interference, the Reds could control all of China in a few months.[59] Chiang Kai-shek was accused of using opium profits to equip his troops against the communists. The editors charged that "if he [Chiang] wins, he has new territories to tax, exploit, and flood with opium."[60] In the midst of this corruption, the communists were praised as good administrators, who had won the allegiance of the masses and were now heroically fighting the Japanese with only captured weapons. Accusing Chiang of being both a puppet of Japan and tool of American capitalism, the *New Republic,* by 1933, was openly advocating a communist victory.[61] By permitting the Reds to fulfill their destiny, China would have a strong government that could act as a counterpoise to Japan and it could serve as a vast market for Western products. The communists had dedicated themselves to improving the standard of living of the masses, while it was feared that humanitarian aid to the Nationalists might be used to purchase weapons.

After predicting that China would soon go communist, the *New Republic* announced glumly that the communist inspired rebellion in Fukien province had collapsed.[62] The editors blamed outside military aid, particularly the assistance given by pro-Nationalist American aviators. These "Hessians" were accused of mercilessly dropping bombs on innocent peasants. The weak resistance of the famous Nineteenth Route Army (defenders of Shanghai in 1931) was explained by an alleged Mexican bribe of six million dollars offered to its military commanders.[63] These setbacks provoked the editors to announce that the Open Door was no longer worth fighting for. America should appease Japan by granting it naval equality.[64] Edgar Snow wrote a series of *New Republic* articles glorifying Mao Tse-tung's heroic valor.[65] Carrying isolationism a step further, the journal insisted on February 26, 1940, that Japan was on the verge of total collapse.[66] This isolationism was designed to enable Japan to destroy the Nationalists and lay the foundation for a future communist victory.

What happened to the promising liberal movement that Dewey's previous visit to China had sought to bolster? It was crushed between reactionary nativism and revolutionary communism. The career of Hu Shih, Dewey's leading disciple, illustrates this predicament. Criticizing the new Kuomintang regime for depriving the people of their democratic rights, Hu lobbied for a new constitution. The Kuomintang policy of relying upon antiquated Confucian traditions and attempting to stifle foreign influences was similarly misguided. Ignorance, not imperialism, was responsible for China's plight. Hu blamed radical intellectuals for instigating disturbances. His anti-communism permitted a partial reconciliation with Chiang Kai-shek. He continued to favor a decentralization program that would have curtailed Chiang's power.[67]

As a pamphleteer and public speaker, Hu struggled to influence public opinion, particularly among the intellectuals. When the league's Lytton Commission proposed non-Chinese control over Manchuria in 1932, Hu praised the commission. He urged his people to remain patient in regaining this territory; they could afford to wait thirty years. In 1935 he advocated the demilitarization and government evacuation of two Chinese provinces in the face of the Japanese military threat. The gravest evil, according to Hu, was not Japanese aggression, but that the Chinese in desperation might utilize militant methods of resistance that would imperil economic and intellectual progress.[68] Hu became an influential member of the Low-Key Club, which advocated negotiation instead of military conflict with Japan. While the problems afflicting Kuomintang China were monumental, the free hand of Japanese aggression unraveled Chiang's legitimacy. Mao was also allowed breathing space for the impressment of peasants. When communists pleaded for full student participation in a "national salvation movement," Hu advised that they employ only verbal protests. The students' pre-eminent responsibility in times of acute crisis was to advance their education. From 1938 to 1942, Hu served as China's ambassador to the United States. He aroused much sympathy in America for China's misfortune.

In October 1938, Dewey was conferred the Blue Grand Cordon of the Order of Jade by the Chinese government.[69] Since he had refused a similar award from the Japanese government in 1919, one can infer that he at least nominally supported the Nationalists. In 1942, American warplanes airdropped a propaganda appeal written by Dewey to assist Chinese solidarity. His active involvement in Chinese relief operations during the civil war evidenced Dewey's commitment to that troubled region. Shortly after the war ended, T. V. Soong, Chinese premier, invited Dewey to visit China as a guest of its universities.[70] It was hoped that Dewey could survey China's problems and become a catalyst in rallying intellectual backing against the communists. The Chinese Embassy secured air priorities for Dewey and his secretary as well as $5,000 for the trip.[71] Unfortunately, this second visit to China was postponed and Dewey never did return. Amidst the power struggle with the communists, Dewey supported Chiang Kai-shek as the "lesser of evils" (Mao being the other possible candidate for support).[72]

The tragedy of modern China, its lost opportunity for free government, epitomized the difficulties of securing democracy in underdeveloped areas. Dewey's approach was squeamish about allowing a transitional period with authoritarian direction to compensate for deficiencies in civil culture. He advocated nonpolitical reform techniques when statesmanly advice to comparatively enlightened leaders was sought in reference to attaining power and holding it within the vortex of political chaos. Once centralized political power was established, as in Turkey under Ataturk, Dewey seemed willing to endorse authoritarian efforts at modernization. Visiting Turkey in 1924, he praised the Ataturk regime despite the fact that it was dictatorial.[73] Dewey also sympathized with the nationalist revolutions in Mexico and in the Soviet Union during the 1920s. He viewed such nationalist dictatorships as "social experiments." The specific point at which such experiments moved from that of a positive to a negative historical force could not be established. Dewey might agree with Herbert Croly that the elevation of the standard of living and education, the expansion of popular support, and the refusal to incite foreign wars might provide some general guidelines.[74] Authoritarian regimes are distinguishable from totalitarian police states. Rather than pure isolation, a viable democratic foreign policy requires the maintenance of relations with a variety of non-democratic regimes. Dewey did not offer much guidance to this netherworld of international politics. Unlike Croly, he was more reluctant to acknowledge that nations may find themselves in a predicament where violence is the only remedy.[75]

Dewey's isolationist-cultural approach to China suffered from democratic purism. When the Marxist-Leninists supplied a messianic ideology to solidify a political movement, the Chinese pragmatists responded by encouraging people to think critically. In itself, this appeal did not offer the emotional vitality that could effectively combine nationalism and democracy. Dewey conceded that Marxism in Russia afforded men "the faith and courage" to challenge the regime.[76] Though reform liberalism represented the forces of political decency, it lost out in the struggle of power. Reform liberalism presupposes an open social order that will enable the gradual implementation of its proposals. Time and events overran Dewey's incremental approach. Exclusive reliance upon persuasive devices in the midst of civil war was marked by failure. This strategy was more appropriate for the schoolroom than the battlefield.

NOTES

1. George Dykhuizen, *The Life and Mind of John Dewey,* p. 187. Charles Howlett's contention that Dewey left for the Far East in order to redeem himself in the eyes of his pacifist friends is very misleading. Neither did Dewey's *Reconstruction in Philosophy* signify his acceptance of pacifism. The book was almost exclusively philosophical in content and the word "pacifist" does not appear. See *Troubled Philosopher,* pp. 44–45.

2. John Dewey, *China, Japan and the U.S.A.* (New York: Holt Co., 1919), p. 9. (Hereafter *CJA*) See Jerry Israel, *Progressivism and the Open Door* (Pittsburgh: University of Pittsburgh Press, 1971), p. 7.

3. John Dewey, *Reconstruction in Philosophy,* p. 204.

4. John Dewey, "Japan and America," *Dial* (May, 1919):503. Dewey, "Liberalism in Japan, Part IV," *Dial* (Nov. 1, 1919):371.

5. John Dewey, "The Student Revolt in China," *NR* (Aug. 6, 1919):16.

6. Dewey praised the Chinese youths' thirst for knowledge, which was the most zealous in the world. He was confident that this enthusiasm would reach fruition in the attempt to gain the facts necessary to implement their ideas. Hu Shih did not share Dewey's enthusiasm for the May Fourth uprising. It destroyed discipline and authority in the schools by disruptive classroom boycotts. Dewey finally warned that continuous disruption might precipitate the collapse of the whole school system. Chinese liberals were hardpressed to sublimate student activism. Dewey, "The Sequel to the Student Revolt," *NR* (Feb. 25, 1920):332. Y. C. Yang, *Chinese Intellectuals and the West (1872–1949)* (Chapel Hill: University of North Carolina Press, 1966), p. 310. Jerry Israel, *Student Nationalism in China (1927–1937)* (Stanford: Stanford University Press, 1966), p. 133.

7. John Dewey, "Is China a Nation?" *NR* (Jan. 12, 1921):187.

8. *CJA,* p. 176.

9. John Dewey, "Industrial China," *NR* (Dec. 20, 1920):39–40. Hu Shih also acknowledged the impossibility of social progress without political stability. See Hu Shih, *The Chinese Renaissance* (Chicago: University of Chicago Press, 1934), p. 23.

10. Jean Chesneaux wrote that ". . . the supporters of federalism expanded about the abstract virtues of federalism, they did not pursue the study of political processes which would have enabled their system to be put into practice." Jean Chesneaux, "The Federalist Movement in China, 1920–23," in Jack Gray, ed., *Modern China's Search for a Political Form* (New York: Oxford University Press, 1969), p. 126.

11. Warren Cohen, "America and the May Fourth Movement: The Response to Chinese Nationalism (1917-1921)," *Pacific Historical Review* (1968):97.

12. John Dewey, *Letters from China and Japan,* Evelyn Dewey, ed. (New York: Dutton, 1920), p. 174. (Hereafter *LCJ*)

13. *LCJ,* p. 176.

14. John Dewey, "The Far East Deadlock," *NR* (March 16, 1921):71-74.

15. "The Unwisdom of Coercing Japan," *NR* (Oct. 19, 1921):202.

16. Ibid., p. 204.

17. John Dewey, "The Far East Deadlock," *NR* (March 16, 1921):13.

18. John Dewey, "The American Opportunity in China," *NR* (Dec. 3, 1919):16.

19. John Dewey, "Chinese National Sentiment," *Asia* (Dec., 1919):1242.

20. *CJA,* p. 61.

21. H. N. Brailsford, "A New Technique of Peace," *NR* (Nov. 30, 1921):12-15. Dewey, "Causes of International Friction," *Baltimore Sun* (16 Nov. 1921), p. 10.

22. *CJA,* p. 62.

23. John Dewey, "Four Principles for China Regarded as Best Framework," *Baltimore Sun* (23 Nov. 1921), p. 1A.

24. "Conferences vs. Alliances," *NR* (Dec. 14, 1921):60-62.

25. "The Far Eastern Concert," *NR* (Dec. 21, 1921):88-9. Dewey, "Three Results of the Treaty," *Baltimore Sun* (11 Dec. 1921), p. 2. Dewey also mentioned that the treaty ended talk of fortifying Guam. American soldiers in both Guam and the Philippines later suffered the consequences of these stipulations. See "American Obligations Under the Treaty," *NR* (Dec. 21, 1921):113-115.

26. "The Culmination of the Conference," *NR* (Dec. 14, 1921):36-38.

27. Raymond Buell, *The Washington Conference* (New York: Appleton & Co., 1922), p. 326.

28. *NR* (Dec. 28, 1921):110.

29. John Dewey, "Race, Prejudice and Friction," *The Chinese Social and Political Science Review* (1922):14.

30. "China's Civil War," *NR* (May 10, 1922):306.

31. *NR* (August 9, 1922):291.

32. *NR* (May 17, 1922):227-28. Ironically, Sun Yat-sen rejected Marxist class struggle in favor of an evolutionary socialism relatively close to Dewey's position. In fact, the 1924 Kuomintang platform endorsed a "child-centered educational program." On March 13, 1927, Dewey spoke at a memorial meeting for Sun and indicated the correlation between Sun's book, *San Min Chin I,* and Maurice William's *The Social Interpretation of History*; William's work influenced Sun's political thinking. Maurice William, *Sun Yat-sen vs. Communism* (Baltimore: Williams & Williams Co., 1932), p. xvii. James Shotwell, "Sun Yat-sen and Maurice William," *Political Science Quarterly* (March, 1932):119-126.

33. *NR* (Jan. 1, 1924):1.

34. *NR* (Oct. 8, 1924):130.

35. *NR* (March 25, 1925):109.

36. *NR* (July 8, 1925):163.

37. Charles Howlett misquoted Dewey in claiming that Dewey was opposed to the Open Door. See *Troubled Philosopher,* p. 57.

38. John Dewey, "We Should Deal with China as Nation to Nation," *Chinese Students' Monthly* (1926):54.

39. Edward Borchard, "How Far Must We Protect Our Citizens Abroad?" *NR* (April 13, 1927):214-216. *The Christian Century* implored Chinese missionaries to forsake military protection and, like David in the lion's den, practice "missionary heroism." *The Christian Century* (June 18, 1925):788. (Hereafter *CC*)

40. John Dewey, "The Real Chinese Crisis," *NR* (April 27, 1927):210. *NR* (May 4, 1927):284. Dewey became involved with the Hands Off China Committee. See V. F. Calverton to John Dewey (April 18, 1927), John Dewey Collection, Morris Library, Southern Illinois University.

41. *NR* (May 4, 1927):287. "Imperialism Is Easy," *NR* (March 23, 1927):133–34.

42. John Dewey, "Intervention a Challenge to Nationalism," *Current History* (May, 1928): 212–213.

43. "The Outlook for China," *NR* (Feb. 27, 1929):51. *NR* (Dec. 19, 1929):77.

44. "The Duel in China," *NR* (Oct. 23, 1929):258.

45. "Child Slavery in China," *NR* (Oct. 11, 1930):182.

46. *NR* (Aug. 26, 1931):29.

47. "Recall of Our Envoy From Tokyo Is Urged," *New York Times* (27 Nov. 1931), p. 2.

48. "Japan Defies Imperialists," *NR* (Nov. 11, 1931):514–16.

49. Stanley High argued that the liberal movement in Japan was an irresistible tide released by the modernization process. He wrote that "not before in history has a nation without revolutionary overturn made such rapid strides in the practice of democracy." Stanley High, "Is Japan Going Democratic?" *Harper's* (Dec., 1928):221.

50. "Dynamite at Shanghai," *N* (Feb. 10, 1932):150.

51. "Can Japan Be Stopped?" *NR* (Feb. 10, 1932):335. The editors simultaneously applauded the Soviet military build-up in Siberia. The journal advocated that the United States strengthen Russia's powers of resistance by every legitimate aid in the name of neutrality. "Why Do We Boycott Russia?" *NR* (March 16, 1932):112–13.

52. "Boycott Leads to War," *NR* (March 2, 1932):59.

53. "The Stimson Letter," *NR* (March 9, 1932):86.

54. John Dewey, "Peace—By Pact Or Covenant?" *NR* (March 23, 1932):147.

55. Raymond Buell, "For a Japanese Boycott," *NR* (March 9, 1932):100–102.

56. John Dewey, "Sanctions and the Security of Nations," in *Intelligence and the Modern World,* Joseph Ratner, ed. (New York: Modern Library, 1939), p. 583.

57. "The Japanese Boycott Again," *NR* (April 13, 1932):222. H. N. Brailsford, "For a Boycott: A British View," *NR* (April 15, 1932):237–38.

58. Felix Cohen, "Pacifists and Manchuria," *NR* (March 2, 1932):76.

59. *NR* (May 4, 1932):310.

60. *NR* (July 27, 1932):222. Herbert Croly's death in 1930 corresponded to the journal's fellow-traveling line. Though Dewey remained an associate editor, he did not comment on the Far East after 1932. The editors also thought that Stalin could function as a mediator to settle differences between China and Japan. *NR* (Dec. 28, 1932):176.

61. "Red China," *NR* (Sept. 27, 1933):171–72.

62. *NR* (Jan. 17, 1934):264.

63. "An Army Betrayed," *NR* (Jan. 31, 1934):331–32. *NR* (May 16, 1932):2.

64. "Decision in the Pacific," *NR* (Jan. 9, 1935):236. "Japan Devours China," *NR* (June 26, 1935):182. *NR* (Oct. 9, 1935):227. "Words About the Open Door," *NR* (Nov. 11, 1938):30.

65. Edgar Snow, "Soviet China," *NR* (Aug. 14, 1937):351–54.

66. "Is Japan Cracking Up?" *NR* (Feb. 26, 1940):260.

67. Y. C. Wang, *Chinese Intellectuals and the West (1922-1949),* pp. 406–409.

68. Jerome Grieder, *Hu Shih and the Chinese Renaissance* (Cambridge, Mass.: Harvard University Press, 1970), p. 257. Barry Keenan, *The Dewey Experiment in China* (Cambridge, Mass.: Harvard University Press, 1977).

69. Hu Shih to John Dewey (June 29, 1939), John Dewey Papers, Morris Library, Southern Illinois University.

70. T. V. Soong to John Dewey (Nov. 15, 1945), John Dewey Papers, Morris Library, Southern Illinois University.

71. Chinese Embassy to John Dewey (March 26, 1946), John Dewey Papers, Morris Library, Southern Illinois University. Also John Dewey to Walter R. Houston (April 22, 1946), John Dewey Papers.

72. John Dewey to Sidney Hook (Sept. 6, 1950), John Dewey Papers, Morris Library, Southern Illinois University. See Lin Yutang, "Communist 'Democracy' in China," *NL* (Jan. 27, 1943):8.

73. John Dewey, "Secularizing a Theocracy," *NR* (Sept. 17, 1924):69–71.

74. Herbert Croly, "Mexico and the United States," *NR* (March 30, 1927):59–63.
75. Herbert Croly, "Liberals vs. Fascism," *NR* (March 7, 1927):33–35.
76. John Dewey, "The Great Experiment and the Future," *NR* (Dec. 19, 1928):135.

7

Pacifism and the Outlawry of War

Dewey's peace activities and their relationship to his pragmatic liberalism warrant careful scrutiny. Charles Howlett, for example, maintains that after World War I pacifism became an integral part of Dewey's political approach.[1] While Dewey participated in the Outlawry of War Movement and educational peace research, in what sense could he be called a "pacifist"? In 1945 he offered the following clarification: "The term 'pacifist' has unfortunately assumed a more restricted meaning during recent years. It used to apply to all persons who hoped and worked for a world free from the curse of war. It has now come to stand almost exclusively for those who are opposed to war under any and all conditions."[2] Dewey clearly identified himself with the more expansive definition. Yet, Howlett persists in connecting Dewey with the absolute pacifism of Jane Addams or Mahatma Gandhi.[3] Dewey's experimentalism does not permit the adoption of doctrinaire pacifism.

The relationship between intelligence and coercive force is extraordinarily complicated, depending upon an examination of specific circumstances. Recognizing this, Dewey repudiated a reliance upon "sheer force" alone.[4] In 1935 he contended that "the emphasis of liberalism upon the method of intelligence does not commit it to unqualified pacifism; but to the unremitting use of every method of intelligence that conditions permit and to search for all that are possible."[5] While Dewey appeared to juxtapose intelligence and violence in *Liberalism and Social Action*, he did not rule out the use of coercive force. For example, minorities who use force to resist the policies of an authorized majority must be subdued.[6] Thus, peace was not simplistically equated with democracy.[7] Dewey advocated nonviolent reform within the democratic domestic environment of twentieth-century America, although no attempt was made to categorically eliminate the use of military force internationally. In fact, Dewey supported World War I, World War II, the Korean War, and the Cold War. Peace without democracy would be very troubling indeed.

During World War I, Dewey affirmed that he was indeed a "pacifist," but, unlike the absolute pacifists, he sought effective ways to construct an enduring peace. In 1914 he became acquainted with Salmon O. Levinson, a Chicago lawyer, who enthusiastically sought to transform the whole nature of international relations. Discovering that war was sanctioned by international law as a legitimate means to settle disputes, Levinson proposed to formulate a new international code that would outlaw war. In its initial version, the plan included the establishment of an international organization authorized to execute, by force if necessary, the decrees of an international tribunal created to adjuciate various conflicts.[8] Endorsing Levinson's plan, Dewey reiterated that pacifists must be willing to fight for the creation of this new social order or admit that their position is merely sentimental.[9] After the debacle at Versailles, the force clause to the Outlawry proposal was deleted by Dewey and Levinson.

While Levinson vigorously recruited notables like Jacob Schiff, Jane Addams, and Raymond Robins, Dewey left for the Far East. The massive destructive power of modern warfare and the recognition that it affected everyone enhanced the prospects for public participation in the Outlawry campaign.[10] The belief that peace could be preserved by preparing for war had temporarily lost credibility. Dewey was convinced that the people as a whole were opposed to war. However, jingoistic propaganda could deflect them from pursuing the simple necessities of life. To combat this threat, Dewey espoused a people-to-people diplomacy that would supplant government-to-government relations.[11]

After Dewey returned from China, Levinson, who had already formed an Outlawry of War Committee in Chicago persuaded him to create a similar committee in New York. Dewey explained to Levinson that "if we can't trust the good will and good faith of the people of the world expressing the common purpose and judgment through law, the only means of expression the world had discovered for all other disputes, no political machinery will hold, and the world is doomed to war and doomed by war."[12] A successful League of Nations would be impossible until the people controlled their governments. Such a political league would reinforce the status quo by sanctioning physical force against recalcitrant nations. World opinion had to be mobilized against the war system, and Levinson's plan was the appropriate agency. However, Dewey did not anticipate any imminent dawning of a new millennium. Years, if not decades, of painstaking education lay ahead before public opinion could begin to constitute an effective nonviolent force in world affairs. How different, then, was Dewey's faith in world opinion from that of the mushy, sentimental pacifist belief in disembodied moral forces that he had earlier criticized and attempted to distinguish himself from? Wasn't Dewey's position just another "moonstruck morality"? Had he not merely replaced one millennial vision in World War I with another equally fanciful one?[13] Dewey was aware of the odds against him as well as the steps necessary for an ultimate solution. This educational crusade was necessarily estranged from immediate politics. Outlawry could cauterize in the public mind a foreboding international issue and challenge politicians to declare forthrightly their intentions.

Through numerous speeches and articles, Dewey stumped the bastions of secular and religious liberalism in behalf of Outlawry. During the 1920s, he joined a working alliance with liberal Protestant and pacifist groups. Norman Thomas was the first editor of the *World Tomorrow,* which sponsored the Outlawry movement through an outpouring of articles. The *Christian Century,* edited by Charles Clayton Morrison, reflected the Social Gospel movement as well as pacifism. Morrison was a prominent spokesman for the Outlawry of War. He published a book on Outlawry for which Dewey wrote an afterword.[14] The movement did not abstain completely from politics, because it sought the cooperation of isolationist senators like Knox, Borah, Walsh, and La Follette. Senator Knox, a former Secretary of State, endorsed Outlawry in the Senate during 1919 and 1920. Despite Dewey's fears, the politicians would again manage to co-opt the Outlawry movement for their own suspect motives.

Levinson endeavored to conscript Senator Borah for Outlawry in December of 1919. Borah was not overwhelmed by the plan since it circumscribed national sovereignty, which he indefatigably fought to protect. He continually temporized with the feverish Levinson, agreeing to launch a campaign in 1922 and then postponing it. In 1923, Borah finally introduced the Outlawry proposal to the Senate and gained its approval. This action greatly augmented its public credibility. Borah utilized Outlawry as a device to undermine other internationalist proposals. For Borah, foreign policy was a conspiracy among eastern big businesses to lead the country into war in order to protect overseas investments.[15] Though Borah may have manipulated Outlawry for political advantage, Dewey publicly defended him against Walter Lippmann's charges of political expediency.[16] Dewey and Borah carried on a limited relationship, largely through correspondence, the former remaining ever hopeful that western and midwestern progressives could provide a political base for his social reforms.

Dewey supported the Borah-Levinson four-step approach to Outlawry. First, a popular upsurge of public opinion would bring pressure upon all countries to draw up an international treaty that would formally declare war to be a crime, thus outlawing it as an institution. National plebescites could effectively register public opinion. Second, an international group of jurists would restructure international law on the basis of the illegality of war. Third, an international court would be instituted with affirmative power to settle disputes likely to breed wars. Its enforcement power would rely solely on the pacific sentiment of world opinion.[17] This court would be modeled after the American Supreme Court. Fourth, each nation would make violations of international law domestic crimes as well. War-breeders would be punished within their own countries. Once the conviction that war is evil is made manifest in law, the militarists will be the criminals and not the pacifists. Public conscience and law will be synchronized. The war system had implanted a professional elite whose members confused militarism with national patriotism. With war outlawed and national security protected, essential conditions for magnanimous "political negotiation" and domestic reform could be established. The international tribunal could arbitrate conflicts and expose the facts to the public. Nationalistic smokescreens would be penetrated. For example, Americans would not fight to preserve the oil interests of big business in Mexico. If American nationals were killed, then war hysteria could reach a militant pitch with national honor and prestige enlisted to favor war. The avowed purposes and actual causes of war were seldom identical. Instead of blaming individuals or nations for war, Dewey attacked the system of law that rendered war a legitimate alternative of last resort.[18]

Walter Lippmann strongly objected to this "utopian proposal." He claimed that Outlawrist proponents, like Borah, were exploiting the movement as a means to find some toothless substitute for the League of Nations.[19] While people might agree that war is horrible, how could the Outlawry proposal cope with specific questions? For example, do colonies have a right to revolt? Would nations allow such issues to be adjudicated by an international body? When the Outlawrists insisted that rights of self-defense and wars of liberation were not to be outlawed, Lippmann added that only wars of openly declared aggression would fail to slip through the loopholes. In genuine war-breeding crises, traditional diplomacy was mandatory. No court could handle it, because immediate action was demanded through compromise, bargaining, and threat of force. And any effort to eliminate politicians from a world organization would be futile because any international legislature would be representative of each nation involved.

In response to Lippmann's critique, Dewey charged him with misrepresentation. Dewey did not oppose the League of Nations, only the war system behind it. Lippmann falsified the history of the Outlawry movement: it was not the machination of the Irreconcilables; rather, it originated out of analysis of the prerequisites for an association of nations that had been debauched at Versailles.[20] Instead of permitting a nation to mask its aggression as "defensive" warfare, Dewey repeated that the right to self-defense meant the right to defend oneself *when attacked*. Such a right could never be abrogated. Wars of liberation and civil wars were strictly domestic and therefore outside the jurisdiction of international law. Domestic legislation would have already declared them illegal. This line between domestic and international war could not be so clearly drawn, however. Outlawrists did not oppose conferences and other noncoercive political techniques for resolving disputes. When such methods fail, however, the courts rather than armies should decide the outcome. The fact that an international court would be conceived through a political process should not condemn it any more than in the case of the American Supreme Court.

At bottom, Lippmann and other opponents of Outlawry accepted the war system as inevitable; war and law were the only two methods to compel a settlement. For the Outlawrists the judicial approach was at least worth attempting. Arbitration might in fact calm the hysteria that provokes most wars. Europe was a "briar patch" of war, employing force at every turn; and although Americans were naive about world affairs, they did not desire to become entangled in the European war system. Toward this end, Dewey had this proposal:

> Minding one's own business is a form of conduct that commends itself even more internationally than domestically. Isolation is not a high ideal but it denotes a better state of things than one of meddling which involved the meddler in unpleasant complications and does no one else any good in the end.[21]

Its unique geographical isolation afforded America the opportunity to use its natural advantages for the welfare of the whole world. Dewey strove to channel American idealism into the Outlawry of War: the positive and negative aspects of the war system should be placed squarely before the peoples of the world.

Dewey and Levinson extended their efforts to recruit influential backers for the Outlawry Plan. James MacDonald, chairman of the Foreign Policy Association, endorsed the plan.[22] Dewey tried to convert Herbert Croly; he eventually succeeded.[23] Meanwhile, Levinson struggled to sway President Coolidge toward Outlawry, and to some extent his aspirations were fulfilled. By 1925, Lippmann told Dewey that he had been convinced by the plan.[24] Lippmann's allegiance was shortlived, however, since by 1928 he had returned to the opposition. Norman Thomas remained critical of the Outlawry proposal because nations were permitted to retain armies and navies, thus allowing for the possibility of self-defense. He did not accept the claim that without defensive capability a country could easily succumb to exploitation by its neighbors; this compromised his pacifist principles. Still maintaining the right of self-defense, Dewey continued to distance himself from the absolute pacifists.[25]

Another wing of the Outlawry of War Movement was headed by Nicholas Murray Butler and James Shotwell. Both men were associated with the Carnegie Endowment for Peace and with Columbia University. Shotwell and Butler favored the League of Nations, hoping that the Outlawry plan could maneuver the United States into a collective security arrangement. A negative alliance, one that ensured the mutual nonbelligerence of two countries toward one another during any conflict, would enable a nation to violate America's neutrality with impunity, much as the British had done in World War I. Butler advocated a deterrence for aggression through massive retaliation. Levinson's plan conflicted dramatically with the latent motive of the Shotwell approach. Levinson sought to eliminate collective security arrangements, particularly those tied to the European balance of power diplomacy, which he believed would perpetuate conditions for war not peace. Under the Geneva Protocol, Shotwell also wanted compulsory arbitration through the World Court. Those nations refusing to abide by its decisions would be condemned as aggressors and subjected to sanctions.[26] This split in the Outlawry ranks was endemic to the peace movement itself. Some wanted to endow international institutions with the same kind of military and police power as nations; other advocates opposed international sanctions and coercion. As a result, the public was very much confused about the implications of the Outlawry plan.

With Dewey assisting as a mediator, Levinson and Shotwell molded a Harmony Plan that could align these two groups and unify the peace movement.[27] This compromise urged the United States to join the World Court with the understanding that an early conference was to be convened to negotiate the Outlawry of War. If the conference was not called within two years, the United States could then suspend its support for the World Court. After five years, it would withdraw from participation altogether.[28] Dewey had previously opposed participation in the World Court because it was a tool of the League of Nations.[29] While Dewey and Levinson might have been willing to forgo criticism of the World Court in order to bolster Outlawry, Borah would not compromise. The differences between the Levinson and Shotwell factions prohibited any lasting cooperation. Even though Dewey remained on speaking terms with both Shotwell and Levinson, pacifist harmony ended in personal rancor as each side viewed the other with suspicion and contempt.

On April 6, 1927, the tenth anniversary of American intervention into World War I, Aristide Briand, foreign minister of France, rekindled the floundering Outlawry proposal. With the help of James Shotwell, Briand proposed to renounce war between the United States and France. Shotwell actually wrote Briand's message, and he undoubtedly violated laws against carrying on state diplomacy.[30] Briand's initiative bore scant resemblance to the Borah-Levinson plan. It was designed to structure a negative security pact that would strengthen France, while assuaging inflamed relations between the two countries. Secretary of State Kellogg was determined not to be cornered, and doggedly requested a multilateral treaty. Many American peace workers seemed oblivious to the diplomatic intrigue. They rallied to the cry of "outlawing of war," and a massive propaganda campaign honed public pressure and expectations to providential heights. Nicholas Murray Butler traversed the country, tirelessly delivering speeches and mobilizing his influential contacts in government and business behind the proposal.

A weird constellation of the Lindbergh flight, peace fever, and diplomatic intrigue culminated in the signing of the Kellogg-Briand Pact on August 27, 1928. While the idea of outlawry, arriving at the level of international negotiations after only ten years, was certainly reason for enthusiasm, Dewey realized that the pact was the result of diplomatic maneuvering rather than an irresistible public demand.[31] The implications of the Kellogg proposal involved a renunciation of the League Covenant, the Treaty of Locarno, and all French defensive alliances. Briand must have been petrified by such a possibility. When he offered to outlaw "aggressor nations," he had in mind only states that could threaten the European status quo. Dewey cautioned the United States not to underwrite this unfortunate result. Walter Lippmann understood the potentially serious implications of Kellogg's proposal; for this very reason he defended Briand.[32] Peace projects, he argued, must be built upon an appeal to the strong status quo powers. Good statesmanship allowed for constructive reform. Lippmann held that no international order could exist without an international government. War would not be abolished until a political rather than moral equivalent could be found. Dewey considered the passage of a multilateral pact to be only a step toward peace, not a final solution.[33] The treaty would remain little more than a scrap of paper unless it was accompanied by an international tribunal and a new international code. Nonetheless, Dewey reasoned that, at the very least, the treaty offered a "breathing spell" and could aid peace initiatives by augmenting existing defensive alliances.[34]

Dewey and Shotwell debated the Outlawry plan in the *New Republic*. Alarmed at Dewey's earlier article, Shotwell demanded that the definition of "aggression" be settled in advance of any future negotiations.[35] Dewey suspected that Shotwell was attempting to commit the United States to the same obligations as league members. No definition should deprive the United States of free action with regard to a future European war. The Shotwell peace group, by undermining Kellogg, had encouraged Europe to continue its ill-fated course. Support for the league signified a commitment to war. Shotwell mentioned the possibility of "League wars."[36] He judged the Borah-Levinson proposal to be a perfect example of the post-war American mentality. It wanted to impose radical reform on international law but did nothing to guarantee enforcement. This struck many Europeans as outright cant and hypocrisy.[37]

The interpretations of the Kellogg-Briand Pact differed from one nation to another, with many attaching reservations to the treaty. During the negotiations, it was conceded that each nation could judge whether a war was founded on self-defense. Dewey observed that the reservations were not explicitly mentioned in the pact's text and had dubious legal status. These contentions would be transferred to an International Court for sanction. While recognizing that these ploys were symptomatic of the traditional diplomacy, Dewey could not countenance Senate ratification of the pact as a rider to a Heavy Cruiser Bill. Such a move would seriously imperil the moral impact of the treaty.[38] The *New Republic* also objected on the same grounds, for the treaty's value rested in altering the moral tone of international relations. The editors had no delusions about the treaty's efficacy; public opinion was its sole power. Rather than its positive benefits, the treaty should be ratified because its rejection would be "calamitous." Without the treaty, American moral influence in Europe would be destroyed.[39] On the day the pact was signed, Dewey told Joseph Ratner that it would hinder rather than help the Outlawry objective.[40] After Senator Borah helped to pass the Kellogg-Briand Pact, he refused to cooperate further with the implementation of the Levinson Plan. Levinson described this abandonment as the greatest disappointment in his life.[41] Dewey boosted Levinson for the Nobel Peace Prize; however, the award went instead to the redoubtable Nicholas Murray Butler.[42]

The Kellogg-Briand Pact was first challenged by the Sino-Soviet conflict over the Chinese Eastern Railway. The Soviet Union defended its imperialist property rights in China. Ideology never seemed less consequential when compared to national interests. American attempts to mediate the crisis under the provisions of the pact failed miserably. The *New Republic* held that if the pact undermined mediation by the League of Nations, it was actually "very harmful."[43] Dewey was still convinced that the Outlawry of War was the best method to end war. In 1933 he praised the pact as "a fruitful source of international cooperation."[44] The doctrine of nonrecognition for gains achieved through aggression had evolved directly from the pact. It gained acceptance by both the League of Nations and the Stimson Doctrine. Dewey warned Outlawrists not even to play in thought with the idea of sanctions or coercive force since both courses of action would reinforce the war mentality.[45] By building an habitual resistance to military conflict, peace lovers would not be seduced by the war hysteria. Unfortunately, this habitual resistance also could obfuscate a realistic appraisal of world affairs in cases where a military response to barbarism was the only prudent option. Dewey temporarily evaded his injunction in favor of critical intelligence in order to assess the utility of coercive force in each situation.

At times Dewey's anti-war activities flirted with doctrinaire pacifism. In the *Ethics* (1932), he mentioned the pledge of war resisters not to engage in any form of military service; and Dewey also called attention to Albert Einstein's contention that if only two percent of the population resisted military service, then war would end.[46] As a member of the Emergency Peace Commission, Dewey signed a letter to President Hoover advocating Einstein's plan for a reduction of world armaments by fifty percent as a step toward total disarmament, the elimination of chemical warfare, and the immediate discontinuation of enlistment and conscription in all countries. By legalizing conscientious objection, the basis for outspoken public opinion against militarism could be fortified and kept out of jail.[47] Along with Jane Addams, Robert Morss Lovett, and James Shotwell, Dewey supported the Griffin Bill, which would exempt no one from citizenship who opposed the lawfulness of war.[48]

During the 1920s and early 1930s the military served as the intellectuals' special brand of anti-Semitism. Pacifist organizations relentlessly investigated for evidence of clandestine military influence in American life. Lewis Mumford's *New Republic* article "Arms and the Baby" typically skewered the "military mind."

> Whatever his initial start in life, we may describe the military man as one whose conduct is professional, fixed on an infantile level; . . . he retains the infant's

unbounded will-to-power, he instinctively desires to eliminate anything that stands in the way of his own plans. . . . All these subterfuges and evasions would be funny, if they did not imply that a military organization is incapable of living anywhere but in Cuckooland. Most of us begin with the same tendencies that characterize the military man; but reality compels us to outgrow them.[49]

In an era when Mahatma Gandhi was canonized by liberals, the *New Republic* carried an eight-part series on "Our Professional Patriots." The Fellowship of Reconciliation labored to promote pacific internationalism in the schools. It examined textbooks for jingoistic references, cursed war toys, opposed conscription, and campaigned against the maintenance of Reserve Officer Training Corps (ROTC) units on college campuses.[50] Reinhold Niebuhr warned that "the ROTC not only challenged the morality of civilization and its jungle-like ethics but it thrusts a type of training and an attitude into the college which is thoroughly incompatible with the spirit of democracy and science."[51] Winthrop Lane's *Military Training in Schools and Colleges* reproached the ROTC's alleged brainwashing tactics. The pamphlet was endorsed by John Dewey, Jane Addams, and Senator Borah.[52] Secure behind its oceanic Maginot lines, the American public pressured Congress to cut back the American military to a skeletonized force, while Europe and Asia became an armed camp.

Despite the reduction of the American army to 50,000 troops, Dewey perceived a dangerous conspiracy afoot to militarize America's public schools, as indicated in official documents. The militarists were "well-organized, energetically active, and relentlessly aggressive." In 1930, Dewey sponsored an appeal by the Joint Peace Council to end military training in the schools. Other signers included Sigmund Freud, Bertrand Russell, Jane Addams, Albert Einstein, and Romain Rolland.[53] Dewey's words were ominous:

> Is he [the reader] aware that militarism has already become a vested interest, economic as well as political and social? Is he aware that the vested interest resorts to methods of aspersion and overt attack in order to intimidate those persons and organizations who oppose its efforts to get a stranglehold on our schools and in order to prevent students from being influenced by the facts and arguments these opponents present?[54]

Dewey was attacked by some military officials for being a communist bent on destroying the public school system. These personal assaults probably contributed to Dewey's intense hostility for the military. In 1920 he joined the League of Mutual Aid, signing a protest against New York State's Lusk Law (an anti-subversive statute). The American Vigilant Intelligence Federation claimed that Dewey headed "more pink organizations than anyone in the country."[55] Filling the void left by the destruction of local community bonds, nationalism was sedulously propagated. It became the new religion of the multitudes. Dewey considered the military to be the locus of political reaction.

In New York, Dewey sponsored the Committee for the Conference on Student Rights. It voiced opposition to the City College of New York's Military Training Program (ROTC). The *New Republic* characterized this anti-war group as a defender of academic freedom.[56] The committee objected to interferences with the students' freedom of expression. A student auxiliary known as the National Committee for the Student Congress Against War was formed. This organization was later captured by communists who subverted its aims to match the configuration of Soviet foreign policy. In April 1934 the student wing of the League for Industrial Democracy sponsored a "National Peace Strike" rallying around the Oxford Pledge, vowing never to fight for God or country. By 1936 the anti-war movement on campus reached a crescendo. Over 500,000 students participated in Oxford Pledge meetings across the country.[57]

Peace activists carefully monitored war-breeding American business activities overseas. The evils of monopoly capitalism were also epitomized by the munitions makers, whose livelihood depended upon war and human suffering.[58] Journeying to Mexico in 1926, Dewey detected an American economic imperialism in which cheap labor was exploited and natural resources confiscated. The Monroe Doctrine had been interpreted to mean protection for American investments and citizens in Latin America. Though American motives may have been benign, this relationship between backward and industrialized creditor nations easily degenerated into imperialism and war. "That imperialism is now in economic form our dominating note seems too evident to need proof," wrote Dewey in 1928.[59] The *World Tomorrow* feared that marines would follow the dollar after American oil interests were expropriated in Mexico.[60]

As an opponent of American entry into World War I, Robert La Follette's populist anti-militarism became fashionable during the 1920s. Dewey and the *New Republic* endorsed La Follette's presidential candidacy in 1924. Praising La Follette for utilizing the scientific method in politics, Dewey defined La Follette's view on foreign policy as "the only sound and realistic one." La Follette demanded: (1) the revision of the Versailles treaty, (2) support for the Outlawry of War, and (3) that international problems be approached from an economic instead of a legislative basis.[61] In addition, La Follette proposed the abolition of conscription, massive reduction in armaments, and a guaranteed public referendum on peace and war. His tentative platform contained the following declaration:

> We denounce the mercenary system of a degraded foreign policy under recent administrations in the interests of financial imperialists, oil monopolists, and international bankers, which has at times degraded our state department from its high service as a strong and kindly intermediary of defenseless governments to a trading post for those interests and concession seekers engaged in the exploitation of weaker nations as contrary to the will of the American people, destructive of domestic development and provocative of war.[62]

Politically aligned with this farmer-labor populism, Dewey adhered to an isolationist outlook throughout the twenties and thirties.

Dewey was suspicious of an eastern power elite leading the nation into war. He wanted to strengthen democracy domestically by avoiding foreign entanglements. If other nations could be left to their own devices, international harmony might be established. However, only the most democratic nations would remain conscientious. The Outlawry of War crusade did not bridge the gap between democratic idealism and international reality. The crisis of World War II revealed the full dimensions of this pretense. During times of relative peace and with a sense of geographical insulation, this isolationist self-deception could easily prosper.

NOTES

1. Charles Howlett, *Troubled Philosopher,* X.

2. John Dewey, "Peace and Bread," *Survey Graphic* (April, 1945):117.

3. Howlett cited an article in 1944 as proof that Dewey reaffirmed pacifism. The article polled seventy-five philosophers, including Dewey, asking them to state their best arguments for and against pacifism. The responses were listed numerically and left totally anonymous. Even if one knew who wrote which specific response, it would be impossible to know whether the author was a pacifist. See George Hartmann, "The Strengths and Weaknesses of the Pacifist Position as Seen by American Philosophers," *Philosophical Review* (March, 1944):125–44.

4. John Dewey, "The Motivation of Hobbes's Political Philosophy," in *Studies in the History of Ideas,* Vol. I (New York: Columbia University Press, 1918), pp. 88–115.

5. John Dewey, "The Future of Liberalism," *School and Society* (Jan. 19, 1935):76. During the middle of Dewey's alleged "pacifist" period, he wrote, in conjunction with John Childs, "as far as experience and reflection indicate that pacifistic measures are not likely to be effective, the philosophy [pragmatism] is pacifist; where the reverse is indicated by the best available knowledge of actual conditions, it is revolutionary. All that the method intrinsically calls for is that neither extreme be made so absolute a doctrine that it obstructs inquiry and pushes the plan of action into prejudged channels. Both absolute pacifism and absolute progress reached only through class struggle suffer from the same disease. Neither of them is consistent with experimentalism." Dewey and Childs, "The Underlying Philosophy of Education," in *The Educational Frontier,* William Kilpatrick, ed. (New York: The Century Co., 1933), p. 314.

6. *L&SA,* p. 87.

7. Howlett has a tendency to treat every Dewey avowal of democratic values as an espousal of pacifism. While conceding that Dewey did claim publicly to be a pacifist during the pre-World War I period, Howlett insists that for Dewey military coercion was incompatible with democratic ethics. Howlett maintains that the relationship between pacifism and pragmatism was so "clearly defined" that no further clarifications were necessary. If Dewey became a devout pacifist after World War I, at least one article announcing his new faith could have been anticipated. Howlett, *Troubled Philosopher,* pp. 24, 25, 61. In a letter to Emily Balch, Dewey reaffirmed that he was not an "absolute pacifist." John Dewey to Emily Balch (Dec. 29, 1944), John Dewey Papers, Morris Library, Southern Illinois University.

8. Salmon Levinson, "The Legal Status of War," *NR* (March 9, 1918):171–73.

9. John Dewey, "Morals and the Conduct of States," *NR* (March 23, 1918):232–34.

10. John Dewey, *Lectures in China,* pp. 163, 219.

11. John Dewey, "The Pacific Conference," *Kaizo III,* No. 10 (Sept. 1921):235–40.

12. John Dewey to Salmon Levinson (Nov., 1921), Salmon Levinson Collection, Joseph Regenstein Library, University of Chicago.

13. John Farrell, "John Dewey and World War I: Armageddon Tests a Liberal's Faith," *Perspectives in American History IX* (1975):332.

14. See Charles Clayton Morrison, *The Outlawry of War* (Chicago: Willett, Clark, and Colby, 1927).

15. Robert James Maddox, *William E. Borah and American Foreign Policy* (Baton Rouge: Louisiana State Press, 1972), p. 139.

16. John Dewey, "What the Outlawry of War Is Not," *NR* (Oct. 3, 1923):149-52.

17. John Dewey, "Political Combination or Legal Cooperation," *NR* (March 21, 1923): 89-91. The *Christian Century* proposed that the churches themselves outlaw law. Borah termed this editorial "magnificent." "Let the Churches Outlaw War," *CC* (Jan. 31, 1924):2024.

18. John Dewey, "If War Were Outlawed," *NR* (April 25, 1923):234-35. Dewey, "War and the Code of Law," *NR* (Oct. 24, 1923):224-26.

19. Walter Lippmann, "If War Were Outlawed," *Atlantic Monthly* (1923):245.

20. John Dewey, "What the Outlawry of War Is Not," *NR* (Oct., 1923):149-52.

21. John Dewey, "America's Responsibility," *CC* (Dec., 1926):1583.

22. John Dewey—Salmon Levinson (Oct. 1, 1923). Salmon Levinson Collection, Joseph Regenstein Library, University of Chicago. Dewey was on the executive committee of the Foreign Policy Association along with Jane Addams, Felix Frankfurter, Frederic Howe, Horace Kallen and Thomas Lamont.

23. John Dewey—Salmon Levinson (Nov. 28, 1923).

24. John Dewey—Salmon Levinson (April 27, 1925).

25. Norman Thomas, "The Outlawry of War," *World Tomorrow* (Jan., 1924):9-11. (Hereafter *WT*) See also Kirby Page, "Senator Borah, Outlawry, and the League," *WT* (May, 1928): 61.

26. Robert Maddox, *William E. Borah and American Foreign Policy*, p. 169.

27. S. Stoner, *Salmon O. Levinson and the Pact of Paris* (Chicago: University of Chicago Press, 1943), Ch. 9. On the Harmony Committee were Kirby Page, Norman Thomas, Salmon Levinson, Charles C. Morrison, James Shotwell, James McDonald and Raymond Robins.

28. Charles Chatfield, *For Peace and Justice: Pacifism in America, 1914-1944* (Knoxville: University of Tennessee Press, 1971), p. 104.

29. John Dewey, "Shall the United States Join the World Court?" *CC* (Oct., 1923):1329-34.

30. Robert H. Ferrell, *Peace in Their Time* (New York: W.W. Norton, 1969), pp. 72, 94.

31. John Dewey, "As an Example to Other Nations," *NR* (March 7, 1928).

32. Walter Lippmann, "A Political Equivalent to War," *Atlantic Monthly* (Aug. 1928): 187.

33. John Dewey, "Outlawing Peace by Discussing War," *NR* (May 16, 1928).

34. John Dewey—Salmon Levinson (April 7, 1928).

35. John Dewey and James Shotwell, "Divergent Paths to Peace," *NR* (March 21, 1928): 194-196.

36. John Dewey—Salmon Levinson (Jan. 27, 1928).

37. James Shotwell, *Was As an Instrument of National Policy* (New York: Harcourt, Brace & Co., 1929), pp. 88-89. James Shotwell, *The Autobiography of James T. Shotwell* (Indianapolis: Bobbs-Merrill, 1961), p. 196. Shotwell became the personal enemy of both Salmon Levinson and Charles C. Morrison. Levinson described him as "not mentally honest" and an "animal." Salmon Levinson—John Dewey (June 28, 1927). Salmon Levinson—John Dewey (March 14, 1928).

38. John Dewey—Salmon Levinson (December 4, 1928).

39. *NR* (Nov. 28, 1929):29. *NR* (Dec. 5, 1928):57. *NR* (Dec. 19, 1928):124.

40. Joseph Ratner, ed., with introduction in *Intelligence in the Modern World*, p. 547.

41. Robert Maddox, *William E. Borah and American Foreign Policy*, p. 181.

42. *World Unity Magazine* (Dec. 4, 1928).

43. *NR* (July 24, 1929):241.

44. John Dewey, "The Outlawry of War," in *Encyclopedia of the Social Sciences,* IX (New York: McMillan Co., 1933), pp. 598–603.

45. John Dewey, "Sanctions and the Security of Nations," in *Intelligence in the Modern World,* p. 579.

46. Dewey and Tufts, *Ethics* (1932), p. 413.

47. *NR* (Feb. 5, 1932):323. Other letter signers were Devere Allen, John Hayes Holmen, Dorothy Detzer, J. B. Matthews, Clarence Pickens, Norman Thomas, and Howard Y. Williams.

48. Dorothy Bromley, "The Pacifist Bogey," *Harpers* (October, 1930):565.

49. Lewis Mumford, "Arms and the Baby," *NR* (Oct. 15, 1924):161. By 1938, Mumford trumpeted the martial virtues.

50. Charles Chatfield, *For Peace and Justice,* p. 152.

51. Reinhold Niebuhr, "The Threat of ROTC," *WT* (Oct., 1926):155.

52. Charles Chatfield, *For Peace and Justice,* p. 397.

53. Otto Nathan and Heinz Norton, eds. *Einstein on Peace* (New York: Simon & Schuster, Inc., 1960), pp. 113–14.

54. R. P. Barnes, *Militarizing Our Youth,* Introduction by John Dewey (New York: Committee on Militarism in Education, 1927).

55. Robert Wohlforth, "Spy-Hunters, 1930," *NR* (Jan. 29, 1930):272.

56. *NR* (Dec. 2, 1927):100.

57. Philip Altbach, *Student Politics in America* (New York: McGraw-Hill Co., 1941), pp. 66–68.

58. *F&C,* p. 45.

59. Robert Ferrell, *Peace in Their Time,* pp. 176–77.

60. John Dewey, "A Critique of American Civilization," in Kirby Page, ed., *Recent Gains in American Civilization* (New York: Harcourt, Brace & Co., 1928), p. 260.

61. "Dewey Aids La Follette," *New York Times* (23 Oct. 1924), p. 2.

62. "The La Follette Program," *WT* (June, 1924):181.

8

To the Finland Station?

Dewey's encounter with the communist movement is a concrete testimony to his intellectual honesty and political courage. Attitudes toward the Soviet Union provided a litmus test for liberals. Initially sympathetic toward the "Soviet experiment," Dewey became an implacable foe of Stalinism as chairman of the Trotsky Commission and the Committee for Cultural Freedom. The 1930s composed an era in which, according to Eugene Lyons, the cultural life of certain cities, particularly New York, was subjected to an "intellectual Red terror." Those who refused to conform to the current wisdom, which replicated the Communist Party line, experienced first-hand the ruthlessness of this terror.[1] Out of this cauldron, Dewey emerged as perhaps the most influential spokesman for democratic liberalism.

He traveled to the Soviet Union in 1928, with twenty-five other educators, for the purpose of examining the Soviet social system.[2] Downplaying the immediate political situation, Dewey focused upon the experimental education program as central to the neophyte regime. He wired back serialized reports on Soviet life, which were then published in the *New Republic*. While other prominent liberals made this pilgrimage to the new collectivist experiment, Dewey's dispatches were probably the most significant appraisal of the Soviet Union in this era. His impressions revealed a far different Russia than that of either doctrinaire critics or Stalinist apologists. Similar to the China trip, Dewey's perceptions in many respects mirrored his own political ideals. Though he did not praise Bolshevism, the actual impact of Dewey's reports stimulated interest and sympathy for the Soviet Union. He obliged critics to withhold judgment until the experiment was completed. This would eventually contravert his admonitions about the inseparability of means and ends. Dewey adorned Stalin's Russia with a positive, progressive image. Yet, Reinhold Niebuhr also toured Russia in 1930. While he was impressed with its accomplishments and its revolutionary enthusiasm, Niebuhr apologized for Soviet brutality by declaring it an approximation of "rough justice."[3] Dewey must bear some responsibility for promoting an intellectual honeymoon with the Soviet Union in the 1930s, but he never glorified barbarism.

The Soviet Union was conceived as a vast social laboratory designed to groom a new cooperative human nature and not an egoistic one. The Russian people exuded a "courage, energy, and confidence in life" that animated the greatest cultural renaissance in history. Dewey described this experiment as "nobly heroic, evincing a faith in human nature which was democratic beyond the ambitions of the democracies in the past."[4] The safety and decorum of the masses cemented the regime's stability. New doors of cultural opportunity were being opened to all. He quoted Lenin to the effect that Russia would soon shift its attention to "pacific cultural work." Dewey envisaged in Russian life something comparable to the moving spirit of primitive Christianity. Educators in Russia were envied because they participated in a common social faith sponsored by the government. They could identify themselves completely with a new constructive social order. Social engineering proceeded unretarded since Russia possessed a comprehensive social purpose.[5] In no other country did the aesthetic aim so dominate educational practice. According to Dewey, "the Russian educational situation is enough to convert one to the idea that only in a society based upon the cooperative principle can the ideals of educational reformers be adequately carried into operation."[6] He exuberantly announced that progressive educational ideas were more fully realized in Russia than anywhere in the world.

Though Russia was undergoing a transitional stage, Dewey radiated optimism about its future. He anticipated that the repressive features of the regime would recede when the Russians no longer feared foreign enemies. American recognition of the Soviet Union could help to allay this fear. European diplomats had instigated a war atmosphere, and Dewey agreed with Lenin that the next European war would incorporate a domestic class struggle in every capitalist country. Yet, he did not sympathize with the Bolshevik stress on class war or world revolution. Increased interchange with the world, particularly cultural and educational contacts, would gradually drain the enthusiasm for class war.

In contrast to his writings on Germany, Dewey minimized the role of ideology in Russia. He routinely apologized for the propaganda in the Soviet schools. This zealotry would disappear, he believed, as experimentalism dominated. Acknowledging that Russia did not yet possess political democracy, Dewey nevertheless insisted that it seemed impossible for an intellectually free education not to "militate against the servile acceptance of dogma as dogma." Dewey was struck more by the proliferation of voluntary cooperatives than by centralized Bolshevik control. With worker's control and management, democratic ideals would reach their highest fruition. He doubted whether the Russian experiment would follow the prescribed course of its leaders. The outcome would probably be cooperative instead of communal.[7] Dewey praised the regime's concern with preserving cultural autonomy for the non-Russian populations and securing freedom from racial prejudice.[8] Although this portrait glossed over the bitter reality of Stalinism, Dewey sincerely believed that he was witnessing the implementation of his ideals on a national scale.

Reliant upon an interpreter and directed by guided tours, Dewey, despite his disclaimers, had been targeted for the "show-window" treatment. Russia was inspiring living proof that a planned collectivist economy could succeed in contrast to the chaotic and collapsing capitalist systems. The Great Depression had proven to be a great catalyst for Soviet sympathizers. Neither the United States nor the Soviet Union were members of the League of Nations. Stalin feared being isolated and attacked by league members. The educational delegations from America served Soviet interests by generating a groundswell of empathy. Prodded by liberal pressure, the United States finally recognized the Soviet Union in 1933. Reviewing three books on the Soviet Union, Dewey praised the agricultural revolution in Russia, which was removing "the obstinately individualist bias" of the peasants. Stalin's agrarian program liquidated millions who were out of step with the dialectic of history. Dewey hoped that America could achieve these ends voluntarily but lauded the "internal democracy" of Soviet cooperatives. Russia confronted America primarily with a "searching spiritual challenge." Regarding a book based upon personal interviews with Russians, Dewey cautioned that in assessing these reports it must be remembered that grumbling was a chronic cultural habit among the Russian people.[9] However, Dewey himself should have been more cautious about swallowing rhapsodic accounts.

He engaged in a running dispute with Mathew Woll, vice-president of the American Federation of Labor, who sought to remove all labor union financial support from A. J. Muste's Brookwood Labor College due to its alleged communist orientation. In 1931, Woll organized a Committee of One Hundred to conduct an anti-Soviet propaganda campaign. At the AFL convention, Woll accused both George Counts and John Dewey of being communists. (Later, Dewey would condemn the infiltration of communists within the labor movement, particularly in the CIO.[10]) Dewey formed a Committee of One Hundred in conjunction with the People's Lobby to counteract Woll's assaults. Fearing a witch-hunt against American radicals, Dewey declared: "Our committee is of the opinion that Mr. Woll's campaign is sowing the seeds of international hatred and war. In contradistinction we advocate a fair and friendly policy toward Soviet Russia, both as the proper attitude toward a great social and economic experiment and as a means of furthering international understanding and peace."[11] Dewey did not maintain this posture for long.

By 1931 the internal ferment of purges within the Soviet Union enforced an iron Stalinist orthodoxy and educational discipline. Though Dewey witnessed experimentalism among his Russian disciples, this approach was now officially denounced as "capitalist-bourgeois" by the Soviet Union. He later reflected upon this alteration as a shift from revoluntary idealism to expedient dictatorship.[12] George Counts still indulgently praised Soviet education for producing a new man cleansed of egoistic trappings.[13] In 1932, Dewey expressed a new skepticism. He desired that the Soviet Union succeed in its ultimate aims but he was wary of its political ruthlessness.[14] He characterized both the Soviet Union and Fascist Italy as social experiments. He was not prepared to condemn these countries outright, but encouraged others to examine the outcomes for themselves.[15] By 1933, Dewey's appraisal hardened: distinguishing between a planned and a continuously planning society, planned societies were autocratic, dogmatic, and repressive of individuality. Both Russia and Italy were listed as planned societies.[16]

What could account for Dewey's shift in attitude? During 1932 the Kremlin attempted to enlist Dewey into the communist ranks through Earl Browder's personal appeals. Browder also tried to cultivate Dewey's colleague, Sidney Hook. During the Popular Front days, the Communist Party knew the importance of collaborating with the intellectuals and the media.[17] Dewey resisted these overtures. As early as the fall of 1932, while serving as chairman of the New York Teachers Union committee, he stood opposed to the communists' obstructionist tactics. But why did Dewey wait three years before publicly exposing the reality of Soviet totalitarianism? He had deemed the Soviet Union a "social experiment" and advised a suspension of judgment until the experiment could assume a definite pattern. He probably found the information to be in such a state of flux that evidence had to mount before rendering a full account. Dewey's full account severely damaged the communist cause during a time when liberal opinion had condoned if not championed Stalin's tactics.

Dewey explained in some detail why he was not a communist. First, the type of communism practiced in Russia was inappropriate to the historical, economic, and political conditions in the United States. The stifling cultural control exerted by the party, the extermination of minority opinion, and the cult of infallible leadership sprang from the historical roots of autocratic Russia.[18] Second, the ideology of official communism adhered to a dogmatic and monistic view of history that refused to recognize cultural differences. The United States did not conform to the classic Marxist view, because it had no feudalistic background and its government and social system rested upon the importance of individuality. Third, Dewey questioned whether class war was a viable means to initiate authentic social progress. He credited fear of a communist civil war with ushering in fascism in Italy and Germany. A dictatorship of the proletariat would suppress the human rights of other parties after violently overthrowing the government. Dewey proclaimed that "as an unalterable opponent of Fascism in every form, I can not be a Communist."[19] Fourth, the tone and methods of the communists were appalling. Fair play and elementary honesty were more than "bourgeois virtues." He objected to the constant slandering and intimidation of liberals and the view that the ends justify the means. Fifth, a class war in modern society would destroy civilization. This indictment of communism, noting its similarity to fascism, prompted a virulent reaction by native Stalinists.[20]

Dewey learned about the nature of communist tactics through personal experience. A disciplined communist minority could prevent a union from functioning by intimidation and through manipulating committees to deny members full democratic franchise. Dewey's American Federation of Teachers Union (AFT) in New York underwent just such an assault. As chairman of the grievance committee in 1935, he petitioned the national union to permit a redrawing of the charter in order to eliminate such obstructionism. The petition was denied, and Dewey, along with the majority of the union, withdrew from the national organization. Both George Counts and Reinhold Niebuhr opposed Dewey in an effort to preserve the Popular Front. In fact, communists eventually gained full control over the Progressive Education Association.[21] In 1939, Louis Hacker and John Childs resigned from the Teachers College Chapter of the New York College Teachers Union because it was controlled by Stalinists.[22] When a local American Federation of Teachers Union was similarly co-opted, Dewey served on the educators' committee that investigated the situation. Other members included Reinhold Niebuhr, John Childs, and Horace Kallen. The committee recommended that the executive council of the AFT drop the local. This policy was adopted.[23]

Social Frontier, the journal of progressive education, included articles by noted communists but remained intellectually autonomous. George Counts, the editor, steered the journal toward popular frontism during 1936 and 1937. The journal opposed a charter revocation of the communist-dominated New York local of the American Federation of Teachers.[24] It argued that there was no hope for genuine education under a capitalist system. Political reform was the first responsibility of progressive educators; they could not be neutral in the class struggle. While Dewey agreed that teachers were not only responsible for intellectual growth but also for promoting democratic values, to adopt the class struggle motif for political action was tantamount to Marxism-Leninism. He urged action based upon a "social" rather than a "class" outlook — a perspective that would accept the democratic idea as the frame of reference. The Marxist approach, on the other hand, would intensify class consciousness and warfare. Schooling would become an instrument of propaganda and indoctrination. Since Dewey also supported an alliance of teachers and workers, John Childs confessed that he failed to comprehend any operational difference between utilizing a "class" or "social" viewpoint. The differences, however, were quite substantial.[25]

In *Liberalism and Social Action* (1935), Dewey expanded his critique of Marxist theory and communist practice. He rejected the invitation to violence, objected to the postulation of fixed classes with unbridgeable differences, and defended both civil liberties and the method of intelligence.

While earlier he had been reluctant to discuss Marx, in this volume Dewey noted that Marx did not advocate the inevitability of violent change in either the United States or Great Britain. In distinguishing Marx from his disciples, Dewey was undoubtedly influenced by Sidney Hook, who highlighted the democratic-scientific Marx.[26] Dewey conceded that democratic-capitalism rested upon veiled coercion, which, when directly threatened, would revert to undisguised violence. If capitalism was founded on coercion, how could it ever be supplanted by peaceful reform techniques? This frank contradiction in Dewey's thought was amended when he acknowledged that capitalism could become socially responsible. Both the *New Republic* and the *Nation* reviewed Dewey's book cooly. Reinhold Niebuhr described Dewey as "the leading philosophical exponent of liberal doctrine." Niebuhr rejected the belief that critical intelligence could engineer social change. Since the power holders in America would never voluntarily agree to reform, they had to be rooted out through violent class struggle. According to Niebuhr, Dewey's emphasis on peaceful reform only confused the "pressing social issue."[27] In assuming the rhetoric of radicalism, Dewey was vulnerable to Niebuhr's critique. However, he revised his political diagnosis. The Seventh Congress of Communists formally endorsed the popular front tactic in August 1935. Dewey's critique of communism was particularly unwelcome and untimely.

Late in 1934, the Kirov assassination provoked a cascade of rationalizations from the popular front press. Stalin utilized Kirov's murder, which he had arranged, as a pretext for a mass purge of all those who were suspected of participating. The *New Republic* commented editorially that "Russia's right to crush Nazi-White Guard conspiracies or other plots of murder and arson no one questions — few have anything but approval of it."[28] Blaming White Guard and Trotskyite plotters, the communist *New Masses* held that the Soviet Union's civil liberties were unequalled anywhere in the world.[29] The journal objected to Horace Kallen's attack on the National Committee for the Defense of Political Prisoners when it refused to protest the Soviet executions.[30] An International Committee for Political Prisoners was formed on January 20, 1935. It issued a letter of protest to the Soviet ambassador; John Dewey, Sinclair Lewis, Roger Baldwin, and Edward Lindemann were among the signers. Though striving to present the question in a "friendly spirit," so as not to render aid to reactionaries, the letter charged that "scores of men were shot, some within a few hours of their arrest, without even the semblance of a trial, merely upon a review of evidence by a special tribunal sitting in secret."[31] Even though he was a committee member, Waldo Frank refused to sign the letter. Undergoing a crisis of loyalties, Frank was reluctant to judge Soviet practices; however, he felt obliged to urge his Soviet comrades to avoid "ambiguous actions" that might tarnish their image.[32]

The *New Republic* commented about the International Committee's action. The editors contended that the absence of civil liberties was "not the sole or major premise" in judging a regime. Liberty was a "relative quantity" and it was "childish" to believe that liberty could escape unblemished during a great social revolution. Fair trials were not possible under conditions of civil war. It was "understandable" that the heroic builders of the new regime did not give suspected plotters and assassins the "benefit of the doubt."[33] Malcolm Cowley compared the victims of the Soviet terror with harmful parasites. Partisans of the Soviet Union should not condemn violations of civil liberty but instead recognize their deeper necessity. No such considerations could be applied to Hitler and Mussolini, because they had no rational goal or ultimate gain to counteract the present loss. No difference in the world could be greater than between a classless society and a racist, militarist autocracy. The editors declared, "it is only fair to call for suspension of judgment against the Soviet authorities when civil liberties are violated in view of the historical and political situation until the facts of specific cases are known."[34] However, William Chamberlain, Russian correspondent for the *Christian Science Monitor,* decried the double standard concerning terror when applied to Germany and Russia. *Common Sense* editors Alfred Bingham and Selden Rodman reviled the Soviet executions, comparing them to Hitler's Night of the Long Knives.[35]

The *New Republic* and the *Nation* hailed the new Soviet Constitution in 1936. Individuals who opposed both the fascist and communist dictatorships had gone "seriously astray."[36] After only fifteen years, the relaxation of restrictions during the transitional stage was a "remarkable achievement," one that signified the birth of constitutional democracy. The *New Republic* editor George Soule stated that during his recent trip to Russia he found no evidence that the Russian masses "felt any lack of freedom or were governed by fear."[37] Amidst the Stalinist terror, he observed: "in Russia, people have the sense that something new and better is going to happen to them. And usually it does."[38] Frederick Schuman reasoned that liberalism and communism germinated from the same humanitarian soil.[39] Max Lerner, editor of the *Nation,* developed further the logic of the Popular Front by expounding the "convergence theory" between liberalism and communism—that in practice the two systems would gradually become identical. Dewey was convinced that these two doctrines were intrinsically incompatible.

Beginning in August 1936, the Moscow Show Trials turned into a parade of Bolshevik revolutionaries, who, with stiff bodies and frozen expressions, confessed to fantastic Byzantine plots of treason and sabotage with Leon Trotsky as the supposed mastermind behind the whole affair. The credulity of the Popular Front's reigning faith was subjected to a rugged test. The outright supporters of the communist line challenged any doubts about the validity of the trials. After all, the confessions were made in open court. One had to accept the Soviet Union in toto. According to the *New Republic*: "Mr. Walter Duranty of the *New York Times* knows as much about Russia as any foreigner. He attended the latest trial and has apparently been forced to the conviction that the confessions are true. If you find them incredible, he says, you don't know the Russian temperament, and he advises you to go and read Dostoyevski."[40] Frederick Schuman reasoned that even if the charges lodged against Trotsky were false, the practical, expedient choice was between Stalin and Trotsky. Trotsky was an international trouble-maker, whereas Stalin would cooperate for peace and freedom.[41] Similarly, Reinhold Niebuhr held: "The present policy of the Communist Party is immeasurably superior to that of the Trotskyites. It is a responsible policy and theirs is an irresponsible one. Trotskyite fanaticism is a peril to the revolutionary cause today."[42] Sidney Hook and John Dewey maintained that Trotsky was accused of specific crimes, not merely opposition to Stalin. Trotsky was therefore entitled to a fair hearing.[43]

In exile, Trotsky sought a hearing for himself and his son before an impartial tribunal. An American Committee for the Defense of Leon Trotsky was formed in March 1936 to enable him to state his case. Freda Kirchwey, editor of the *Nation,* originally joined the committee. After she had resigned from it, the *Nation* lapsed into silence about the Show Trials.[44] The communist press excoriated the committee, accusing it of aiding fascism and meddling in Soviet internal affairs. Corliss Lamont, a Columbia philosophy professor, declared that "liberalism toward Trotskyism is stupidity border-ing on treason to the working class."[45] In February 1937 an "Open Letter to American Liberals" defended the Show Trials and attempted to dissuade any liberals from joining the Trotsky inquiry. Among the letter signers were Heywood Broun, Lillian Hellman, Robert Lynd, Corliss Lamont, Malcolm Cowley (editor, the *New Republic*), Max Lerner (editor, the *Nation*), Robert Morss Lovett (editor, the *New Republic*), Louis Fischer (editor, the *Nation*), Theodore Dreiser, Granville Hicks, and Raymond Robins.[46] Robins wrote a personal letter to Dewey urging him not to participate in the inquiry. In an effort to shipwreck the committee, bribes, personal threats, and harassments, plus free trips to Moscow were offered as inducements. Slandered as a Trotskyite, a fascist, and senile, Dewey would confound his assailants by shortly publishing his master work, *Logic: The Theory of Inquiry.* Soviet Ambassador Troyanovsky also attempted to sabotage the inquiry. Nine original members of the committee did resign due to communist-inspired pressure. After being subjected to such treatment, Dewey redoubled his resolve and courageously agreed to participate as chairman of the Trotsky Inquiry Commission.

At the age of seventy-eight, Dewey traveled to Coyacan, Mexico, where the hearings opened on April 10, 1937. The cement barricades, sandbags, boarded-up windows, and police guards at the scene illustrated the pre-cariousness of open inquiry in a sinister world.[47] A week after the inquiry commenced, Carlton Beals resigned from the commission, sighting partial-ity among its members. The *New Republic* pounced upon Beals's statement as evidence that any potential usefulness of Dewey's inquiry would be adul-terated.[48] The inquiry supporters dispatched a letter challenging the *New*

Republic's contention that a counter-trial was futile. The editors of the *New Republic* responded that the trial could not be objective and would be a propaganda soapbox. They advised that a neutral, agnostic position be adopted toward the Show Trials. The dispute was none of America's business; it would divide liberal forces.[49] Attention should be shifted to domestic concerns.

The editors sought to vitiate the inquiry further by mailing official reports of the Show Trials, along with published material defending Trotsky, to an arbiter, Professor Fred Rodell of Yale Law School. Rodell concluded that the two sides "canceled each other out." To reach a valid conclusion at this juncture was impossible and such an attempt should not be undertaken.[50] However, the editors had refused to question the verdict of the Moscow Trials after already intimating the defendants' guilt. Dwight MacDonald accused Malcolm Cowley, literary editor of the *New Republic,* of credulously accepting the whole Stalinist line that Trotskyism led directly to fascism. Sidney Hook mentioned that Cowley contradicted himself by saying that judgment must be suspended on the testimony of Radek and Pyatakov. Cowley then contended that this testimony demonstrated Trotsky's guilt.[51] The *New Republic* reacted by warning that it would print no more letters on the Moscow Trials unless they were sustained by new information. Within a month, it published Walter Duranty's apology for Soviet efforts to ferret out Trotskyite saboteurs in Russia.[52]

After a diligent investigation, Dewey returned to New York and pronounced the Trotsky Inquiry Commission's verdict of "not guilty." He defended the inquiry's objectivity, disclosing that those convinced of Trotsky's guilt were not only invited to the hearing but offered full rights of cross-examination. Dewey reiterated that Trotsky's theories, with which he disagreed, were not on trial; only the specific crimes attributed to Trotsky in Moscow were at issue. Dewey thought that the Sacco and Vanzetti case had been one in which two men were convicted for what they believed and for being "dangerous nuisances" regardless of whether they committed any criminal act. He was disheartened that professed liberals would now adopt this approach in Trotsky's case. Genuine liberals must freely seek the truth instead of expediently concealing the grim facts about Russia. How could liberals blindly accept such behavior by the Soviet Union when they would vociferously condemn it everywhere else? Either Trotsky was guilty or he was not. If he was innocent, the Soviet Union stood condemned for deliberate deceit. Dewey remarked that the cowardly incapacity of liberals to face unpleasant facts was their "standing weakness."[53]

The final committee report, entitled *Not Guilty: Report of the Commission of Inquiry into the Charges Made against Leon Trotsky,* was published on September 21, 1937. The *New Republic* and the *Nation* squirmed evasively after the verdict was announced. The former declined to review the report; it claimed that the real issue was whether there was a conspiracy against the Soviet Union and not whether Trotsky was guilty of some specific act.[54] The *Nation* conceded that some discrepancies had been uncovered but the findings were still inconclusive. Again, discrediting the Dewey Commission, the journal appealed for new evidence.[55] No matter how much subterfuge they might employ, these two journals could not ignore the impact of Dewey's inquiry on public opinion. The *New Republic* termed the Show Trials "a major disaster." In their exasperated struggle to preserve the Popular Front, the editors refused to confront the issue of Stalinism. The trials, however, had presented the world with a fearful glimpse of this totalitarian regime.

The ordeal of the Trotsky Trial reaffirmed Dewey's belief that means could not be divorced from ends. A fatal tendency of the totalitarian mentality consisted in its predilection to utilize any tactics (terror, deceit, violence) in order to obtain a utopian end. Rule by terror could never lead to economic justice, peace, or freedom. Promises of future good behavior notwithstanding, the Machiavellian means defeated the end. On this basis, Dewey crushingly refuted both Stalin and Trotsky because, theoretically, their tactics were identical.[56] The Trotskyites, who hoped that they had gained an ally, condemned Dewey for his puristic pursuit of truth.[57] Alfred Bingham agreed that the Moscow Trials exposed the bankruptcy of both branches of Marxism. Earl Browder, Communist Party chief, explained it this way: "Trotskyism is treachery reduced to a science. Defeated and driven out everywhere it shows its face openly. Trotskyism now works in a hidden manner, especially making use of confused liberals and socialists like John Dewey and Norman Thomas who have lost their bearings in the chaos of capitalist disintegration."[58] Dewey asserted that his view, not that of the Marxists, was the most radically democratic.

Dewey admitted his disappointment over the course of the Soviet revolution. Initially conceiving the Soviet Union as a social laboratory from which capitalist America could learn, he watched hopeful signs destroyed by repressive terror and purges. He repudiated the Soviet Union as an economic model and as an ally against the fascists. Democracy in Russia was a monstrous hoax; communism and fascism were becoming identical in practice. He predicted the likelihood of a Nazi-Soviet alliance months before the fact.[59] Dewey's activities earned him the undying enmity of Stalin's worldwide legions.

In May 1937, in the midst of the Trotsky inquiry, Dewey resigned as contributing editor to the *New Republic*. The journal never mentioned the reasons for this resignation from a man who had contributed more to its columns than anyone, except perhaps Herbert Croly. Dewey resigned to protest the *New Republic*'s pretense of impartiality and the journal's liberal masquerade, even though it routinely aped the communist line. It no longer encouraged "independent, critical thought."[60] In a letter to Bruce Bliven, the *New Republic* editor, Dewey objected specifically to: (1) the jaundiced apologetics regarding the Kirov assassination, (2) its suspended judgment on the Show Trials coupled with articles arguing for the defendants' guilt,

(3) its efforts to discredit the Trotsky inquiry, and (4) its idealization of the Soviet Union as a democratic model.[61] He was especially irritated at Malcolm Cowley, the literary editor. In 1932, Dewey informed Cowley that he was distressed to see him join the World Congress Against War, since it was a communist front group.[62] Cowley praised the Show Trials, solicited contributions for the communist *New Masses,* and smeared every liberal book that was skeptical of the Soviet Union. Edmund Wilson maintained that "during the last five years when the *New Republic* slid from progressivism to Bolshevism, Malcolm Cowley has served as the unofficial representative of the Communist Party line in literature on its editorial board."[63] Never forsaking hopes of conversion, Dewey wrote to Cowley explaining that the American radical movement must immediately cut all ties with Soviet Russia. Cowley responded by endorsing the Popular Front. He felt that Russia was generally proceeding in the right direction and should be protected from the fascist powers. Cowley also accused Trotsky of splintering the Left.[64] Yet, his *New Republic* never revealed how the Communist Party had systematically besieged the social democratic movement.

After the bizarre spectacle of the Moscow Trials, a group of prominent liberals, under Dewey's chairmanship, formed the Committee for Cultural Freedom (CCF). The committee outlined its principles and purposes in a letter to the *Nation.* Against the rising tide of totalitarianism, it defended creative and intellectual freedom as the "least common denominator" of a civilized culture. The committee placed the Soviet Union within the camp of totalitarian states, directly challenging the Popular Front. The reaction among leftist circles was electric. Freda Kirchwey, editor of the *Nation,* conceded that the communists had their faults but they performed a "necessary function" in the confused struggle of the time.[65] They had the same hopes and fears as liberals, and they also supported New Deal programs. Communists possessed admirable personality traits such as bravery, zealousness, and stoic determination. Like the Soviet Union, they were plucky defenders of "justice and nonaggression" in international affairs. Kirchwey pleaded for unity on the Left, an era of "good will and decency." She suspected some clandestine political motive behind the committee.

Sidney Hook answered Kirchwey's allegations. He reaffirmed that the committee had no political motive beyond a defense of intellectual freedom, a point that the letter specifically mentioned.[66] Kirchwey's slander was itself "morally reprehensible" and a threat to intellectual freedom. Was deceit necessary in order to preserve the Popular Front? Should not communists be differentiated from other leftist groups if they are found to be guilty of disgraceful practices? Every tactical weapon employed by the fascists was also utilized by the communists, Hook charged. Hiding behind the anonymity of various front groups, the communists were routine violators of democratic practices. This aided the forces of reaction. Hook stressed that the loyalty of the American Communist Party was to the Kremlin and not to peace, democracy, or intellectual freedom.

The *Nation* agreed to publish the committee's letter; the *New Republic,* on the other hand, refused to print it despite the renown of its sponsors. The editors contended that it was too lengthy; its full length was not justified by its "naive" comments. Instead, they selected excerpts from the document. Complete liberty was desirable but "liberty" was ticklish to define. In a deft verbal shuffle, the *New Republic* faulted the committee for contrasting the "entire liberty" of the United States with none at all in Russia, Germany, and Italy. This was obviously unfair. While America was free from "government coercion," few nations contained as much social pressure for conformity. According to the editors: "In lumping together Fascist powers and the USSR the committee showed a regrettable lack of historical perspective. It clearly implies that fascism and communism are both completely incompatible with the freedom of the individual. But while this charge is true of fascism, it is certainly not true of the theory of a socialist commonwealth."[67] Not only was the committee accused of aiding the fascists, it was linked to an "anti-Moscow communist splinter group," the Trotskyites. In a world of reality rather than absolutes, the *New Republic* urged a higher practicality.

Dewey wrote a letter complaining that the *New Republic*'s decision not to publish the committee's entire statement was indeed significant; for only then could readers judge for themselves whether the editor's attack was accurate. The committee's primary concern related to the threat of alien totalitarian doctrines subverting cultural freedom within the United States. Since numerous socialists, including Norman Thomas, signed the letter, it was nonsensical that the committee would juxtapose individual freedom and socialism. Dewey was not concerned about the *theory* of a socialist commonwealth, only its *actual practices.* He repeated that there was not a Trotskyite among its signers. In fact, the committee was actually assailed by the Trotskyite press.[68]

The *New Republic* continued to malign the Committee for Cultural Freedom in an undisguised campaign to destroy it. Accusing the committee of red-baiting, the editors praised Soviet foreign policy as a "steady influence for peace. Failure to differentiate between the Soviet Union and fascist states was "calamitous." Ferdinand Lundberg, secretary of the committee, replied to these allegations. The defense of American liberalism did not necessitate a whitewashing of Stalin. Terming the Lundberg letter "boring," the editors repeated that they had seen "no evidence that the political trials were frame-ups, at least on the whole. . . ."[69] They also parroted the *New Masses'* line that General Kritivsky was an imposter. Kritivsky, head of Soviet military intelligence for twenty years, brought corroborated charges against Stalin.[70] Corliss Lamont and Donald Ogden Stewart, head of the frontist League of American writers, acted in concert with the Communist Party in trying to stampede resignations from the CCF. They began to circulate a letter designed to torpedo the committee.[71] On July 6, 1939, the *Daily Worker* announced that William Carlos Williams and Countre Cullen had bolted the committee. The two stated that their action was prompted by the League of American Writers. Williams earlier dissociated himself from a magazine that had been blacklisted by the Communist Party. He excused himself by explaining that further contact would prevent his verse from being published in the communist *New Masses.*[72]

On August 26, 1939, the letter sponsored by Corliss Lamont surfaced at last. Addressed to "All Active Supporters of Democracy and Peace," it scathingly denounced the Committee for Cultural Freedom as fascist-oriented. The letter was signed by over 400 distinguished intellectuals including: Waldo Frank, Max Lerner, I. F. Stone, Frederick Schuman, James Thurber, Robert Morss Lovett, and, of course, William Carlos Williams. The committee had perpetuated the "fantastic falsehood that the USSR and the totalitarian states are basically alike." The manifesto listed ten fundamental ways in which communism and fascism differed. The Soviet Union would continue "as always to be a bulwark against war and aggression."[73] While eliminating racial and national prejudice, the Soviet Union had effected a great educational advance by providing the Russian masses with the best thought from Aristotle to Lenin. They replaced myths with the sanction of experimental science. Democratic freedom was being rapidly extended as the transitional dictatorship was consummated by the new epoch-making Soviet constitution. The mutual aims and ideals of the United States and the Soviet Union had begotten a sound cooperative basis for peace and collective security. The letter indicted the Committee for Cultural Freedom for deviously twisting anti-fascist into anti-Soviet sentiment.

The *New Republic* deemed the letter to be less than candid about the Soviet dictatorship and its violations of civil liberty. Nevertheless, the "general tendency" of the document was correct. Continued American-Soviet friendship was commendable in light of the current world situation.[74] These remarks were printed one day before the signing of the Nazi-Soviet Pact. The *Nation* later published the letter and commented that it constituted an "unqualified endorsement" of the Soviet system.[75] Though the majority of its editors opposed the letter, two did sign it. The journal now contended that the international events of the previous week served as an "effective commentary" on the letter.

Complaining that European affairs were mined with "insincerity, devious methods, secrets, and surprises," the *New Republic* struggled to rebound from the shock of events.[76] Adopting the new communist isolationist line, the editors held that like the United States, much could be said for Russia's isolation.[77] They denied rumors about a secret agreement partitioning Poland, indicating that Russia could still sell arms to Poland under the terms of the Nazi-Soviet Pact. When the Soviets mobilized on the Polish border, the editors clung to the view that Russia was merely protecting its own border and would not launch an attack on Poland.[78] After the Soviet attack, they confessed that Soviet power throughout the world rested on force rather than moral trust. The Soviet Union was just like other great powers. However, Poland did possess a reactionary government.[79] Practically none of the Soviet sympathizers who signed the letter engaged in any public recantation. Dewey wrote a letter to all 400 signers asking them if the Nazi-Soviet Pact provoked them to reconsider their allegiances. Only two expressed a change of sentiment.[80]

The implacable hostility between communism and fascism was the bedrock premise of a generation of intellectuals. Shortly after the attack on Poland, the Communist Party held a mass rally at Madison Square Garden. James Wechsler recalled that the packed house did not know for whom or what they should be rooting. No speaker tried to explain the party line on foreign policy. The only safe target was Leon Trotsky whose name brought jeers from the crowd. Finally, the meeting was reduced to singing old revolutionary songs. Not one heckler was in the audience. Some seemed relieved that tenuous fellow-travelers had been exposed, leaving only the hard core of genuine loyalists.[81] The untimely events of August 1939 caused a temporary moratorium on the Popular Front. Dewey believed that Stalinism had "self-destructed." Sidney Hook offered the following warning: "Crypto-Stalinism has been the curse of American culture for the last few years. . . . It is already retreating from its mild criticism of the Stalinazi Pact."[82] Hook identified the *New Republic* editor, George Soule, as the prototype crypto-Stalinist; later they engaged in a heated polemical exchange in the *New Leader*. The Nazi-Soviet Pact, coupled with the Russian attack on Finland in November 1939, did cripple the Popular Front. Frederick Schuman had defended the "Stalinazi Pact" as successful *realpolitik,* but the invasion of Finland was "utterly indefensible." Even the *New Republic* admitted that the Soviet invasion of Finland was the clearest case of "calculated and unprovoked aggression" against a small neighbor.[83] Vincent Sheean and Louis Fischer, both articulate apologists for Stalin in the past, turned against him after the pact.

Dewey and the Committee for Cultural Freedom addressed an open letter to the League of American Writers. The league operated as perhaps the most effective communist-front group. It had refused to invite Dewey to a symposium, citing his dissident pro-fascist tendencies.[84] Since the "Stalinazi Pact," an eerie reticence had fallen over the league. Dewey asked if it still existed and outlined a series of questions on which members might deliberate.[85] One-third of its officers had resigned; it did not meet again till June 1941 when the political atmosphere was more propitious. The Committee for Cultural Freedom persevered in its efforts to expose communist-front groups. (When in 1940 Dewey refused to join Franz Boas's front group, the American Committee for Democracy and Freedom, he was again branded a "fascist."[86]) Dewey lectured at the CCF's first public meeting.[87] While the committee relentlessly monitored communist activities, it remained sensitive to civil liberties. Dewey and Hook signed a committee letter to Congress demanding the replacement of Martin Dies on the House Committee on Un-American Activities. Dies seemed incapable of distinguishing aliens from subversives.[88]

Dewey's book, *Freedom and Culture* (published in late 1939), represented his most graphic response to the rise of Marxist totalitarianism. Without equivocation he formulated the differences between totalitarian and democratic cultures.[89] In the midst of a complex and at times overwhelming world, totalitarianism was able to simplify problems by reducing them to one causal factor. This was the source of its romantic appeal, which was very seductive to intellectuals in search of a dogmatic faith. Marxism offered a monistic vision that ignored or condemned those who quarreled with its central dogmas. By removing the contingent human factor in history, it obviated the need to observe the world critically.[90] The final answer had already been given; human responsibility had evaporated and dissent was intolerable. Marxist science was not scientific. In an effort to demonstrate this, Dewey analyzed the strange dialectic of Truth, negating the negation, when it was controlled by the party. It jumped from a denigration of democracy as middle-class capitalism, labeling all democratic socialists as social fascists, to the policy of the Popular Front, presenting Bolshevism as twentieth-century Americanism. Then, it switched from a denunciation of Nazi Germany to a virtual alliance with Hitler.[91] Peace was promoted by a succession of wars. Previously de-emphasizing the role of Marxist ideology, Dewey insisted that it animated Stalin's regime and found a receptive environment in Asiatic Russia.

Peter Viereck observed that the glory of the intellectuals during the thirties consisted in their opposition to fascism, while their shame was a blindness towards communism. By this standard, Dewey emerges as a monumental figure. With courage and integrity, he stood firm against the pocket-sized Stalins of the literary-academic world. No one contributed more to desanctifying the workers' paradise.

NOTES

1. Eugene Lyons, "Where the News Ends," *NL* (July 1, 1939):8.

2. In 1926, Charles Clayton Morrison and Kirby Page visited Russia and warmly praised the "colossal Soviet experiment." They wrote President Coolidge urging diplomatic recognition. *WT* (Oct., 1926):180. Roger Baldwin, director of the American Civil Liberties Union, toured Russia. He wrote a book, *Liberty Under the Soviets* (1928), which hatched a distinction between political and economic freedom. Though no political freedom existed, something more basic was being accomplished — genuine economic freedom. The repressions were necessary as a foundation for unprecedented levels of civil liberty. The divisibility of liberty became a leading instrument for Soviet apologists.

3. Reinhold Niebuhr, "Russia Makes the Machine Its God," *CC* (Sept. 10, 1930):1080–81. Niebuhr, "The Church in Russia," *CC* (Sept. 29, 1930):1144–46. Niebuhr, "Russian Efficiency," *CC* (Oct. 1, 1930):1178–80. Niebuhr, "The Land of Extremes," *CC* (Oct. 15, 1930):1241–45.

4. John Dewey, "A Country in a State of Flux," *NR* (Nov. 21, 1928):14.

5. John Dewey–Sidney Hook (July 25, 1928), John Dewey Papers, Morris Library, Southern Illinois University.

6. John Dewey, "New Schools for a New Era," *NR* (Dec. 17, 1928):91.

7. John Dewey, "The Great Experiment and Its Future," *NR* (Dec. 18, 1929):135-6. Dewey noted how trade unions had voluntarily created a cultural center. In fact, trade unionism was liquidated in the Soviet Union.

8. William Brickman argued that Dewey could not have obtained first-hand knowledge of what was happening to non-Russian populations. Brickman expressed amazement that Dewey could tacitly approve of Lenin's vocabulary of class struggle. William Brickman, "Soviet Attitudes Toward John Dewey as an Educator," in Douglas Lawson and Arthur Lean, eds., *John Dewey and the World View* (Carbondale: Southern Illinois University Press, 1976), p. 79.

9. John Dewey, "Surpassing America," *NR* (April 15, 1931):241-43. In 1929, Dewey wrote an introduction to Maurice Hindus's *Humanity Uprooted* (New York: Cope and Smith, 1929), pp. xv-xix. He praised the book's objectivity. Hindus would claim that certain inequities did exist in Russia but, "in revolution as in war, it is the objective that counts, and not the price, whether in gold or in blood." The extermination of the Kulaks and the terror were acceptable revolutionary acts. See Maurice Hindus, *The Great Offensive* (New York: H. Smith & K. Haas, 1933), pp. 28-29.

10. Heywood Broun, "Dr. Dewey Finds Communists in the CIO," *NR* (Jan. 12, 1938):280.

11. John Dewey, "Politics and Labor Education," *NR* (Jan. 2, 1929):213. *NR* (Aug. 26, 1931):48.

12. Dewey reminisced about his Russia trip in a series of letters to Robert V. Daniels published in *The Journal of the History of Ideas* (1959):576-77.

13. George Counts, *The Soviet Challenge to America* (New York: John Day Co., 1931).

14. *NR* (June 8, 1932):104.

15. John Dewey and Tufts, *Ethics* (1932), pp. 477-78.

16. John Dewey and John Childs, "The Social-Economic Situation in Education," in William Kilpatrick, ed., *The Educational Frontier* (New York: Century Co., 1933), p. 72.

17. In recollecting the situation Hook stated that "[the Communist Party] realized that it could not capture the liberal movement unless it had John Dewey in tow. So long as he stayed out of its chief fronts or was critical, the hegemony of the Communist Party over large sections of American liberal opinion was threatened. Until this time, he had not taken a hostile position to the Soviet Union and was one of the earliest public figures to call for its recognition." Sidney Hook, "Some Memories of John Dewey," *Commentary* (1952):251.

18. John Dewey, "Why I Am Not a Communist," *Modern Monthly* (April, 1934):135.

19. Ibid., p. 137.

20. Paul Salter and Jack Libronne, "Dewey, Russell, and Cohen: Why They Are Anti-Communist," *New Masses* (July 17, 1934):24-27.

21. Bruce Bliven, *Five Million Words Later* (New York: J. Day Co., 1970), p. 173. When the American Civil Liberties Union became infiltrated with communists, Dewey also resigned in protest from this organization. Dykuizen, *The Life and Mind of John Dewey*, p. 173.

22. "Four Prominent Columbia Professors Quit: Teachers' Union Score Stalinists," *NR* (Jan. 7, 1939):2.

23. "Local Five and Communism," *NR* (April 5, 1941):472.

24. "A Plea for Unity," *SF* (Oct., 1935):3.

25. "Teachers and Labor," *SF* (Oct., 1935):7. Dewey, "Class Struggle and the Democratic Way," *SF* (May, 1936):241-42. John Childs, "Democracy, Education, and Class Struggle," *SF* (June, 1936):274-78. Earlier, Dewey acknowledged that social science would develop only if social planning was effected. Dewey, "Social Science and Social Control," *NR* (July, 1931):276-77.

26. *L&SA*, p. 85. In 1930, Dewey wrote that he did not know enough about Marx to discuss his philosophy. This is a startling admission for a philosopher of Dewey's stature. Max Eastman noted that Dewey admitted that he never read Marx. However, Dewey listed *Das Capital* as the most influential book in the last twenty-five to fifty years. "News and Notes," *English Journal* (1936):497. Dewey, "Social Change and Its Human Direction," *Modern*

Quarterly (Winter, 1930):424. See Max Eastman, *Einstein, Trotsky, Hemingway, Freud and Other Great Companions* (New York: Collier Books, 1959), p. 280.

27. Reinhold Niebuhr, "The Pathos of Liberalism," *N* (Sept. 11, 1935):303-4. See frontist Kenneth Burke's review, "Liberalism's Family Tree," *NR* (March 4, 1936):115-6.

28. *NR* (Jan. 9, 1935):233.

29. *New Masses* (March 5, 1935):4-5.

30. *New Masses* (Jan. 29, 1935):5.

31. "The Russian Executions," *NR* (Feb. 27, 1935):77.

32. Waldo Frank, "The Russian Executions," *NR* (Feb. 27, 1935):77.

33. "The Conditions of Civil Liberties," *NR* (Feb. 27, 1935):60-2.

34. *NR* (Jan. 9, 1935):233.

35. "Liberals and Soviet Russia," *NR* (Feb. 27, 1925):76. *CS* (Jan., 1935):5.

36. "Russia's New Constitution," *NR* (Dec. 9, 1936):160-1. Louis Fischer, "The New Soviet Constitution," *N* (June 17, 1936):722.

37. George Soule, "Does Socialism Work? Judging the Soviet Union," *NR* (Feb. 12, 1936):13.

38. George Soule, "Does Socialism Work? III," *NR* (Feb. 19, 1936):41.

39. Frederick Schuman, "Liberalism and Communism Reconsidered," *Southern Review* (Autumn, 1936):326-28.

40. "Another Russian Trial," *WR* (Feb. 3, 1937):400.

41. Frederick Schuman, "Leon Trotsky: Martyr or Renegade?" *Southern Review* (Summer, 1937):51-75. See Sidney Hook's rejoinder, "Liberalism and the Case of Leon Trotsky," *Southern Review* (Winter, 1937):267-82.

42. Reinhold Niebuhr, "Against Carl Browder," *NR* (June 9, 1937):132. Niebuhr was also a member of the American Committee for the Defense of Leon Trotsky.

43. Sidney Hook, "Both Their Houses," *NR* (June 2, 1937):104. Dewey, "Dewey Rebukes Those Liberals Who Will Not Look into Facts," *NL* (May 14, 1937):4, 7.

44. *N* (Aug. 29, 1936):226.

45. *Soviet Russia Today* (March, 1937):7.

46. "An Open Letter to American Liberals," *Daily Worker* (Feb. 9, 1937), p. 2. Reprinted in *Soviet Russia Today* (March, 1937):14-15.

47. John Dewey, "Pravda on Trotsky," *NR* (March, 24, 1937):212.

48. *NR* (April 21, 1937):343. Carleton Beals, "Mr. Beals Resigns From Trotsky Commission," *Soviet Russia Today* (May, 1937):38.

49. "Trotsky and the Russian Trials," *NR* (May 17, 1937):169-70.

50. "Agnosticism in the Moscow Trials," *NR* (May 19, 1937):33-34.

51. Dwight MacDonald, "Trotsky and the Russian Trials, *NR* (May 19, 1937):49-50.

52. Walter Duranty, "The Riddle of Russia," *NR* (July 14, 1937):220-22. *NR* (June 2, 1937):187.

53. John Dewey, "Dewey Rebukes Those Liberals Who Will Not Look into Facts," *NL* (May 15, 1937):7.

54. *NR* (Dec. 22, 1937):181-2.

55. *N* (May 22, 1937):578.

56. John Dewey, "Democracy Is Radical," *CS* (Jan. 1937):10-11. Dewey, "Means and Ends, Their Interdependence" and Leon Trotsky's "Essay on Their Morals and Ours," *New International* (Aug., 1938):232-33. Dewey, "Country Warned by Dewey of Dangers in Any Communism," *NL* (Dec. 25, 1937):1, 5. See Trotskyite George Novack's critique of Dewey in *Pragmatism vs. Marxism* (New York: Pathfinder Press, 1975). Dewey was a member of the Workers Defense League, which aided eighteen convicted Trotskyites. "Aid Labors Eighteen Political Prisoners and Their Families," *Fourth International* (1944):1. For Dewey's involvement in other Workers Defense League Appeals, see "Dewey Voices Protest Over Jersey Gag Rule," *The Call* (Jan. 14, 1939):3. "Save Odell Waller," *CS* (Dec., 1941):375.

57. James Burnham and Max Schactman, "Intellectuals in Retreat," *New International* (Jan., 1939):6.

58. Earl Browder, "Toward an American Commonwealth," *SF* (Feb., 1938):164. Sidney Hook, "The Logic of the Moscow Trial Condemns Stalin's Brutalitarian Dictatorship," *NL* (April 7, 1939):5.

59. Agnes Meyer, "The Significance of the Trotsky Trial: Interview with John Dewey," *International Conciliation* (Feb., 1938):54. Writers in both *Common Sense* and the *New Leader* predicted the Nazi-Soviet Pact well in advance. See Peter Drucker, "That Coming Nazi-Soviet Pact," *CS* (March, 1939):16-17. *CS* (April, 1939):26. Boris Shub, "Stalin Speech Leaves Way Open For Accord With Hitler Regime," *NL* (March 18, 1939):4. According to Eugene Lyons: "If the Nazi-Soviet rapprochement did not take place, the fault will certainly not be Stalin's. He has been begging for the embrace." Eugene Lyons, "Where the News Ends," *NL* (Jan. 14, 1939):8.

60. John Dewey – John Dos Passos (June 12, 1937), University of Virginia Collection, University of Virginia Library, University of Virginia.

61. John Dewey – Bruce Bliven (May 26, 1937), Sidney Hook Collection, Morris Library, Southern Illinois University.

62. John Dewey – Malcolm Cowley (July 21, 1932), John Dewey Papers, Morris Library, Southern Illinois University. Instead of agnosticism, Cowley, along with 150 educators and artists, signed a letter to the *Daily Worker* proclaiming that the trials by the "sheer weight of evidence" established the guilt of the defendants. It called upon liberals to assist the efforts of the Soviet Union to liberate itself from "insidious internal dangers," which constituted the chief threat to democracy and peace. Other signers included Lillian Hellman, Granville Hicks, Corliss Lamont, V. J. McGill, and Maxwell Stewart. "Leading Artists and Educators Support Soviet Trial Verdict," *Daily Worker* (April 28, 1938), p. 4.

63. Edmund Wilson, "Cowley and the Literary GPU," *NL* (Jan. 27, 1940):8. See Malcolm Cowley, "Stalin or Satan?" *NR* (Jan. 20, 1937):349. Eugene Lyons, "Where the News Ends," *NL* (Oct. 29, 1938):8.

64. John Dewey to Malcolm Cowley (June 2, 1937), Malcolm Cowley to John Dewey (June 4, 1937), John Dewey Papers, Morris Library, Southern Illinois University.

65. Freda Kirchwey, "Red Totalitarianism," *N* (May 27, 1939):605-606.

66. *N* (June 17, 1939):711. See Hook, "The Anatomy of the Popular Front," *Partisan Review* (Spring, 1939):429-462.

67. "Liberty and Common Sense," *NR* (May 31, 1939):89.

68. "The Committee for Cultural Freedom," *NR* (June 14, 1939):161-2.

69. "In Reply to Mr. Lundberg," *NR* (June 28, 1939):202. Ferdinand Lundberg, "The Committee for Cultural Freedom," *NR* (June 28, 1939):216-18. See Boris Shub, "Culture in a Straitjacket," *NL* (June 17, 1939):3. Victor Riesel, "New Culture Committee Grows Rapidly," *NL* (June 10, 1939):1. Ferdinand Lundberg, "Stalinoid Literary Triggermen Barrage Cultural Committee," *NL* (July 29, 1939):5.

70. Suzanne La Follette, "The *Nation* Hedges on Anti-Krivitsky Drive," *NL* (July 15, 1939):5.

71. Victor Riesel, "Stalinites Smear Cultural Committee as 'Fascists,'" *WL* (Aug. 5, 1939):1.

72. "Sinclair Lewis Joins Cultural Committee," *NL* (July 9, 1939):1.

73. *N* (Aug. 26, 1939):228.

74. *NR* (Aug. 23, 1939):63.

75. *N* (Sept. 2, 1939):231.

76. "Stalin's Munich," *NR* (Aug. 30, 1939):88.

77. *NR* (Sept. 6, 1939):118.

78. *NR* (Sept. 20, 1939):175. I. F. Stone and Richard Rovere blamed Chamberlain for the Nazi-Soviet Pact. I. F. Stone, "Chamberlain's Russo-German Pact," *N* (Sept. 5, 1939):313-16. Richard Rovere, "What Every Appeaser Should Know," *New Masses* (Sept. 5, 1939):5-6. "Why the Red Army Marched," *New Masses* (Sept. 26, 1939):3-4.

79. *NR* (Sept. 27, 1939):197-8.

80. "Hook Replies," *Commentary* (Dec., 1949):600.

81. James Wechsler, *Age of Suspicion* (New York: Random House, 1953), pp. 145-46.

82. Sidney Hook, "The Art of Crypto-Stalinism," *NL* (Nov. 18, 1939):5. See Hook and Soule, "The USSR and the *New Republic*," *NL* (Dec. 16, 1939):5. Soule wrote a foreword to Chenodanov's *Building a New World*, published by Stalinist Workers Publishers. See Hook, "The Anatomy of the Popular Front," *Partisan Review* (Spring, 1939):429-462.

83. *NR* (Dec. 13, 1939):218. Frederick Schuman, "Design for Chaos," *Events* (Jan. 1940): 6. Vincent Sheean, "The Summer Soldier," *New Masses* (Dec. 19, 1939):21-22.

84. *NL* (Nov. 11, 1939):8. Babette Deutsch resigned from the League of American Writers, citing the league's harsh treatment of Dewey.

85. "An Open Letter to the LAW," *Partisan Review* (1939):127-28. Dewey asked the following questions: "(1) What is the character of the present war? Is it an imperialist war or a war of the democracies against fascism? (2) What is the role of the Stalin regime in this war? Did the Stalin-Hitler Pact advance the cause of world peace or did it provoke fascist aggression? Does the league approve of the partition of Poland between Germany and Russia? (3) Does the league still hold that the United States should cooperate with the Soviet Union in order to stop the onward march of fascism? (4) Does the league still maintain that the United States should adopt a 'collective security' policy? If so, what countries should be included in such a common front? (5) Does the League of American Writers still consider the Communist Party to be a force for peace, democracy, and socialism?"

86. *NL* (April 27, 1940):2. For a listing of Boas's members see "Letter to FDR," *New Masses* (April 2, 1940):21.

87. John Dewey, "Democratic Ends Need Democratic Means for Their Realization," *NL* (Oct. 21, 1939):3.

88. *NL* (Jan. 6, 1940):7. Clarence Karier accused the Committee for Cultural Freedom of engaging in McCarthyite tactics. See Karier, "Liberalism and the Quest for Order," *History of Education Quarterly* (Spring, 1972):75.

89. Clarence Karier did not mention Dewey's Freedom and Culture when proclaiming that Dewey could not distinguish between totalitarian and free societies. John Diggins accused pragmatic liberalism of a "debilitating relativism," which was responsible for its alleged failure to meet the challenge of totalitarianism. After Dewey refused to predict the outcome of the war in December 1939, Diggins faulted pragmatism for providing "the most useless knowledge possible." Apparently, Diggins craves not knowledge but prophecy. See John Diggins, *Mussolini and Fascism: The View From America* (Princeton: Princeton University Press, 1972), p. 474.

90. See Sidney Hook, *Reason, Social Myths, and Democracy* (New York: John Day Co., 1940). Hook, *The Hero in History* (New York: John Day Co., 1943). Hook determined what was living and dead in the Marxist tradition.

91. *F&C*, p. 97.

9

Neutralism and the Depression

The thirties arrived with the Great Depression and were escorted out by World War II. During this tumultuous period, Dewey intensified his direct political activities. He sought solutions to both the foreign and the domestic challenges facing liberal democracy. He struggled to fend off his leftist revolutionary critics, while offering radical proposals for social change. By 1940 his political outlook had fully matured.

The Depression convinced Dewey that the traditional two-party system was bankrupt. He campaigned energetically through speeches, letters, and articles for an alternative, liberal third party. The prospect existed for such a party to stir a political realignment similar to what the British Labour Party had accomplished. Democratic labor groups would vie with reactionary business forces for political power. Since both the Democratic and Republican parties were the instruments of bosses and big business, Dewey termed expectations for change within these parties "an infantile illusion." In 1933 he functioned as chairman of the Seabury Investigation, which exposed the corruption of big city machine politics in America.[1] Dewey was convinced that the common people had been disenfranchised. Only a radical new party could effectively cope with the nation's economic distress. While a middle-class intellectual elite must initially provide the leadership and construct a unified program, farmers and workers would be integrated into the party and assume a dominant role. Like Thorstein Veblen, Dewey predicted that the cumulative impact of technology would foster a rational, secularistic middle class, one that could spearhead social reform toward economic planning.[2]

In May 1929, Dewey was elected as national chairman of the League for Independent Political Action, a group comprised of Social Gospel clergymen, socialists, reform liberals, and pacifists. Other members of the executive committee included Paul H. Douglas, Oswald Garrison Villard, Reinhold Niebuhr, Stuart Chase, Sherwood Eddy, Norman Thomas, and Howard Y. Williams. The purpose of the league was to act as a clearing-house for progressive opinion and then formulate a coherent set of principles upon which to launch a third party. Dewey set for himself the task of establishing this unified program. In addition, he was appointed president of the People's Lobby. Through its bulletin and the pages of the *New Republic,* he castigated the policies of the Hoover and Roosevelt administrations. Benjamin Marsh worked as executive secretary of the People's Lobby. On its council were Harry Laidler, Oswald Villard, Rexford Tugwell, and Harry Elmer Barnes. By 1932 the lively journal *Common Sense* began operating as the official outlet for the movement's policies, with Dewey listed as a contributing editor.

Through an extensive educational campaign, it was hoped that grass-roots support among intellectuals, workers, and farmers could be marshalled. The *New Republic* and the *Nation* endorsed the third-party approach.[3] On May 19, 1932, Dewey addressed the National Association for the Advancement of Colored People and urged blacks to join his new movement.[4] However, the league's effort to organize a widespread following resulted in only 10,000 members by 1932. Organized labor, blacks, progressive politicians, and other leftist groups were largely unresponsive.

Encouraged by the early success of league-supported Farm-Laborite candidates in Minnesota, Dewey wrote an open letter on December 25, 1930, to George Norris, senator from Nebraska. He implored Norris to become a presidential candidate for the third-party movement. Norris rejected the offer. Dewey criticized progressives like Borah and Norris for their lack of political courage. He later chastized them for their failure to persuade Hoover to call a special legislative session to deal with the economic crisis.[5] Dewey condemned Borah's nationalistic refusal to abolish World War I reparations, despite Borah's opposition to the war itself.[6] Outside of Minnesota and Wisconsin, league efforts to enlist support from politicians floundered miserably. The league was not even invited to attend a Conference of Progressives, held in Washington, D.C., in 1932. Both George Norris and Fiorello La Guardia (another league prospect) contended that the electoral college system institutionally stultified any possibility of a third party.[7]

On July 9 and 10, 1932, the League for Independent Political Action held a National Progressive Conference in Cleveland, Ohio. Dewey refrained from identifying the league's program as "socialist" since the term possessed doctrinaire and alien European connotations. At the conference, the league endorsed by many Socialist Party nominees — among them Norman Thomas for president — but the league avoided an endorsement of every aspect of the Socialist program.[8] Thomas polled only two percent of the total votes cast in the 1932 election. His poor showing was attributed to doctrinaire socialism; the league looked once more to midwestern labor and farm groups. Four new Farmer-Labor Party candidates were elected to Congress in 1932. Dewey viewed the western agrarian rejection of the Republican Party as a hopeful sign.[9] Norman Thomas reacted to league criticisms by blasting Dewey's "watered-down socialism and fence straddling." Many league members tacitly decided to vote for Roosevelt in order to prevent Hoover's re-election.[10] For this Thomas accused the league of being elitist. Its members possessed a hidden class interest and discretely avoided contact with the working masses. Dewey replied by reaffirming the need for a united political program and a strong third party. However, he doubted whether the Socialist Party could furnish a sufficiently broad political base. A successful political movement must not exclude the middle class and must also represent native American radicalism. The league's experimental program offered a concrete and comprehensive approach for radical reform.[11]

The league's "Four-Year Presidential Plan" was formulated out of the Cleveland Conference. This eighty-four point plan was jointly conceived by over one hundred political economists and experts and incorporated practically all of Dewey's recommendations. It advocated a socially planned economy considerably more expansive than New Deal reformism. While the *Nation* under Villard praised the document's advanced thinking, the socialist *World Tomorrow* objected to the plan's lack of cohesion. It betrayed "the meeting of many minds that didn't quite meet."[12] The journal argued that this program could not be implemented without a much more radical social reorganization than its gradualist philosophy permitted. In essence, the *World Tomorrow* wanted the league to assimilate with the Socialist Party. It was argued that the league lacked a "thoroughgoing social philosophy." In other words, it did not espouse doctrinaire socialism. Dewey did not search in vain for his one central issue. One word could describe this volatile social concern: money.

As chairman of the Joint Committee on Unemployment, Dewey was impressed by the fundamental need to change the basic economic system to one emphasizing social control.[13] The income of the nation must be redistributed to encourage general consumption. To accomplish this, the rich should be taxed heavily.[14] He advocated unemployment insurance; a massive federal relief program; federal credit for public works and construction; a six-hour work day; abolition of child labor; a full social insurance program; nationalization of banking and credit; repeal of consumption taxes; old age pensions; and public ownership of utilities, railroads, and eventually natural resources.[15] In addition to Dewey's specific proposals, the league's domestic plan included an investigation of the New York stock exchange, reorganization of the Federal Reserve System, public regulation of the securities market, outlawing holding companies, repeal of the syndicalist and Espionage Acts, guarantee of labor's right to strike, abolition of yellow dog contracts (whereby employees agreed not to join labor unions), abolition of the Electoral College, and a constitutional convention. These proposals outdistanced the New Deal, though some were subsequently adopted by Roosevelt. Dewey considered Roosevelt's program to be "blind and half-hearted." It was designed to patch up the present system with power remaining in the hands of the same vested elite. The captains of finance were the central targets of Dewey's reform program; they manipulated money while the common people labored for practically nothing. His proposals assumed a populistic tenor.

The league's foreign policy proposals also mirrored Dewey's isolationist anti-militarism. He objected to the Smoot-Hawley tariff, which afforded manufacturers protection at the expense of farmers and invited the world to engage in economic warfare.[16] The league suggested that the tariff's rates be reduced by twenty-five percent. An International Economic Conference should be convened to ease world tariffs and eventually establish free trade. International debts and reparations should be readjusted or, better still, liquidated altogether. The league urged a drastic fifty percent cut in military spending, ending federal subsidies on ships and planes that could be converted to war use, curtailment of industrial preparedness, abolition of conscription, consolidation of the armed services to facilitate complete disarmament, abolition of ROTC, safeguards for conscientious objectors, and a referendum on war. The league's platform also promised full cooperation with the League of Nations, entry into the World Court with affirmative jurisdiction, clarification of the Kellogg-Briand Pact to prevent warmaking, along with repudiation of the "Sole Guilt" clause and recognition of Soviet Russia. Regarding American imperialism, the league opposed military intervention in all countries (particularly Latin America), no protection for foreign investors, reorganization of the Pan-American Congress, military withdrawal from China, termination of extra-territorial privileges, and independence for the Philippines.

Dewey thought that the special interests of finance and monopoly conspired to involve the country in imperialistic adventures. This destroyed natural markets abroad, promoted underconsumption at home, and severely damaged European economies. Basic changes in the economic systems of all nations, excluding Russia, were necessary to subdue worldwide chaos.[17] Only the cooperative world management of resources would bring a stable peace. This prospect was dim: amidst a worldwide depression, the league's proposals embodied both the prevailing intellectual climate and the visceral isolationism of the midwestern states, where the league had its greatest appeal.

During September 1933 the league met in Chicago with other progressives to form the Farmer Labor Federation. Dewey became its honorary chairman. He recognized the odds against political success but did not lapse into disillusion.[18] With Congressman Thomas Amlie's assistance, the federation earned the support of Minnesota Governor Floyd Olson as well as Senator Robert LaFollette of Wisconsin. These men promised to bring their parties into a national campaign for the presidency in 1936.[19] The effort for a unified, national progressive party floundered as another conference in 1935 merely resulted in the formation of another umbrella group, the American Commonwealth Political Federation.[20] Factionalism, Roosevelt's popularity, and communist intrigue disintegrated this federation by the 1936 election. As a result, the third party Dewey had hoped for was never established. While many league members backed Roosevelt, Dewey voted instead for Norman Thomas. He contended that little difference existed between the two major parties.[21] Dewey's third-party political activities were an obvious failure since they scarcely approached national power. However, it may have been Dewey's most effective and available means to influence the country. His league did become a sounding board for new approaches to economic relief.

Rhetorically, Dewey despaired of peacemeal policies. This was uncharacteristic of his political tendencies. By 1935 he endorsed Alfred Bingham's proposal to absorb the capitalist system gradually by capturing the allegiance of the middle classes.[22] Like Edward Bellamy's transition plan, a production-for-use system with a shadow organization, the Cooperative Commonwealth, would demonstrate its superiority in practice to the capitalist system.[23] Private enterprise would continue in many small businesses, like the production of specialties, arts and crafts, and luxuries. Foreign trade would become a government monopoly. The commonwealth could buy out private industries as businesses joined the cooperative system voluntarily. Professional associations would direct the activities of various functional economic groups, encouraging democratic control. "I have read the proposed plan and I heartily agree," Dewey concluded.[24] This plan was incorporated into the platform of the American Commonwealth Political Federation. Though its actual implementation was highly improbable, the plan enabled Dewey's followers to reconcile democracy, voluntarism, and cooperative planning into one theoretical framework.

Bingham's *Common Sense* beseeched Roosevelt not to listen to the big army and navy crowd. It observed that "the armaments racket is assuming almost a determining character in international politics."[25] The Nye Investigation into the munitions industry stirred a torrent of "merchants of death" rhetoric from liberal journals.[26] They eagerly endorsed the investigations. *Common Sense* discovered in the hearings a springboard to fail-safe neutrality legislation.[27] Charles Beard praised the Nye Committee, comparing its revelations favorably with the diplomatic exposés following World War I.[28] A new deluge of revisionist writings on World War I appeared, of which Walter Millis's *Road to War* was the most popular.

Dewey and *Common Sense* called for the termination of all military and political support for the Machado regime in Cuba. He wrote an appeal for Cuban Revolutionary Youth expressing outrage at the American indifference to the crimes against humanity only ninety miles away.[29] Describing an uninhibited reign of terror with persecution of students and execution without trial, Dewey demanded action, although he did not specify whether that action should be in the form of arms, men, or moral sympathy. Since he also signed a letter admonishing Roosevelt to withdraw 600 American marines from Haiti, one can presume that Dewey was opposed to military intervention.[30] Earlier, as president of the People's Lobby, he wrote a letter to Hoover condemning a proposed forty-two million dollar sugar loan to Cuba. Dewey charged that "it is not the primary function of the United States to maintain power in areas subject to malign interpretations of the Monroe Doctrine pliant nominal rulers to operate governments by direction of Wall Street financiers."[31] The United States propped up the Machado regime by threatening its opposition with armed force. The sugar loan was nothing more than a conspiratorial plot hatched by an international cartel to boost sugar prices. Eventually, President Roosevelt did withdraw American support from the Machado regime, which was then replaced by Batista.

Charles Beard articulated a comprehensive foreign policy approach that synchronized with Dewey's isolationist outlook during the 1930s. After the failure of the London Economic Conference, liberals deemed it impossible to secure cooperation from national economies bent on capitalist profiteering. Concern for domestic problems and national self-sufficiency therefore took priority. This was the flip-side of idealistic internationalism. John Maynard Keynes proposed that "a greater measure of national self-sufficiency and economic isolation among countries than existed in 1914 may tend to serve the cause of peace rather than otherwise."[32] By October 1934 the *Nation* was openly relieved that the London Conference had failed.[33] Instead of curtailing foreign trade and concentrating his efforts on intranational consumption, Roosevelt constructed a large navy to protect foreign markets for American surplus goods. Beard correlated Roosevelt's policy with the Hamiltonian program of constantly expanding the industrial sector by artificially managing foreign trade through protective tariffs and subsidies.[34] He shared Jefferson's fear of the rise of an urban proletariat resulting in a vast disparity of wealth between capitalists and workers. Beard hypothesized that the probability of American involvement in a European or Asian war related directly to the economic interests of American nationals in the area. Dewey was also convinced that economic aid and loans had brought America into World War I.[35] Alarmed that Roosevelt might employ a foreign war to escape domestic crises, Beard opposed any extension of the American military presence beyond its continental waters. His continentalist approach was premised on America's capacity for a relatively self-sufficient economy. At the time, only seven percent of the gross national product was dependent on foreign trade. The prime source of national rivalry originated from an inefficient and unjust distribution of wealth at home. Beard did not categorically oppose international cooperation, but he did recognize that American policy and economic planning could not depend upon it.

By clarifying the national interest, Beard strove to lessen the likelihood of stumbling into another war. However, he did not completely rule out American participation in a future war. He favored a program of neutrality legislation designed to ensure that such involvement would not pivot around executive discretion or protection of neutral rights. Neutrality could be preserved by severely limiting the munitions trade and restricting foreign loans to belligerents. A genuine neutrality policy precluded any alteration favoring either of the belligerents after a war had commenced. The American public should retain the opportunity to air the issue of war and peace thoroughly before leaping into the abyss.[36] Discounting prospects of any miraculous invasion from either Europe or Asia, Beard could discover no justifiable reasons for the United States to fight beyond its hemispheric zone. Dewey agreed that America's physical isolation protected it from European conflicts.[37] He enthusiastically reviewed Beard's *America at Mid-Passage,* which elaborated the continentalist approach. In late 1939, Dewey concluded that he "should have greater confidence in the healthy development of the American ideal of humanistic democracy in the coming years if every editorial writer, every radio commentator, every legislator, and every administrator in the United States had beside him and used for constant reference the Beard account of our unfinished mid-passage course. A substitute title might well be 'Lest We Forget.'"[38] America was engaged in a unique political experiment. Divorcing American from European culture, Dewey portrayed the world crisis as between New and Old Worlds. America should concentrate on cultivating democracy here at home.

Was hemispheric defense a feasible policy? In the late 1930s, Roosevelt redoubled his efforts for better Pan-American relations. He utilized arguments for hemispheric defense as a backdoor justification for his rearmament program. Edward Mead Earle was convinced that with a coastal naval superiority the United States was practically invulnerable. In *The New Western Front* (1939), Stuart Chase attempted to demonstrate that the New World could become economically self-sufficient. Therefore, hemispheric defense was also viable. Hanson Baldwin, military editor of the *New York Times,* agreed. He further insisted that the United States could outbuild the rest of the world in a naval race. As stories of fascist intrigues in Latin America circulated, Nicholas Spykman indicated the inherent difficulties of Pan-American unity and hemispheric defense. In 1940–1941, the Phi Kappa Delta National Forensic Honor Society selected the hemispheric defense issue as the national debate question. At the time, the question was hardly self-evident. Unfortunately, Dewey assumed axiomatically that America was geographically invulnerable without ever exploring the military strategic parameters. America's security could best be preserved by engaging the enemy as far away from our shores as possible. Dewey eventually realized that a totalitarian Europe would necessitate a "fortress America" garrison state. The United States could not insulate itself from the plight of the rest of the world.[39]

The rise of Nazism strained the liberals' fetish for nonintervention. The book burnings, the Reichstag fire, the prison camps, and uniforms petrified the liberal community. As refugee scholars streamed in from Central Europe, Dewey helped to create the university-in-exile. Five weeks after Hitler rose to power, a "Provisional Committee for Protest Against German Fascist Atrocities" was formed. Along with Reinhold Niebuhr, Dewey was a committee member. At Cooper Union, Dewey spoke at a mass rally to honor Carl Von Ossietzky as a Nobel Prize winner. Sponsored by the International Relief Association, other speakers included Niebuhr and Mayor La Guardia. Dewey was a member of the International League for Academic Freedom, which recommended Ossietzky for the Nobel Prize. Ossietzky was convicted of high treason by exposing German rearmament in violation of the Versailles treaty.[40] In 1936, Dewey declined to participate in the celebration of a philosophical institute in Berlin. Both Dewey and Beard did not flavor their neutrality with any Nazi sympathies. For example, Dewey was honorary chairman of the "Joint Committee for Political Refugees," and Beard was chairman of the International Relief Association.

Many refugee scholars (Thomas Mann, Albert Einstein, and Auriel Kolnai, for example) were instrumental in converting the liberals from peace to war. By shifting the blame for fascism from the Versailles treaty to the spiritual depravity of German culture, the basis for reassessing the history of the previous twenty years was established. Books like Hans Kohn's *Revolutions and Dictatorships* and J. F. C. Hearnshaw's *Germany, The Aggressor Throughout the Ages* fingered Germany as the major enemy of Western civilization. Its criminal record was traced back to Attila.

When Adolf Hitler commenced his liquidation of the Versailles treaty through rearmament, liberal guilt initially inspired a policy of appeasement. The *Nation* blamed the Allies' continuous blundering for Hitler's decision to rearm. This "bold" defiance exemplified the utter futility of World War I and the total failure of violence to alter men's minds.[41] The encirclement of Germany would merely arouse even greater hatred and distrust. Ruling out any preventive war, the *Nation* proposed full equality for Germany among nations as a means to take the wind out of Hitler's rhetoric. The *New Republic* observed that Hitler was made "almost inevitable" by the Allied policy of enforcing the inequitous Versailles treaty, collecting impossible reparations, and perpetuating economic misery for Germany.[42] The *People's Lobby Bulletin* ridiculed any posture of righteous indignation: "America has been horrified at the stories of Hitler's oppression of the Jews in Germany. America has no right to expect anything different in Germany, for cruel and vicious as have been Hitler's policies, they are exactly what American financiers have brought about using Woodrow Wilson as their agent to get America into the war."[43] After a trip to Germany, Alfred Bingham characterized fascism as a middle-class movement against capitalist insecurity and the panic of a proletarian revolution. Instead of a capitalist war conspiracy, fascism's economic goal was self-sufficiency. Nazism was a highly unstable system of government that had the potential to evolve in a number of directions. According to Bingham, in 1935, the most likely direction was toward a truly "cooperative and classless" socialist society.[44] Bingham consistently underplayed the military threat of fascism, analogizing it to the Red Scare. He hoped to harness the sources of fascist appeal in America to secure social democratic ends. Isolationist anti-militarism could not dwell on Hitler's demonic character without evoking moral cries for some action.

On August 31, 1935, Roosevelt signed into law the first Neutrality Act. The *New Republic* supported this legislation, desiring to remove any presidential discretion in defining "the aggressor." When Mussolini attacked

Ethiopia, the editors reiterated Dewey's contention that sanctions were useless; they opted for even more stringent neutrality legislation. Charles Beard offered the following reminder to Americans: "We tried once to right European wrongs, to make the world safe for democracy. Mandatory neutrality may be no better, for not anyone actually knows. But we nearly burnt our house down with one experiment, so it seems not wholly irrational to try another line."[45] *Common Sense* chided the British and the French for condemning imperialist policies, which both of these countries had perfected for centuries.[46] Not to be outdone, the *Christian Century* published an article entitled "Hitler as Pacifist." It noted that Hitler was preoccupied with domestic problems and did not want war. Since he was revising the ignoble Versailles treaty without military conflict, Hitler was being promoted for the Nobel Peace Prize.[47] In a 1935 symposium on America's war involvement, Dewey stated that he would first try to keep the country out of war and then keep himself out if war occurred. Not even a prospective victory by Hitler over most of Europe could, at that time, persuade Dewey to advocate American participation. Avoidance of war was seemingly the highest priority, even if convinced, like Charles Beard, that the Nazis would soon commit aggression.[48] This was fundamentally a European problem.

The outbreak of the Spanish Civil War in July 1936 supplied crypto-Stalinists with a unique opportunity to press for a Popular Front. Liberals almost universally sympathized with the Loyalists. A democratically elected government was embattled by a reactionary, clerical minority. The issue could not have been more unequivocal. At first, both the *New Republic* and the *Nation* favored a policy of neutrality with nonintervention of all European powers in the conflict.[49] They anticipated a quick, decisive victory for the Loyalists. By January 1937, after the tide of battle worsened, the *New Republic* jettisoned neutrality for a special cash-and-carry plan to the Loyalists.[50] Louis Fischer, the *Nation's* correspondent in Spain, charged that neutrality and pacifism bred war by encouraging aggression. He pleaded for munitions shipments to the Loyalists.[51] Max Lerner, Frederick Schuman, and Lewis Mumford condemned the Spanish embargo because it indirectly aided the fascists. According to Archibald MacLeish this was definitely "America's War." I. F. Stone praised the Soviet Union as the only genuine anti-fascist state. The communists fighting in the streets of Madrid formed a frontline defense of the United States. Stone speculated about an Italian air raid on America's eastern seaboard.[52]

John Dewey, Norman Thomas, and other social democrats were confronted with a curious dilemma. They empathized with the Loyalists but recoiled from direct intervention or collective security. Objecting to the *Christian Century's* posture of complete isolation from Spain, Dewey, like Beard, proposed that the United States continue normal commercial relations with the Spanish Loyalists. It was the recognized government, and maintaining trade was in accord with international law. The embargo was illegal because this was a civil war. All private aid should be unrestricted. Legal objections to the recruitment of men in the United States were instigated by those with fascist sympathies. Dewey complained that the journal belittled the issue of democracy versus fascism. While an international war between fascist and democratic states would be a battle of "rival capitalisms," this civil war symbolized the effort to defend the democratic method under a properly elected government. If the Loyalists won, Dewey had faith that the resulting government would not be dictatorial. To keep America out of a future European war, the aggression of the fascist states must be stymied. Spain was the testing ground for the impending struggle against fascism.[53] Dewey was vice-chairman of the American Friends for Spanish Democracy, along with Ernest Hemingway, Albert Einstein, and frontist Malcolm Cowley. In January 1937, Dewey presided over an 18,000 strong Madison Square Garden Rally for Loyalist Spain, during which he shared the podium with Reinhold Niebuhr and communists like Ralph Bates.[54] The judicious line drawn between a civil war and international war was hopelessly tenuous. The sanctity of this popular cause would shortly be impugned.

Early into the Spanish Civil War, *Common Sense* analyzed the battle as comprised of communism and fascism, not fascism and democracy. It revealed that the Russians were masterminding the Loyalist regime. A communist dictatorship would be the probable result of a Loyalist victory. Opposing any lifting of an arms embargo, John Don Passos reported that the Loyalists were ruthlessly purging all anti-Soviet liberals from their ranks. Instead of joining the Abraham Lincoln Brigade, he implored Americans to remain at home and work for democratic reform.[55] Anarchist and Trotskyite forces in Spain battled against Stalinists in the streets of Barcelona. Yet, the *New Republic* and the *Nation* accepted the Soviet version of events because they were dependent upon Popular Front correspondents. Both Louis Fischer and Malcolm Cowley accused the anti-Stalinists of cowardice before the enemy and working in league with the fascists. Bertram Wolfe, an eyewitness to the scene, contested Fischer's report. Fischer applauded Soviet moves to purify and discipline leftist forces.[56]

Alfred Bingham warned that hatred and fear of fascism were almost as menacing as fascism itself. The conflict in Europe was a religious war between fascism and communism. America possessed its own unique faith. While intellectuals were inflaming the public for another war to make the world safe for democracy, democracy was not the issue. Capitalist democracy could not effectively serve as a bulwark, because fascism was more economically advanced. Only socialist democracy was a viable alternative. The real threat to civilization was war. The entry of America into a European war would signal the demise of the last democracy. Dewey accepted the essentials of this analysis. (Sidney Hook, Alfred Bingham, Norman Thomas, Lionel Trilling, Edmund Wilson, and several others signed a letter of protest to the *Nation*. After the *Panay* incident in China, the journal espoused a collective security approach and denied that the neutrality laws should be applied to China. While the *Nation* hoped to play upon sympathy for China to back into the Popular Front, the letter charged that the neutrality laws were passed democratically and should not be circumvented by executive discretion.[57])

After the Munich settlement, Roosevelt and his collective security supporters began the drive to revise the neutrality legislation. *Common Sense* favored a policy of appeasement and called for even stronger neutrality legislation. It suggested a world congress to revise the Treaty of Versailles by offering concessions to the have-not nations. Bingham defended the Munich settlement for staving off war.[58] Quincy Howe, associate editor of *Common Sense,* concluded that if the alternatives narrowed to that of a Hitlerized versus a Stalinized Europe, German domination was preferable. *Common Sense* believed that this was the conclusion reached by British and French diplomats at Munich.[59] Bingham insisted that Czechoslovakia was a geo-political monstrosity concocted at Versailles; such small, weak states were expendable for the overall goal of an integrated Europe. The Germans only desired territories guaranteeing their economic self-sufficiency. They would be absorbed with the effort to organize the Balkans, consolidating *mittel Europa*.[60] The *Nation* supported a revised neutrality but criticized Roosevelt's acquiescence in Chamberlain's Munich policy. Editor Freda Kirchwey advocated a collective economic boycott of fascist powers by England, France, Russia, and the United States.[61] However, Oswald Villard judged the collective security approach to be damaged irreparably. After Munich, who would ever want collective security with Britain or France?[62] The *New Republic* condemned Hitler's coup; but since it was still subject to pacifist Bruce Bliven's influence, it did not advocate an alteration in either the neutrality policy or armed preparedness.[63] Bliven admitted that he could not fight to defend a status quo, which for twenty years he had denounced as "unjust and unworkable."

Hitler took all of Czechoslovakia on March 16, 1939, cynically violating the terms of the Munich settlement. During that same month, *Common Sense* conducted a symposium on war, involving Lewis Mumford, Max Lerner, Charles Beard, John Dewey, John T. Flynn, Bertrand Russell, and Harry Elmer Barnes. All except Mumford and Lerner defended neutrality. Dewey remarked that under modern circumstances, war molded even democratic stages into totalitarian ones. He therefore agreed with Beard, Bingham, and Herbert Hoover: policy should be shaped by America's needs, not by European sentiments. If America entered the next war, it would possess a fascist government, a military-financial autocracy, which would suppress all of the democratic values for which it allegedly fought. Liberals who only recently had resolved that they would never support another war were now talking as though war was inevitable. Dewey pleaded, "if we make up our minds that it is not inevitable, and if we now set ourselves deliberately to seeing that no matter what happens we stay out, we shall save the country from the greatest social catastrophe that could overtake us, the destruction of all the foundations upon which to erect a socialized democracy."[64] This unpragmatic statement was written before the stark reality of a Hitlerized Europe.

After Hitler and Stalin attacked Poland and European armies mobilized for war, Dewey still defended a strict neutral policy. Anti-war sentiment was more entrenched than in World War I but the work had to be maintained. In *Freedom and Culture,* Dewey stressed that the most serious threat was internal, in the American attitudes and institutions that reverted back to old emotions and habits of Europe. The battlefield was really within ourselves.[65] This conflict was not to be waged with arms; it involved the extension of democratic methods to every aspect of community life. At the first public meeting of the Committee for Cultural Freedom (October 23, 1939), Dewey reaffirmed that "resort to military force is the first sure sign that we are giving up the struggle for the democratic way of life, and the Old World has conquered morally as well as geographically."[66] Freedom could not be furthered by adopting a totalitarian regime to fight totalitarianism.[67] America could best assist the world by offering a model for democracy. In 1937, Dewey made this acknowledgment: "The only time dictatorships seemed superior is in the abnormal conditions created by war and internal economic crises. I can think of nothing more fundamentally wrong than use of such pathological conditions as a criteria of the excellence of a government."[68] This admission concedes too much. If democracies are less militarily efficient than dictatorships, the only alternative is isolation. Democratic freedoms do not prosper in wartime but they are not necessarily destroyed either.

What can account for Dewey's liberal isolationism between the two world wars? His position was motivated by the following considerations: (1) rejection of the League of Nations and the World Court for fear of a European entanglement as a result of the Versailles treaty; (2) condemnation of nationalism, militarism, and imperialism; (3) acceptance of the revisionist historical thesis about war guilt; (4) endorsement of the merchants-of-death conspiracy hypothesis; (5) advancement of cultural particularism and geographical isolation of America from Europe (like Beard), and (6) suspicion that the war would destroy democracy at home. This outlook would eventually be transformed by the pressure of world affairs.

After Hitler's invasion of Poland, *Common Sense* contended that Hitler did not want an extension of the war. His peace terms were "intelligent and reasonable."[69] The preservation of the British Empire and Europe's small states was not worth American intervention. Though neither side should expect a total victory, the prospect of a German unification of Europe did not signify the end of civilization.[70] Irresponsible national sovereignty was at the root of Europe's plight. By July 1940 a policy aimed at giving Britain all-aid-short-of-war was being advocated by the editors of *Common Sense.* America's defensive preparations should be accelerated along with more efficient social organization at home. The editors stressed that the people's faith in democracy was more important in the long run than armed resistance. Eleanor Roosevelt praised this policy, and the journal endorsed

Roosevelt for president in 1940.[71] The editors called for a definition of Allied war aims and suggested a world federation founded upon a general economic settlement. Alfred Bingham fought to preserve neutrality and to pressure both sides to negotiate at the earliest opportunity. Repeating the war liberals' "peace without victory" policy, he proposed a negotiated settlement. Only a negotiated peace and a reformed Nazi regime could establish the stable federated Europe that Bingham desired. If American entrance could assure a speedy Nazi defeat, he favored American involvement. However, Bingham rejected any protracted conflict. He saw Hitler as impregnable on the continent and wanted to prevent a British defeat.[72] The *New Republic* also claimed that the defeat of Hitler was not sufficient in itself as a war aim. The *Nation*'s Freda Kirchwey rejected any possibility of negotiation with Hitler.[73]

In the December 1939 issue of *Common Sense,* Dewey delineated "the basis for hope" during the world crisis. Mentioning the possibility of a United States of Europe (Bingham's plan), Dewey searched for a silver lining.

> I think there are dependable signs that both in Europe, and in this country, belief in war and sheer force as the source of production for needed social change has suffered greatly. There is even a possibility that belief in war as an agency for this will have received a mortal wound by the time the war is over.[74]

These sanguine remarks were offered during the "phoney war" period when it appeared to some that Hitler would not attempt a wholesale conquest of Europe. The "Stalinazi Pact" had cleared the air of liberal illusions and revealed the common methods of totalitarians. Democracy could be reinvigorated by recognizing its unequivocal antagonism to totalitarianism. The hypnotic faith in political panaceas was discredited. While Dewey again emphasized the internal state of democracy in America, he insisted that wars could be resorted to, not as an agency of civilization, but to prevent the relapse into barbarism. Nazism would epitomize this barbarism. Dewey had thus qualified his unconditional neutrality.

American socialists were badly divided on the war issue. The international conspiracy of finance capitalism was the diabolical enemy according to the *People's Lobby Bulletin*. "Vicious as is Hitlerism," wrote Benjamin Marsh, "how much better or less dangerous to Americans is Morganism?"[75] The lobby seemingly despised British and French imperialism more than either Hitler or Stalin. It enforced a neutral position up to the bombing of Pearl Harbor. The lobby opposed Lend-Lease, sought an investigation of war profits, and advocated a war referendum. A transfer of government to the British Labour Party was a pre-condition for substantive American aid. Norman Thomas detailed his neutralist-pacifist foreign policy in *Keep America Out of War* (1939). He argued that modern war required totalitarian methods. When war arrived, truth yielding to advantage. All doubts and opposition were silenced. Reminding his readers of the treachery of

Versailles, Thomas considered this war merely another chapter in the age-old European game of power politics. This battle between old and new imperialisms should not involve America. America had no worry of foreign invasion. How could one fight beside Britain and France when both had racially oppressed their colonial peoples? Was Nazi aggression any more degrading than Britain's Opium War? By such reasoning, Thomas strove to display the total moral ambiguity of the conflict. He proposed a referendum on war with eighteen-year-olds being allowed to vote. Neutrality legislation must force impartiality and extend the arms embargo. The Industrial Mobilization Plan should be terminated, the military budget reduced, and war plotters driven from public life.[76] Thomas participated actively in the America First Committee rallies in New York City. Though his political judgment was blindly doctrinaire, Thomas was unfairly condemned for collaboration with Silver-Shirt Fascist elements.[77]

The *New Leader,* organ of the Social Democratic Federation, vehemently disputed Norman Thomas's approach to the war. Dewey sanctioned the *New Leader* as his chief source of information on foreign affairs. He became a contributing editor in 1942. In September 1939 the journal offered the Allies all-aid-short-of-war. Not yet advocating American participation as a full belligerent, the editors hoped that the Nazis could be defeated by cash-and-carry aid to Britain and France.[78] On October 21, 1939, editor William Bohn wrote an open letter to Charles Beard, repudiating isolationism.[79] The journal stayed two or three steps ahead of Roosevelt's policy, urging that planes rather than fireside chats would save the Allies.

Sidney Hook, Dewey's close colleague, became a key formulator of social democratic policies toward the war. Like Dewey, he also accented the defense of democracy through democratic procedures. The most radical differences among peoples was between experimentalists and absolutists. In October 1939, Hook declared: "Personally, I believe that the cause of democratic socialism will suffer if we become involved in war. But support or opposition to war is not the acid test of differentiation among socialists but rather the kind of method we have used in reaching our conclusion."[80] Having already divorced himself from the dogmatic pacifism of Norman Thomas, Hook suggested that the Ludlow Amendment (requiring a national referendum on war involvement) be included with proposed neutrality legislation. In 1938 this war referendum bill failed in Congress by a single vote. The amendment was consonant with the American democratic ideal and provided a truth test for these politicians who professed a desire to keep America out of war.[81] It could also mobilize public support behind the war effort. Neither Dewey nor Hook indicated at that time whether they supported military aid to the Allies.

After the fall of France in July 1940, Hook publicly challenged Norman Thomas's war policy. Nazism was "counter-revolutionary" to socialist ideals. No imaginable possibility existed for socialism to be introduced in a Nazi-dominated Europe. The socialists should lead the fight against the

Nazis.[82] By attempting to undermine capitalist governments, socialists would assist in the triumph of Hitler and commit suicide. Rather than fixing blame on who was ultimately responsible for the war, socialists should be concerned about the consequences of an Allied versus a Nazi victory. The American Socialist Party supported the government against actual invasion but ridiculed the possibility of any such attack. Hook reasoned that if war actually brought totalitarianism, then this defensive position was untenable as well. Hitler now possessed the intent to conquer. With a few technological developments after Britain's fall, he could also possess the means to launch an invasion after consolidating Europe. A hemispheric or quarter-hemispheric defense was insufficient. The Socialist Party policy was a tragic error stamped with "the hallmark of political unrealism."[83] Hook did not advocate a declaration of war on the Nazis; instead, he supported massive military and economic aid for Britain. The Socialist Party was already advocating aid for Loyalist Spain against the fascists. Why would they not support aid for Britain? Hook fully conceded that military aid might lead to war; but war, even with the risk of a dictatorial government, was preferable to a Nazi victory, which would guarantee the destruction of democratic freedoms. He defended his policy as "the lesser evil," the only viable plan in an imperfect world. Despite Thomas's misbegotten foreign policy, Hook still pledged to vote for him in 1940.

During 1940 the liberal community pivoted toward an interventionist foreign policy. The air was filled with public recantations as intellectuals voiced a sudden patriotism and shifted from anti-militarism to war. Isolationists were hounded off the staffs of the *New Republic* and the *Nation.* John T. Flynn resigned under pressure from the *New Republic.* He charged that Roosevelt was leading the country into war in order to maintain domestic political power. Flynn persisted in voicing a twenty-year *New Republic* posture that had now become unfashionable.[84] Oswald Garrison Villard, a long-time editor of the *Nation,* was dropped unceremoniously because he symbolized "escape and appeasement." Freda Kirchwey commented editorially that Villard and his ilk lived in a fantasy-world and their writings were a more present danger than fascism itself.[85]

Coupled with the fall of France, Archibald MacLeish's article "The Irresponsibles" mobilized liberal war opinion. He vilified the skeptical, apolitical stance of post-war writers and scholars. The anti-war novels of Dos Passos and Hemingway bred cynicism rather than authentic resolve in America's youth. These writers were insulated from the real world; they allowed evil to run unchecked, refused to accept personal responsibility, and cultivated an "antiseptic air of objectivity."[86] Dewey described MacLeish's manifesto as "moving"; however, it also embodied a prevalent revolt against reason, which was a major source of democracy's current ailments.[87] America needed a fighting faith, and MacLeish was eager to supply the orchestration. The jaundiced material-economic attitude toward war had to be supplanted by emphasis upon heroic valor and spiritual values.

By October 1940, the progressive *Social Frontier* had reasoned its war policy. "These are days," John Childs said, "when stubborn events are calling into question many social and political doctrines which for several decades have enjoyed almost the status of axioms among liberal thinkers. One of these controlling beliefs is that a war involving European imperialistic nations is by its inner essence necessarily an affair of no concern to American liberals."[88] He repudiated the military defeatism of many neutral liberals. Those who snickered at patriotism and neglected national defense left the reactionaries with no opposition. War mobilization against fascism would not provoke America to become fascist any more than freedom was destroyed in Britain during wartime. Editor William Kilpatrick now spoke gravely about the threat to civilization. Jesse Newton of Teachers College demanded aid for Britain. Educators should assume the leadership in the campaign for war preparedness. George Counts proposed that the schools indoctrinate democracy as a new fighting faith.[89]

Pacifist George Hartmann of Columbia University sent a letter of protest to *Social Frontier,* asking, "Has the Progressive Education Movement Become Militarist?" He indicated the new hostility of progressive educators to the Committee on Militarism in Education, which had collapsed due to lack of support. He mentioned that Dewey opposed the draft and backed Norman Thomas for president, while many of Dewey's disciples were agitating for combat. "The failure of all but a handful of liberals to stick by Dewey in these unpopular expressions of a living faith," Hartmann said, "indicates that organized progressive education is today on the verge of intellectual bankruptcy."[90] Since Dewey was eighty years old, in a year's retirement, and suffering from prostatitis, he was not an active participant in the war debate. Like most Americans, he desired both the defeat of Nazism and the avoidance of direct American belligerency.

During the 1940 presidential election, Dewey declared his support for Norman Thomas. In a letter to the *Nation,* signed by Dewey, the Independent Committee for Kreuger and Thomas outlined its foreign policy approach. Thomas rejected any compromise with the "slightly lesser evil." Instead of tagging after the nationalist-militarist pied-pipers of war, implanting domestic socialism was the appropriate answer to totalitarian Europe.[91] Hook also signed the Thomas letter, which, by the way, specifically repudiated his own position. One can not infer that Dewey gave Thomas's foreign policy a blanket endorsement. However, as acting president of the League for Industrial Democracy (1940–1941), Dewey did echo the themes of defending democracy at home and providing the world with a model of freedom and cooperative peace.[92] In a letter to the *Progressive* (February 15, 1941), he repeated this message.[93] Defense was merely negative, an "armed quarantine" against infection from abroad. Dewey stressed hopes for progress toward a fuller democracy. The fate of democracy took precedence over the issue of whether America should or should not enter the war. It is noteworthy that Dewey did not repeat his earlier plea for America to stay out of the conflict no matter what. Liberal isolationist journals employed Dewey's message as a sanctification of their policy.[94] La Follette's *Progressive* was a final refuge for die-hard isolationists. Stuart Chase, Harry Elmer Barnes, and Oswald Villard became regular contributors.

Dewey was concerned about the erosion of civil liberties and reactionary nationalism stimulated by the war crisis. When Harold Rugg's history books were banned in 1940 for their alleged anti-patriotic content, Dewey defended Rugg.[95] Under the sponsorship of the Committee for Cultural Freedom, Dewey joined Bertrand Russell in his fight to teach at the City College of New York. Russell was removed due to Episcopal Bishop William Manning's charges of "atheism" and "hedonism." This case jeopardized not only academic freedom but the separation of church and state.[96] Dewey and 240 other educators, including Harry Elmer Barnes, Oswald Villard, George Hartmann, and Morris Cohen, opposed a peace-time draft in July 1940.[97] This campaign was sponsored by the Committee on Militarism in Education and chaired by William Kilpatrick of Teachers College. Its statement emphasized that an unprecedented peace-time draft smacked of totalitarianism and was contrary to voluntaristic American democratic traditions. While the European crisis was grave, voluntary recruitment procedures could be sufficient. A smaller, highly trained force with modern technological weapons had proven superior to a partially trained civilian force. However, with armies on the march, the logic of defense strategy should not rest upon a minimalist program. *Common Sense* also attacked the Burke-Wadsworth Conscription Bill as an imminent threat to democracy.[98] Though many outspoken pacifists signed the anti-conscription manifesto, no neutralist policy was advocated toward the war.

Nicholas Murray Butler, Nobel Peace Prize winner, again declared war on Germany. He warned faculty members at Columbia University to resign if their convictions brought them into conflict with that institution's wartime ideals. Academic freedom was subordinate to the war effort, which promoted the "higher freedom" of the university. While the *New York Times* embraced Butler, the *New Republic* censured him because "it [the pro-war position] is the worst possible advertisement for the anti-Hitler cause when its leading proponents act as Hitler would in their place."[99] Pro-war liberals were sensitive to the charge that a new war would destroy democracy at home. Dewey wrote a letter of protest to the *New York Times,* expressing incredulity at Butler's statement. To enforce conformity of beliefs on students and faculty as Butler proposed would be tantamount to totalitarianism.[100]

Dewey sympathized with the Allies but he was reluctant to advocate full belligerency unless it was a last resort. At the time, Dewey was on the board of directors of Leo Birkhead's interventionist group, the Friends of Democracy. Other members included Thomas Mann, Will Durant, and Van Wyck Brooks. This group opposed efforts to appease the Nazis.[101] When it published a pamphlet entitled "America First: The Nazi Transmission Belt,"

John T. Flynn, the New York chairman of America First, wrote Dewey seeking a disclaimer and Dewey's enlistment into America First. On March 17, 1941, Dewey answered by refusing to repudiate the pamphlet. He insisted that Germany was "the greatest menace to civilization since Genghis Khan."[102] While Charles Beard and Harry Elmer Barnes joined the America First Committee, Dewey did not cooperate with it. He proclaimed on May 20, 1941, that "nationalism expressed in our country in such phrases as America First, is one of the strongest factors in producing existing totalitarianism, just as the promise of doing away with it has caused some misguided persons to be sympathetic with Nazism."[103] In a letter to Selden Rodman, editor of *Common Sense,* Dewey reaffirmed that he was not an absolute pacifist; he did hope, however, that America might enter at the "latest possible time." He admitted that "it is now clear that unless the Nazis are beaten this country will be permanently militarized."[104] Clearly, the gradual change in Dewey's attitude toward the war was a response to the evolving complexity and seriousness of the predicament.

The summer of 1941 witnessed a consensus among the liberal community that it was time to rally behind the war. The *New Leader* promoted a full declaration of war by April, before Hitler's Russian campaign.[105] After the attack, aid to the Soviets was endorsed, but the journal harbored no illusions about Stalin's beneficence. Hook implored Moscow to order the dissolution of the American Communist Party as a gesture to obtain public approval for aid. He further suggested that Stalin release liberal political prisoners held in concentration camps.[106] After pacifist Bruce Bliven and popular frontist Malcolm Cowley had been converted to war, the *New Republic* proposed a war declaration on June 20. The *Nation* found a formal declaration of war to be unnecessary, because the United States was already at war.[107]

In supporting Roosevelt's declared policy, *Common Sense* struck a middle course: that of seeking peace without victory, while sensing that peace with Hitler could only be an armed truce. American military power must be sufficient to stop him. Declared peace terms could loosen the Nazi grip on the German people. Only the German people could destroy Nazism through an internal rebellion.[108] America could play a more constructive role if it formally remained a nonbelligerent. *Common Sense* called the Atlantic Charter's commitment to a total Axis defeat and disarmament "revenge." The editors offered this prophecy:

> As the Red Army marches across Europe, and the German regime crumbles, perhaps permitting Britain belatedly to help in the liberation of France and the low countries it will be communism that will write the peace and unite Europe, rather than democracy. Will our institutions be much more secure if Moscow rather than Berlin dictates the peace?[109]

Common Sense repeated its plea for a negotiated peace in September 1941. But how could one negotiate with Hitler?

Among educational circles, the role of citizenship training and patriotism replaced the former emphasis upon criticism and protest. In February 1941 the Educational Policies Commission of the National Education Association, of which Dewey was honorary president, decried the stress upon the problems in American life. This hypercritical cynicism and faithlessness in the American way of life confused facts and weakened national morale. By July 1941, shortly after Hitler attacked Russia, *Social Frontier* formally answered Roosevelt's call to man the battle stations. Ratifying a policy of full belligerency, the editors defined the battle not as one between rival imperialisms, but a conflict between two ways of life. The triumph of totalitarianism in Asia and Europe would imperil America and civilization itself.[110] John Childs was astonished by Norman Thomas's persistent attempts to underplay the differences between Britain's parliamentary democracy and the Nazi political system. After America's entrance into the war, both John Childs and William Kilpatrick headed war commissions on education.

Roosevelt had already made a mockery of neutrality. The Greer and Kearney incidents at sea were utilized to stoke the war fever. Roosevelt gave British agents free rein in America. He completed the destroyer deal and the occupation of Iceland.[111] Each new escalation was offered as an argument to keep out of the war. Isolationists saw these actions as a self-fulfilling prophecy, while interventionists defended Roosevelt's policy of leading the country into war as a case of sound *realpolitik*. Charles Beard testified in the Senate against Lend-Lease and continued his personal vendetta against Roosevelt. Harry Elmer Barnes wrote an article on December 6, 1941, entitled "No War with Japan."[112] On December 10th the pacifist *Christian Century* concluded that "every national interest and every moral obligation to civilization dictates that this country shall keep out of the insanity of a war which in no sense is America's war."[113] Events had clearly overtaken the liberal isolationists.

On the night of the Japanese attack on Pearl Harbor, Dewey delivered a speech at Cooper Union entitled "Lessons from the War [World War I]: In Philosophy." He commented that the present war was more than simply a military conflict; it constituted a major turning point in history with respect to whether free government could survive. He had learned that the rise of the totalitarian threat must be met with force.[114]

NOTES

1. John Dewey, ed., *New York and the Seabury Investigation* (New York: The City Affairs Committee of New York, 1933).

2. John Dewey, "Who Might Make a New Party?" *NR* (April 1, 1931):177–79.

3. "Program Making vs. Power Politics," *NR* (March 18, 1931):111–12. "The Position of Progressives," *NR* (Feb. 4, 1931):327–29. "A Four-Year Presidential Plan," *N* (Feb. 17, 1932): 185–6. "Do Americans Want a Third Party," *WT* (July 1, 1930):294–6. For a criticism see Edmund Wilson, "Two Protests," *NR* (July 22, 1931):251.

4. Karel Bisha, "Liberalism Frustrated: The LIPA, 1928-1933," *Mid-America* (Jan., 1966):24, 28.

5. "Dewey Raps Progressives," *NL* (March 14, 1931):2. Dewey, "An Open Letter to Senator George Norris," *New York Times* (Dec. 26, 1930). "Norris Declines to Head New Party: Still a Republican," *New York Times* (Dec. 27, 1930), "Dewey on Norris's Rejection to Form a Third Party," *New York Times* (Dec. 31, 1930):3. Dewey, "Full Warehouses and Empty Stomachs," *PLB* (May, 1931):1.

6. "Dewey Contradicts Borah on Debt Revisions," *New York Times* (July 15, 1931), p. 17.

7. Edward Bordeau, "John Dewey's Ideas About the Depression," *Journal of the History of Ideas* (Jan., 1971):72.

8. *N* (July 20, 1932):46.

9. "News Bulletin of the LIPA (Nov.-Dec., 1932):1.

10. Norman Thomas, "Reply to Gabriel Heatter," *N* (Dec. 14, 1932):585. Gabriel Heatter, "The Future of the Socialist Party—Open Letter to Norman Thomas," *N* (Dec. 14, 1932):584.

11. John Dewey, "The Future of Radical Political Action," *N* (Jan. 4, 1933):8. Howard J. Williams, "LIPA Replies," *WT* (June, 1933):191. "Third Party or Fourth?" *WT* (Aug., 1932): 223-24.

12. "A Four-Year Presidential Plan," *N* (Feb. 17, 1932):185-6. "A Four-Year Plan," *WT* (March, 1932):67-68. The entire plan was published in *N* (Feb. 17, 1932): Section II.

13. John Dewey, "Superficial Treatment Must Fail," *PLB* (June, 1933):1, 2.

14. John Dewey, "The Real Test of the New Deal," *PLB* (May, 1933):1. Dewey, "Imperative Need: A New Radical Party," *CS* (Sept., 1933):6-7.

15. John Dewey, "The Banking Crisis," *PLB* (March, 1933):1-2. Dewey, "The Duty of Congress," *PLB* (Dec., 1932):1. Dewey, "Facing the Era of Realities," *PLB* (April 1, 1934):1-2. Dewey, "America's Public Ownership Program," *PLB* (March, 1934):7.

16. John Dewey, "The Need for a New Party," *NR* (May 25, 1931):151.

17. John Dewey, "Policies for a New Party," *NR* (April 1, 1931):204.

18. John Dewey, "Intelligence and Power," *NR* (April 25, 1934):306-7.

19. "On Obtaining Power," *CS* (Jan. 1935):2-3. "Toward a New Party," *CS* (Dec., 1934): 2-3.

20. "Platform of the American Commonwealth Federation," *CS* (Aug., 1935):8-9.

21. "How They Are Voting," *NR* (Oct. 9, 1936):249.

22. John Dewey, "Review of Alfred Bingham's *Insurgent America*," *CS* (Dec., 1935):73.

23. "For a Commonwealth Party," *CS* (May, 1935):2-3. "A Plan of Transition," *CS* (May, 1935):6-10. Bingham, "Further Light on Transition," *CS* (June, 1935):13-16. Thomas Amlie, "The American Commonwealth Federation," *CS* (Aug., 1935):6-7.

24. "The Transition Plan—Pro and Con," *CS* (July, 1935):25. Franklin Wood, "Burying the Profit System with Profit," *CS* (Dec., 1935):18-19.

25. *CS* (March 16, 1933):3-5.

26. *N* (Sept. 16, 1934):313. *NR* (Jan. 16, 1935):259.

27. *CS* (March, 1936):4.

28. Charles Beard, "Solving the Domestic Crisis by War," *NR* (March 11, 1936):127-29.

29. John Dewey, "Appeal to Cuban Youth," *School and Society* (1968):444-46.

30. *CC* (June 14, 1933):795.

31. "People's Lobby Hits Sugar Loan to Cuba," *New York Times* (Nov. 24, 1930):10-2.

32. John Maynard Keynes, "National Self-Sufficiency," *Yale Review* (1933):75-77.

33. *N* (Oct. 31, 1934):494-95.

34. Charles Beard, *The Idea of National Interest*, with G. H. E. Smith (Chicago: Quadrangle, 1934), p. 436.

35. John Dewey, "Aid for the Spanish Government," *CC* (March 3, 1937):292.

36. Charles Beard, "The Supreme Issue for America," *Events* (April 7, 1938):275.

37. *F&C*, p. 173.

38. John Dewey, "Review of America at Mid-Passage," *Atlantic Monthly* (July, 1939).

39. *CS* (Oct., 1938):4-5. Hanson Baldwin, "What of the British Fleet?" *Reader's Digest*

(Aug., 1941):1–5. Nicholas Spykman, *America's Strategy in World Politics* (New York: Harcourt, Brace & Co., 1942), pp. 340–41.

40. *NR* (Dec. 16, 1936):II.

41. "Hitler Liquidates Versailles," *N* (March 27, 1935):348.

42. *NR* (March 27, 1935):169.

43. "The Hitler Boomerang on Wilson's Policies," *PLB* (April, 1933):1–2.

44. *CS* (Sept., 1935):5.

45. "Dress Rehearsal for Neutrality," *NR* (Nov. 13, 1935):4–5. Hook, "Radicals in War Against Sanctions," *Modern Monthly* (April, 1936):15. Beard, "Heat and Light on Neutrality," *NR* (Feb. 2, 1936):8–9.

46. *CS* (Sept., 1935):5.

47. "Hitler as Pacifist," *CC* (Aug. 22, 1934):1005–7.

48. "When America Goes to War," *Modern Monthly* (1935):7.

49. *NR* (Aug. 26, 1936):62. *N* (Aug. 29, 1936):228–29.

50. *NR* (Jan. 13, 1937):200.

51. Louis Fischer, "Can Madrid Hold On?" *N* (Jan. 16, 1937):62. "18,000 Jam Garden for Spain Rally," *Daily Worker* (Jan. 5, 1937), p. 1.

52. I. F. Stone, "1937 Is Not 1914," *N* (Nov. 6, 1937):494–7. Alfred Bingham took issue with Stone's remarks. See "Refuting Mr. Stone," *N* (Nov. 20, 1937):571.

53. John Dewey, "Aid for the Spanish Government," *CC* (March, 1937):292–3. Norman Thomas, "Spain, A Socialist View," *N* (June 19, 1937):200.

54. *NR* (Dec. 23, 1936):IV. Fischer, "What Can Save Spain?" *N* (March 26, 1938):348–50.

55. *CS* (July, 1937):8–10.

56. Louis Fischer, "The Loyalist Dilemma," *N* (Aug. 8, 1937):148–50.

57. "War and the *Nation,*" *N* (Jan. 22, 1938):11. "Why Commit Suicide?" *CS* (May, 1938): 5. Bingham, "Communism vs. Fascism," *CS* (June, 1937):15–18. Bingham, "War Mongering on the Left," *CS* (May, 1937):8–10.

58. *CS* (Oct., 1938):4–5.

59. Quincy Howe, "After Munich—What?" *CS* (Nov., 1938):21–23.

60. *CS* (Oct., 1938):4. *CS* (May, 1939):17. Robert Hickert, "Can Germany Unite Central Europe?" *CS* (Sept., 1938):8–11. See Alfred Bingham, *The United States of Europe* (New York: Duell, Sloan, and Pearce Co., 1940).

61. "A Challenge to America," *N* (Sept. 24, 1935):285–6.

62. *NR* (Oct. 15, 1938):381.

63. "Nemesis Postponed," *NR* (Oct. 12, 1938):255–7. *NR* (Oct. 18, 1939):381.

64. John Dewey, "No Matter What Happens—Stay Out," *CS* (March, 1939):11.

65. *F&C*, pp. 175–76.

66. John Dewey, "Democratic Ends Need Democratic Methods for Their Realization," *NL* (Oct. 23, 1939):1. Dewey's biographer, George Dykhuizen, claimed that Dewey switched from a policy of neutrality to support for Lend-Lease and making America the "arsenal for democracy" in September, 1939. Dewey's interventionism evolved more slowly than this suggests. On November 28, 1939, Dewey wrote Max Otto that he was eighty years old and the job of promoting democracy must be placed in the hands of his younger colleagues. See Dykhuizen, *The Life and Mind of John Dewey,* p. 291. John Dewey—Max Otto (Nov. 28, 1939), Max Otto Collection, Wisconsin Historical Society, Madison, Wisconsin.

67. Morton White interpreted Dewey's remarks as implying outright pacifism. See White, "From Marx to Dewey," *Partisan Review* (1940):64.

68. John Dewey, "The Future of Democracy," *NR* (April 28, 1937):351.

69. *CS* (Nov., 1939):18.

70. "What Are They Fighting For?" *CS* (Nov., 1939):16–17.

71. "A Foreign Policy for American Democracy," *CS* (July, 1940):16–17. In November, 1939, a group called The New Western Front was formed to resist American entry into the war. It was comprised largely of *Common Sense* writers—John Chamberlain, Selden Rodman, Quincy Howe, and W. Fleming MacLeish.

72. "Generosity and Intolerance," *CS* (Oct., 1940):16–17.

73. *NR* (Nov. 18, 1929):1–2. *N* (Jan. 27, 1940):87–88.

74. John Dewey, "The Basis for Hope," *CS* (Dec., 1939):9.

75. Benjamin Marsh, "In War Who Can Remember?" *PLB* (Sept., 1939):3. The People's Lobby mailed out copies of a Lindbergh speech. See *NL* (April 26, 1941):18.

76. Norman Thomas and Bertram Wolfe, *Keep America Out of War* (New York: Frederick Stokes Co., 1939), p. 11.

77. Norman Thomas, "The Mecca Temple Meeting," *NR* (March 17, 1941):375.

78. *NL* (Nov. 4, 1939):8.

79. *NL* (Oct. 21, 1939):8.

80. Sidney Hook, "Dewey at Eighty," *NL* (Oct. 28, 1939):5.

81. "Hook Urges Inclusion of Ludlow Clause in Neutrality Act," *NL* (Nov. 4, 1939):8.

82. Sidney Hook, "Is Nazism a Social Revolution?" *NL* (July 20, 1940):4.

83. Sidney Hook, "Socialism, Common Sense, and the War," *NL* (Aug. 31, 1940):7. *NL* (May 13, 1940):5. *NL* (June 1, 1940):1.

84. "Mr. Flynn and the *New Republic*," *NR* (Dec. 9, 1940):293–4.

85. *N* (June 29, 1940):223–4.

86. Archibald MacLeish, "The Irresponsibles," *N* (May 18, 1940):618–623. For critical responses, see Edmund Wilson, "Archibald MacLeish and 'The Word,'" *NR* (July 1, 1940):36 37. Roscoe Burton, "The Tough Muscle Boys of Literature," *American Mercury* (Nov., 1940): 369–74. Rexford Tugwell, "The Crisis of Freedom," *CS* (October, 1941):30–32.

87. John Dewey—Max Otto (Jan. 23, 1940), Max Otto Collection, Wisconsin Historical Society, Madison, Wisconsin.

88. John Childs, "Liberalism and National Defense," *SF* (Oct., 1940):5.

89. Jesse Newlon, "How Shall We Aid England?" *SF* (Jan., 1941):100. George Counts, *The Schools Can Teach Democracy* (New York: John Day, 1939), pp. 15–16.

90. *SF* (Nov., 1940):43–44.

91. *N* (Sept. 28, 1940):283.

92. John Dewey, "Address of Welcome," in *Thirty-Five Years of Educational Pioneering* (LID Pamphlet Series) (New York: League for Industrial Democracy (Jan., 1941), pp. 3–6.

93. John Dewey, "Here at Home," *Progressive* (Feb. 15, 1941):20.

94. John Dewey, "A Philosopher Writes on Defense," *Call* (March 1, 1941):3. Dewey, "Here at Home," *PLB* (April 8, 1941):8.

95. John Dewey, "Investigating Education," *New York Times* (May 6, 1940), p. 16.

96. John Dewey, "The Case of Bertrand Russell," *N* (June, 1940):732–33.

97. "Declaration Against Conscription," *New York Times* (July 9, 1940), p. 4.

98. *CS* (July, 1940):13–15.

99. "No, Dr. Butler," *NR* (Oct. 14, 1940):507. *Common Sense* declared, "some of our educators may have forgotten what happened to democracy during the last war to save democracy, but not enough to let the Good Gray Reactionary get away with that." *CS* (Nov., 1940):129.

100. *New York Times* (Oct. 5, 1940), p. 7.

101. "The Friends of Democracy, Inc.," *NL* (June 9, 1941):804.

102. John Dewey to John T. Flynn (March 17, 1941), John T. Flynn, MSS, University of Oregon Library, University of Oregon.

103. John Dewey, "The Basic Values and Loyalties of Democracy," *American Teacher* (May 20, 1941):8–9. Reprinted in *NL* (July 26, 1941):197.

104. John Dewey to Selden Rodman (May 24, 1941), Selden Rodman, MSS, University of Wyoming Library, University of Wyoming. *Common Sense* also felt that a Nazified Europe would compel America to become a garrison state. "The Wave of the Future," *CS* (Feb., 1941):86–7.

105. *NL* (April 11, 1941):1.

106. Sidney Hook, "Moscow Order Dissolving CP in U.S. Would Swing Wide Public Support to Aid for USSR," *NL* (Oct. 1, 1941):4.

107. "One Day That Shook the World," *NR* (June 20, 1941):871-2. Kirchwey, "Shall We Declare War?" *N* (July 26, 1941):64.

108. "The Aim Is Peace," *CS* (Sept., 1941):272-73.

109. *CS* (Sept., 1941):272-73.

110. "Progressives for War," *Time* (July 7, 1941):48. "This War and America," *SF* (Oct. 15, 1941):11. See the debate on the war referendum with Norman Thomas's last gasp for isolation. *SF* (Nov. 15, 1941):43.

111. See Douglas Norton, "The Open Secret U.S. Navy and the Battle of the Atlantic, April–December, 1941," *Naval War College Review* (Jan.-Feb., 1974):63-83. Beard brought up the case of Tyler Kent who was jailed because he stole copies of secret exchanges between Churchill and Roosevelt, which discussed for two years how America might be maneuvered into the war. Beard accused the Rockefeller Foundation and the Council of Foreign Relations of attempting to muffle post-war historical revisionism. Beard, "Who's to Write the History of the War," *Saturday Evening Post* (Oct. 4, 1947):172.

112. Harry Elmer Barnes, "No War With Japan," *Progressive* (Dec. 6, 1941):10.

113. *CC* (Dec. 10, 1941):1538.

114. "John Dewey: America's Good Fortune," *NL* (Oct. 16, 1948):3. The editor of the *New Leader* recalled Dewey's speech very differently from Howlett's account in *Troubled Philosopher.* "Lessons from the War in Philosophy," Dewey Collection, Morris Library, Southern Illinois University.

10

Dewey's Critics: The Revolt Against Scientific Reason

The economic and military catastrophes of the thirties stirred many philosophers to probe for some root cause behind the apparent decline of Western civilization. The rise of totalitarianism was not considered to be accidental but rather a manifestation of the basic intellectual assumptions of the age. Dewey's pragmatic liberalism was targeted as the noxious inner disease corrupting Western society. Pragmatism was thought to be too shallow, optimistic, and tentative to provide meaning to the tragedies of the era. It epitomized the denial of universal truth when taken to its logical conclusion, which spawned totalitarianism. A chorus opportunistically rang out for a new faith and for religious certitude.

Was America living in an age dominated by Dewey's influence? Dewey acknowledged that those who sought to blame naturalism for the current crisis, as if to say it was an "ideological incarnation" of the fascists, had greatly profited from the wartime situation.[1] After the Pearl Harbor attack, some intellectuals detected a paradigm shift away from Dewey's age of innocence and toward Niebuhr's era of power politics. Collectively, Dewey's critics rejected pragmatic liberalism's faith in science and its incapacity to understand or adequately defend the foundations of Western civilization.

The relationship between a general philosophical approach and concrete political orientations inspired impassioned polemical exchanges. Brand Blanshard challenged the notion that any essential connection existed between empiricism and liberalism, or rationalism and conservatism. He pointed to instances in which "liberal" philosophers were politically "conservative." Blanshard also jibed the pragmatist school by noting Mussolini's close affinity to pragmatism.[2] Sidney Hook could not permit such a slur to pass unchallenged. Pointing to the rise of science and the corresponding dissolution of feudalism, he defended the claim that there is a significant relation between philosophy and social movements. The dominant philosophies of an epoch are integrated into the entire culture.[3] Absolutistic metaphysical systems tend either to apologize for existing social power or to sponsor dogmatic revolutionism. The critical, experimental approach undermined the ideological authority of the ruling class and revealed specific social injustices. Despite an individual's idiosyncracies, one could meaningfully examine the history of philosophical ideals and their relation to politics.

At times Hook also maintained that abstract religious or metaphysical doctrines of human nature could not prescribe any specific social policy. This policy could be established only through empirical procedures. Neo-Thomism could lend itself to authoritarianism, but no concrete social philosophy could be logically developed from supernatural premises. For example, Reinhold Niebuhr's politics was not deducible from his theology; and the same theory of original sin could lead to either a Hobbesian authoritarian state or a Madisonian balance of power politics.[4] Religious obscurantism could permit authoritarianism, while empirical investigation demonstrates that democracy and scientific methods are logically related. Thus, despite the ambiguity surrounding the relation between metaphysics and concrete political commitments, the combatants in these intellectual debates certainly believed that something ideologically significant was at stake.

The Neo-Thomist perennialist movement (i.e., those who sought to restore the predominance of the classics in intellectual life) clustered around Robert Maynard Hutchins at the University of Chicago. In order to obviate the aimlessness of modern educational practice, Hutchins sought to inculcate a body of fixed, authoritative truths that could buttress social stability. These metaphysical first principles furnished the kernel for a liberal education that disregarded vocational training altogether. Dewey acknowledged that Hutchins had pinpointed many genuine problems. However, he wondered who would determine these ultimate verities. The Hutchins approach typified an authoritarianism that capitalized on a rampant, worldwide escape from freedom. Dewey qualified his statement to avoid any implication that Hutchins was personally sympathetic to fascism.[5] Yet, Hutchins's rejoinder suggested that pragmatism contained the seeds of fascism. "As a matter of fact," he charged, "fascism is the result of the absence of philosophy. It is possible only in the context of the disorganization of analysis, and the disruption of the intellectual tradition by immediate practical concerns."[6] Dewey was disappointed that such a crucial discussion of the value of a classical education in comparison to one emphasizing experience and scientific method had ended in recriminations.

When the Conference on Science, Philosophy, and Religion convened in New York City on September 10, 1940, the polemics between pragmatists and perennialists became rancorous. Mortimer Adler, a Hutchins disciple and former student of Dewey, provoked a sensation by blaming professors for instigating the West's spiritual decline. Since culture controls the vicissitudes of politics, Hitler, Mussolini, Stalin, and Chamberlain were little more than symptoms of the disarray in modern secular culture. Naturalistic professors had relegated religion to superstition and philosophy to mere opinion; obstinately they asserted that science was the sole source of genuine knowledge. Adler claimed that democratic values could be defended against totalitarian attack only if they were grounded in supernatural dogma. Capitalizing on the war emergency, Adler captured headlines with the following remark:

> . . . the most serious threat to democracy is the positivism of the professors, which dominates every aspect of modern education and is the central corruption of modern culture. Democracy has much more to fear from the mentality of its teachers than from the nihilism of Hitler. It is the same nihilism in both cases, but Hitler's is more honest and consistent, less slurred by subtleties and queasy qualifications and hence less dangerous.[7]

Adler abstained from differentiating relativism from nihilism or pragmatism from positivism.

Adler accused professors of avoiding basic issues; since fundamental questions of value were beyond the competence of science, these intellectuals reduced all contending views to arbitrary opinion or sentiment. While professors ritualistically espoused the need for dialogue, an attitude of open-mindedness was preserved indefinitely because they could never accept the possibility of a universal truth. The tentativeness of scientific knowledge stimulated "mental libertinism." Anyone who denied philosophy's claim to knowledge also denied that objective moral principles could be demonstrated. Hence, they denied that one could prove democracy to be the best political system. If the academic community preferred democracy, sentiment and not rational commitment was the reason. In rejecting the model of man as a rational animal, these positivists undermined human dignity. Their beliefs sank to the same level of prejudice as that of Hitler. Furthermore, the chaotic brand of democracy emotively sanctioned by professors was an inherently corrupt liberalism, without hierarchy or authority. Individual freedom was made into a fetish. Referring indirectly to Dewey, Adler charged that, by making democracy a way of life instead of a form of government, the professors were propagating a false religion that was no better than fascism. Democracy could be saved only by radically reforming American culture, starting with the schools. Culturally speaking, Hitler's victory or defeat was inconsequential; the primary enemies of democracy were infesting America's classrooms. Adler judged the logic to be inescapable: a successful defense of democracy could only be launched by accepting his metaphysics.

Were the beliefs held by professors actually worse than those of Hitler only because the former disagreed with the views of Mortimer Adler? Sidney Hook labeled Adler's speech as "not merely false, but irresponsible."[8] If Adler's metaphysical propositions were self-evident, why after centuries was there no consensus about them? Scientific methodology should be extended to more disciplines as a means of establishing more universal agreement. No tangible evidence existed to prove that positivism was the chief cause of Nazism. On the contrary, Nazism was expressly anti-scientific. Had Catholics been any more effective in resisting the Nazis than non-Catholics? Hook maintained that no philosophical "fifth column" existed in America—except perhaps among Adler's disciples.

Adler and Hutchins were both sufficiently astute to comprehend Dewey's philosophy. When writing for academic audiences, Hutchins distinguished Dewey from the progressive education movement. Hutchins slurred over this distinction when appealing to popular audiences. After polls revealed that only four percent of the college student population wanted to fight in the war, Adler attributed this cynicism to their failure to take moral issues seriously. Positivistic science fostered this irresponsibility by disjoining facts from values. Adler located the enemy: "The corruption begins at the lower levels. . . . The public school system of the country at both elementary and secondary levels, whether explicitly progressive in program or not, is Deweyized in its leadership. I use the name of Dewey to symbolize what Lewis Mumford describes as 'pragmatic liberals.' "[9] Hutchins also asserted that Americans were losing their sacred moral principles. He stated that pragmatic liberals were "confused Hitlers," incapable of defending or understanding what few principles still remained.[10] The rhetorical linkage between Dewey's pragmatism and Hitlerism constituted both intellectual grandstanding and deceit.

Dewey was not a positivist: he expressly endeavored to apply scientific method to human values. After spending his entire life clarifying the nature of democracy, Dewey was to be condemned for being a greater threat to democracy than Hitler or Stalin. Sidney Hook detected that the ultimate denial of academic freedom was implicit in Adler's viewpoint. Those heretics who dissented from Adler's orthodoxy should not be permitted to teach, because they had no knowledge to impart. By indoctrinating an absolute creed, Adler proposed in effect a state religion, reinforced by the Catholic clergy. His proposal required the creation of a select group of interpreters, whose existence portended both elitism and authoritarianism.[11]

Ironically, Robert Maynard Hutchins joined the America First Committee, while Mortimer Adler was a dedicated interventionist. This illustrates the problems involved in deducing specific political measures from abstract first principles. Hutchins desired to fight the scientific naturalists first, since America was not morally prepared for war. He insisted that Roosevelt's "Four Freedoms" were unachievable and embodied another White Man's Burden. Civil liberties would be eliminated if America entered the war, and the world's last great opportunity to construct a genuine democracy would be lost. Hitler could be defeated only by subduing the "materialism and progressivism" that had produced him. With a unified national spirit, America's influence and the example she set would be more powerful than the Axis armies.[12] War was a false path to freedom, resulting in national suicide. Dewey expressed similar isolationist convictions in 1939, and two years later, in April 1941, Hutchins continued to trumpet publicly this political myopia.

Walter Lippmann, who to some degree shared Hutchins's classicism, directed his polemical attack at the Nazis and at modern education simultaneously. He joined the traditionalists in warning that the prevailing form of education was destined to destroy Western civilization. Those who formulated its controlling philosophy were "answerable for the results." Modern education denied the utility of implanting the classical and religious heritage. This vacuum was filled by the accidental improvisations and idle curiosities of students and teachers. With instincts determining the ends of activity, these ends inevitably drifted into the accumulation of power over men in order to obtain crass material possessions. Students were self-centered, cynical, pacifistic cowards who would willingly promote a policy of appeasement. The spiritual heritage of Europe and America was indissolubly linked. Without this tradition, civilization would wither and die, eventually to be replaced by sheer barbarism.[13] Unlike Hutchins, Lippmann advocated a full defense of the British Empire. Hoping to groom an aristocratic, educated elite, he advised minimal popular democracy and strong executive leadership in foreign policy. Dewey had begun his critique of progressive education ten years earlier. He was one of the first to warn against both pandering to the whims of children and education's lack of social commitment. By neglecting to differentiate Dewey's position from that of progressive education, Lippmann unfairly held Dewey answerable for an approach that the latter repudiated.

The protracted conflict between traditionalists and pragmatic naturalists persisted throughout the war. Hutchins and Adler formed a group called Education for Freedom, Inc., whose membership included Stringfellow Barr, Mark Van Doren, Alexander Meicklejohn, Walter Lippmann, and Jacques Maritain. Employing the coast-to-coast facilities of the Mutual Broadcast System, this group received a substantial public hearing. The editors of the *Humanist* complained that not one speaker in the Mutual radio series espoused a Deweyan point of view. In an attempt to respond to such a one-sided view, Sidney Hook wrote a digest and critical commentary on the series.[14] The Conference on Science, Religion, and Philosophy met annually during the war. It was dominated by those who held that, in order to survive, democracy required a supernatural faith. To counter this conference, Dewey and Hook organized a Conference on the Scientific Spirit and Democratic Faith. It was convened in New York City on May 29, 1943, with Dewey as its honorary chairman. Later, he opposed the Educational Development Act of 1947 because it offered federal support to both parochial and public schools. The public school, he argued, was the focal point of democracy and community life. Local control and the separation of church and state must be preserved. Ecclesiastical (Catholic) and educational authoritarianism had "no place in American democracy" and should not be subsidized by the state treasury. Again, Dewey advocated individuality rather than pluralism as the chief value of democracy. As one manifestation of the American melting pot, the public schools habituated each student to democratic attitudes and procedures. The public school system was an instrument for democratic consensus.[15]

Alexander Meicklejohn's *Education Between Two Worlds* comprehensively maligned Dewey's philosophy. Meicklejohn agreed with Hutchins that since human nature is constant, all human beings should have the same basic education. He was convinced that Dewey's approach promoted a scattered and fragmented education, totally devoid of a unifying purpose. Rather than attempting to ground his universal system of values on Neo-Thomism, Meicklejohn returned to Rousseau for inspiration. Universal brotherhood could become the basis for a new world community. Despite Dewey's critique of John Stuart Mill's brand of liberalism, Meicklejohn accused Dewey of adhering to a negative view of freedom. The state should encompass the absolute and infallible social authority of the General Will. It should not merely reflect the power struggles of interest groups. Sympathy and common purpose could be cemented universally through the vehicle of a global state wherein everyone would become a citizen of the world.[16] Meicklejohn did not believe that Dewey's relativism could supply a constructive program of action to meet a global emergency head on. Pragmatism was nothing more than a negative method of criticism; it could explain neither the detestable nature of dictatorship nor the social value of democracy. In other words, it was simply "irrelevant."

Dewey struggled to clarify several serious distortions in Meicklejohn's critique; however, his attempts to communicate with Meicklejohn ended in frustration.[17] Dewey rejected the hackneyed dualism between the sciences on the one hand and the humanities on the other, as well as the degradation of technical vocational training. A reversion to the immutable principles of the Greeks would stultify the experimental observation designed to reinforce tolerance, compromise, and cooperation all of which are necessary for democracy. Dogmatism flourishes when the moral authority that undergirds individual conduct is independent of natural facts. Nothing could be more relevant to a comprehension of modern life than science and technology. Dewey did not advise intentional neglect of historical studies, but he did refuse to sanction them as the exclusive moral authority. Ernest Nagel wondered whether Meicklejohn's views were implicitly totalitarian.[18] Most certainly, Meicklejohn considered himself to be a defender of democracy, though his doctrines could logically imply authoritarianism. These charges and countercharges reflected the bitterness of the debate between religionists and secularists during the war. In 1945, Mortimer Adler described Dewey as "public enemy number one."[19]

Lewis Mumford merits recognition as the ideological critic with the most inveterate antipathy to the pragmatic temper. Throughout this era, he conducted his "private blitzkrieg" against pragmatic liberals. Eventually, pragmatism would surface as the degenerate source of virtually everything that he despised, both culturally and politically. Mumford fashioned a unified metaphysical-religious vision designed to extricate the world from its current travails. This was accompanied by a grandiose scheme for world reconstruction. In 1940, Lewis Mumford, Reinhold Niebuhr, Thomas Mann, Hans Kohn, and Herbert Agar collaborated to produce *The City of Man,* an ambitious tract for world government that posited an American global trusteeship.[20] Only a world union could justify the sacrifices of the war. This government would be administered by an elite group of experts who would solve all existing economic, political, and spiritual problems. The manifesto represented perhaps the apex of Mumford's checkered career as a political enthusiast.

Mumford pictured modern civilization as being engulfed in a manichaean struggle between man and the machine. Pursuing material security and comfort, Western man utilized technology to control nature. Yet, this scientific enterprise has not liberated but instead has enslaved man in a lifeless, mechanical order. An unsightly urban-industrial jungle has been the result. Poetry, religion, and the arts have been suffocated in a vain quest for external aggrandizement and power. As producer of the catastrophe, the scientific mind threatened first to control and then to destroy humanity itself. According to Mumford, science flourishes in totalitarian regimes. Countless Eichmanns roam the universities, laboratories, and bureaucracies.[21] The detachment of the Nazi experimental doctors in the concentration camps was a natural extension of the modern scientific enterprise.

Mumford yearned to restore the classical man whose place of importance had been taken by the onslaught of hydra-headed technology. Ideal liberalism was contrasted with a bankrupt pragmatic liberalism, the former seeking a return to the great Western tradition founded by the Greeks with their emphasis on the common values of humanity. These universal values were the real objects of fascist attacks. Mumford observed that during the eighteenth century the Rousseauistic belief arose concerning man's basic goodness and his natural affinity for the proper ends of life. Reflection upon these ends was neglected, while liberal thinkers became preoccupied with the anesthetic machinery that provided material well-being. The larger questions of life and death were ignored. The essence of bourgeois man centered upon his refusal to face death and destiny. This also led to an evasiveness about war. Mumford disclosed that "a life sacrificed at the right moment is a life well-spent, while a life too carefully hoarded, too ignominiously preserved, is a life utterly wasted."[22] Pragmatic liberals were incurably optimistic about human progress and convinced that the fascists would respond to utilitarian appeals. Incapable of coping with the crucial problem of human evil, i.e., the inevitability of sin, pragmatic liberals failed to contain evil men. The necessary remedies rested beyond a purely rational solution. Only a pre-rational, religious conversion could save civilization. Mumford prophesized a new humanistic world religion, based upon love, and referred to as "organic syncretism."

Ridiculing the pre-eminence of reason and modern man's intoxification with his power over nature, Mumford condemned liberals for neglecting the dark forces of instinct, emotion, and tradition. Vainly priding themselves on their vaunted scientific objectivity, the pragmatic liberal's emotional neutrality has proven disastrous when confronted with crisis situations. Embodying David Hume's passive empiricist, the modern liberal does not experience initial hatred and fear when confronted with totalitarianism. Mumford charged that "the cold withdrawal of human feeling by the liberals today is almost as terrible a crime as the active inhumanity of the fascists."[23] Liberals seemed color-blind to moral values and unable to distinguish civilization from barbarism. Both Mumford and Niebuhr sought to vilify Charles Beard for his alleged callous indifference to the plight of Europe. Unfortunately, moral sentiments have often been very selective and fickle.

In the early thirties, Mumford repudiated the American capitalist order. The money economy enforced a wholesale perversion of human values and should be overthrown by a domestic upheaval. Advocating "basic communism," he endorsed William Z. Foster, the Communist Party candidate for president in 1932. Mumford mocked liberal reform efforts, and he accused Horace Kallen of being a fascist because Kallen was impressed with Roosevelt's National Recovery Act program. According to Mumford, this program instituted a deep class bias that would smother revolutionary pressures. The Roosevelt Administration was "pragmatism in action." Pragmatism signified aimless experiment, uncritical drift, and the ultimate restoration of capitalism. Pragmatism would ultimately kill democracy and implant fascism; thus, Mumford linked pragmatism to Mussolini. "I can see," Horace Kallen responded, "that, in common with many other permanent adolescents of this generation, he [Mumford] hates pragmatism and loves, perhaps, communism."[24] Mumford's caricature of pragmatism was diametrically opposed to Dewey's specific critique of the New Deal.

Through his "call to arms," in the *New Republic* (May 18, 1938), Mumford formally declared war on fascism. Bitterly assailing the editors' position of neutrality, he accused his colleagues of preparing for peace on the fascists' terms because the editors feared war more than any other possibility. Negotiation with nihilistic barbarism was impossible, merely another example of the intellectuals' credulous self-deception. Fascism could not be cured from within; rather, it required a radical surgery performed by superior military force.[25] Some described Mumford as an "excited surgeon." Mumford's militancy was still premature, according to a consensus of the intellectual community.[26] However, frontists, Louis Fischer and Frederick Schuman, praised Mumford's war declaration.

Though heroic military exertion was ultimately necessary to destroy fascism, Mumford's primary concern in 1938 was with purging fascist tendencies in American life. This spiritual disease had to be treated by the total cessation of political and economic intercourse with Germany, Italy, and Japan. Communism was a "false bogey." At this time, he opposed collective security with England and France because these countries were already terminally afflicted with fascism. By 1940, Britain would assume transcendent virtue. Mumford proposed national registration and surveillance of all active fascists, particularly the Roman Catholic hierarchy. All Germans and Italians were suspect. He suggested that a National Board of Censorship be created to prohibit any favorable references to the Axis powers and to outlaw pro-fascist speakers and journals. His definition of "fascist" seemed sufficiently elastic to silence most everyone who disagreed with him. "We must become a national propaganda department," he wrote to Van Wyck Brooks, "a worthier if more amateurish one than the old Creel Bureau."27

After jettisoning free speech, the next democratic freedom to be abandoned was freedom of assembly. The leaders of all pro-fascist groups were to be jailed or exiled. In addition, every girl and boy reaching military age should spend a year in a labor army. Men should work an extra hour a day. For the women, Mumford recommended more time cooking and having babies. (He warned the fairer sex not to engage in frivolous, unfeminine activities.) Laborers could not strike and businesses were subject to confiscation. Even cigarette smoking did not escape Mumford's moral regimentation: he advocated its prohibition. In order to save democracy, Mumford implored the majority to utilize any amount of coercion necessary to bring minority groups into regimented formation.28 Undoubtedly, Mumford's well-publicized views heightened Dewey's fears about militarism if America entered the war.

After the Nazis ended the "phoney war" period by occupying Norway and Denmark in April 1940, Mumford again upbraided the liberal community in order to mobilize them for combat. Intellectuals were effete, moral cowards who lacked the necessary courage to defend any belief with firm determination. They would sacrifice every scruple in order to survive. In the face of imminent danger, liberals would react with "passive barbarism." When confronted with brute aggression, they would side with appeasement and spin facile rationalizations.29 Sanctimoniously wishing for the best, pragmatic liberals were hopelessly unprepared for the worst. In times of peace and stability, pragmatism might cultivate a "boring and tepid" life. In a hostile world, its doctrines were suicidal.

Pacifists became the special objects of Mumford's polemical scorn. Only force or religious transformation could initiate social change. Rational persuasion was basically impotent, particularly in a crisis. Those who refused to sanction force under any circumstances abandoned the world to the ruthless will of the barbarians. Preserving moral hygiene by loathing war was a defeatist gospel of despair. Such pretentious virtue constituted the typical moral perversion of modern liberalism.

Mumford reserved pure contempt for those who proposed that the United States assume a defensive posture in the conflict. If Americans waited till their own lives were threatened, nothing would be left to save; their souls would already have perished. Even if the Allies were to win without American belligerency, the country would be fatally and ignominiously shamed. Mumford charged that "the isolationism of a Charles Beard or a

Stuart Chase or a Quincy Howe is indeed almost as much a sign of barbarism as the doctrines of a Rosenberg or a Gottfried Feder."[30] He accused the editors of *Common Sense* with "more than a sneaking admiration for Nazi barbarism."[31] National security was a demeaning notion when Western civilization and the world were imperiled. In July 1940, Mumford advocated a union between the British Empire and the United States as a means of prompting full military involvement. Efforts to induce the British to define their war aims were deemed "pro-Nazi." Joining the Fight for Freedom Committee, Mumford demanded unconditional surrender. Thirsty for battle, he scolded Roosevelt for poll-watching and for a lack of presidential leadership. He offered the Allies advice on military strategy, explaining to the British how they could have knocked out Italy with a single decisive blow. In 1941, Mumford opted for an immediate American war on Japan. The fear of a two-front war should never sanction any compromise with evil.[32]

Mumford's relentless indictment predictably aroused the liberal community. The *New Republic* editors wondered about exactly which liberals Mumford was chastising. He never referred to Dewey by name in his assault on "pragmatic liberals." Sidney Hook playfully suggested that Mumford must be earmarking crypto-Stalinists.[33] Noting Mumford's systematic program for suppressing civil liberties, the *New Republic* offered this observation: "The Nazis themselves are guilty of setting primitive emotional impulses against reason, and glorifying the former by contrast. This gives rise to an obscurantist and destructive mysticism. Critics like Mr. Mumford are in danger of making the same mistake."[34] Others termed Mumford "the Fuhrer of anti-Fascism" and an "ideological drill sergeant."[35] They implored him to emigrate to Canada and join the Royal Air Force as a means of venting his hostilities. In *Common Sense,* Fleming MacLeish warned that "the word mongers and war mongers were joining hands."[36] Mumford expanded his second war manifesto into a book entitled *Faith for Living.* James T. Farrell, Dewey's long-time friend, described the book as a "bible for war intellectuals."[37] Reviewing the book in the *New Republic* at a time when Russia adopted an isolationist line, Malcolm Cowley countered Mumford's anti-rationalism: "Dr. Goebbels often speaks in the same vein, using often the same words. Behind Mumford's patriotic vista one can see the barbed wire of concentration camps."[38] Pragmatist Irwin Edman berated Mumford's inability to comprehend even the rudimentary tenets of liberalism. However, Reinhold Niebuhr praised the book for being as important as the political and military measures taken to retrench the last remnant of democracy.[39] While many of his colleagues jousted with Mumford, Dewey regarded as quite distant the possibility for a constructive dialogue. In this judgment, he was undoubtedly correct.[40]

Failing to convert the *New Republic* to war in June 1940, Lewis Mumford and Waldo Frank resigned from its editorial staff in disgust. Frank had published a companion piece to Mumford's "Corruption of Liberalism." In it he described Dewey as an anti-philosopher whose empirical rationalism had both infected modern man and resulted in fascism.[41] Mumford and Frank compared the *New Republic* editors to the "discredited bankrupt personalities" who paved the way for fascism's cheap triumph in Europe.[42]

Mumford's attacks on pragmatists and Germans continued unabated, even after America entered the war. On the cultural front, he developed a special Humanities Department at Stanford University to resist the spectre of modern science. Betraying an elitism, he proposed that young artists (embryonic thinkers and creators) be exempted from the military draft in order to nurture America's cultural heritage.[43] When the Allies employed massive bombing of populated areas as a tactic to defeat the Nazis, the cause became both tarnished and dehumanized in Mumford's eyes. America had adopted the methods of the enemy. It had emerged in a worse light than the Nazis, since the United States had perfected the techniques of mass annihilation. America's moral disintegration had cleared the path for the ultimate symbol of nihilism, the atomic bomb.[44] In 1946, Mumford insisted that scientific research be firmly repressed because the search for truth had displaced "human values and wishes." After calling for an all-out war to defeat Hitler, Mumford had misgivings because modern technology was effectively utilized to prosecute the war. He was torn between Germanophobia and technophobia.

Mumford easily kept pace with Vansittart in his castigation of the German people. Deploring apologetic books offering socio-economic explanations for the rise of Nazism, he reiterated that the demented German soul never rested within Western civilization. Germans almost uniformly displayed the characteristics of servility, militarism, and sadism. Unlike Reinhold Niebuhr, Mumford rebuffed any distinction between the German people and the Nazi leadership. Debunking the myth of the good German or the German opposition to Hitler, he repudiated the idea that Christian charity should be extended to the defeated German people. They should be treated no better than their victims.[45] In fact, the Allies had been exceedingly indulgent to the Germans after World War I. He opposed the Nuremberg Trials because they supplied a scapegoat for the German people, who were collectively guilty of being willing accomplices in the Nazi horrors. Mumford endorsed Stalin's approach to the question by affirming that the Nazis should never have been permitted an open trial. Orders should have been given to shoot all of them on sight. The Germans were a devil race of political irresponsibles who should be interned through occupation for an indefinite number of years. The racist argument had been fully inverted.

When Charles Beard was awarded a medal of distinction by the Institute of Arts and Letters, Mumford resigned from the institute in protest. Beard, more than any other writer, was held responsible for breeding a cynicism into youth that crippled their ability to comprehend the reasons for fighting.[46] Mumford charged that Beard was an "intellectual Quisling" who functioned as "an active abetter of tyranny, sadism, and human defilement."[47] Beard practiced intentional intellectual dishonesty by not abandoning isolationism.

His self-betrayal was comparable to Knut Hamsun's perverse decision to side with the Nazis. Beard should have been read out of every scholarly society long ago.[48] Since he had achieved a large measure of intellectual prestige, the danger of Beard's work was compounded. He furnished a "respectable intellectual front" for pro-Nazis in our midst. Mumford had grave difficulty distinguishing a scholar's work from the potential political exploitation it may undergo at the hands of others.

Mumford epitomized those literary writers whose political tastes hinged upon personal aesthetic impressions and subjective intuitions. His seasonal postures vacillated wildly. Instead of appealing for evidence, he quickly grew impatient with critics who failed to share his vision. They were not simply mistaken but morally depraved. As a self-styled cultural prophet, he relied upon neither empirical facts nor a vulgar public opinion that circumscribed the range of political possibilities. Mumford practiced a politics of the impossible. Though his caricature of modern culture was quite fashionable, Mumford insisted that only a small band of visionaries have penetrated the gravity of the cultural malaise. The scientific-pragmatic temperament provided no spiritual pathos for those seeking utopian solutions.

Reinhold Niebuhr, by contrast, possessed more political sophistication as well as philosophical substance in his criticisms of pragmatic liberalism. Niebuhr's objections to Dewey's political philosophy were rooted in the theology of original sin, Marxism, and a critique of science. He formulated an alternative theoretical basis for democratic politics, one that pivotally influenced the "realist" or "power politics" school of thought. War and the revelations from the death camps added substance to the belief in human evil. Niebuhr's outlook harmonized with the mood of the era. Dewey and Niebuhr sometimes shared the same political causes. They both joined the League for Industrial Democracy, the Socialist Party, the League for Independent Political Action, and the Liberal Party. Niebuhr's parody of modern liberalism ill-accorded with Dewey's specific viewpoint. Dewey was irritated by Niebuhr's "sweeping generalizations."[49] Unfortunately, Niebuhr seldom addressed Dewey's politics directly. Their occasional political cooperation should not obscure the fundamental philosophical differences that separated them.

Niebuhr delineated his philosophy by juxtaposing it to Dewey's pragmatic naturalism. The application of scientific intelligence could not eliminate the coercive features of government. Coercion was an inexorable element in political and economic life. Failure to understand this harsh fact lay at the center of much moral confusion.[50] The Pollyanna liberal belief in progress and the inherent reasonableness of man was inapplicable to a precarious world where violence was incessant. These sentimental illusions could only flourish in a stable and geographically isolated America. Niebuhr termed Dewey "incredibly naive," and he insisted that "no one expresses modern man's uneasiness about his society and complacency about himself more perfectly than John Dewey."[51] All social problems were not reducible to problems of education. Impartial or disinterested knowledge cultivated by organized inquiry was unattainable. Scientific reason itself was tainted with subjectivism and could be easily serviced for ideological subterfuge. Niebuhr claimed that the worst injustices in history emanated from the pretense of absolute and impartial truth. Scientific experts reflected a middle-class bias. Politics could not be converted into science. Hans Morgenthau, Niebuhr's disciple, accused Dewey of attempting to transform moral problems into "engineering issues."[52] However, Dewey fully recognized the tentativeness of scientific knowledge and was a lifelong critic of absolutism.

Niebuhr portrayed human nature as riddled with selfishness, finitude, and self-deception, which fomented a ceaseless struggle of interests. The tragic bloodletting of human history was not explainable in solely environmental terms. Politics was not the residue from a pre-rational period of human history, a cultural lag. Races and nations would not simply dissolve before the dawning of universal values. Stressing ingrained egoism, Niebuhr contended that the use or nonuse of violence should be judged not by an absolute moral law but by expediency. Democracy was not an end in itself. Social change required fanaticism and not merely critical intelligence. Dewey's new party was unrealistic because membership in an economic class determined political allegiance; i.e., farmers would not cooperate with workers. Niebuhr embraced temporarily the revolutionary movement within the Socialist Party. He also engaged in fellow traveling and participation in Popular Front causes. However, his intellectual independence finally proved decisive.[53] An Augustinian conception of human nature conditioned his skepticism about peaceful social change within a democracy.

Dewey agreed with Niebuhr's ideal of a cooperative society dedicated to the self-fulfillment of its citizenry. However, Niebuhr's analysis in terms of an inclusive, neo-orthodox crisis theology stifled constructive social action by looking toward divine intervention and a historically determined future. Rather than seeking agreement on some esoteric metaphysics of history, Dewey wanted to reverse the procedure and concentrate on the urgent needs of the present. He found Niebuhr deplorably vague about specific recommendations.[54] Dewey was confused by Niebuhr's tendency to oscillate between violent class struggle on the one hand and a euphoric peaceful triumph of social righteousness at the millennium on the other. If man was naturally depraved and no one group would voluntarily relinquish power, how could the dialectic of history be magically transcended? Occasionally, Niebuhr did admit that some conciliation was possible but it rested upon spiritual conversion and not rational persuasion.[55] He could not easily reconcile his Marxist emphasis on concrete economic forces with the power of spirituality to overcome these conflicts. How could Niebuhr's insistence upon fanaticism as a force for historical change be synthesized with the conviction that all ideologies were nothing more than self-serving idolatry? Dewey suggested that liberals unite behind a common program instead of relying on moral pontification.

Niebuhr's foreign policy earned him widespread notoriety but it differed from Dewey's position primarily in terms of rhetorical tone. During the twenties, Niebuhr was a pacifist and at that time he became executive director of the Fellowship of Reconciliation. Although he resigned from this organization in 1934, Niebuhr did not repudiate "international pacifism." Defending strict neutrality along with Dewey, he held that war under modern conditions would be suicidal. The United States should be preserved as a relative sanctuary for sanity.[56] Since nations were inherently motivated by predatory egoism, moral distinctions between combatants were elusive. The capitalist elite within each country must be overthrown. The plague of war could be relieved by this internal reordering since capitalism bred conflict. But wouldn't civil wars also be devastating?[57]

After Mussolini's invasion of Ethiopia, Niebuhr proposed collective security for Europe but neutrality for America.[58] Like Dewey, he opposed the Spanish embargo. After first supporting a nongovernmental boycott of Japan, Niebuhr approved sanctions when that nation renewed its attack on China. Nonetheless, Niebuhr did not endorse military aid for China.[59] He objected by saying that neutrality legislation was reckless; it prohibited a distinction between aggressors and victims. Yet, as late as the middle of 1938, Niebuhr opposed American military preparedness and urged nonmilitary pressures to stem the cancer of fascism. For a socialist to support a capitalist war economy was the ultimate act of ideological heresy. Capitalists would enlist war to destroy democracy at home and to advance their predatory economic interests.

The Munich crisis illustrated the confusions latent in democratic liberalism.[60] Liberals still had faith that conflicts could be amicably adjudicated. They spinelessly negotiated with an enemy who intended to destroy them. Liberal culture was too comfortable and individualistic to be aroused for collective action in the face of barbarism. It could not fathom the monstrous, implacable evil of Nazism. Niebuhr expected the British Labour Party to develop a realistic foreign policy; instead, the party embraced appeasement as much as the ruling classes. His Marxist faith in the working class was betrayed. Gradually, he recognized that only the arch-Tory Winston Churchill understood the gravity of the Nazi menace. He alone could offer the leadership needed to rally the beleaguered democracies.[61] In May 1940, Niebuhr resigned from the Socialist Party after repudiating its pacifist-isolationist stance. Socialists of the Norman Thomas type were incapable of coping with the "roughstuff" of politics. Collective action always caused an overlapping between the guilty and the guiltless. Life was a contest of power. Those who were unable to digest this fact should "retire to the monastery where medieval perfectionists found their asylum."[62] Liberalism spawned a utopianism that could not decipher the lesser of evils or the differences between the Western democracies and Nazism. While the people might at least possess some common sense, Niebuhr charged that "the fools were the intellectual leaders of our democracy who talked utopian nonsense in a critical decade in which the whole of Western civilization faced 'its hours of doom.' "[63] Endorsing Roosevelt for president in 1940, Niebuhr advised military and economic aid to Britain, just short of American involvement in the war. He testified before a Senate committee in favor of Lend-Lease. His social radicalism was supplanted by a realism that preferred to defend an imperfect democracy against totalitarianism.

Niebuhr founded and edited *Christianity and Crisis* in 1941 in order to combat Christian pacifism and isolationism. Despite his impassioned polemics, he still remained firmly committed to American neutrality. He believed that Americans were not united on intervention. The people had not realized that their vital interests were at stake. Democratic nations entered wars only as a last resort.[64] War under modern conditions would lead to a dangerous erosion of civil liberties, and Niebuhr feared the repressive, reactionary tendencies of the interventionists.[65] Niebuhr alerted the public that Nazism would not collapse from internal contradictions but that the movement must be resisted. A victorious Hitler would threaten American economic and political interests throughout the world. On July 14, 1941, Niebuhr urged repeal of the Neutrality Act.[66] America must accept its international responsibilities rather than remaining complacent and in selfish insulation. Events would determine whether aid or full belligerency was required to defeat the Nazis. Niebuhr's specific policies did not differ substantially from those of Dewey. The ideological struggle between pragmatic and hardboiled liberalism signified verbal posturing more than practical politics.

Though Niebuhr adhered to a pragmatic fallibilism, his post-Depression social theory contained sharp limitations on pure democracy. He accepted the inevitability of oligarchic rule. His Madisonian balance-of-power approach was also conditioned by the necessity of decisive leadership. Niebuhr was impressed by the statesmanship of both Churchill and Roosevelt. He professed no sentimental faith in the wisdom of the masses. Regarding a referendum on the war, Niebuhr argued that foreign policy was the area where pure democracy was least applicable and most perilous.[67] Ordinary people could never become statesmen. Incompetent leadership during the thirties catered to the appetites of the public. The firmest test of a statesman is whether he can inspire the people to sacrifice their private and immediate interests to the common good. They must be shaken out of their moral lethargy.

After the attack on Pearl Harbor, Niebuhr acknowledged that Roosevelt's tactics were devious but imperative, due to the incapacity of the public to face reality. The issue was not whether America would become involved but when the people would overcome their self-deception.[68] While democracies possessed inherent weaknesses in foreign policy, Niebuhr also advocated Fabian intellectual, elite control over the British Labour Party. The workers required expert guidance.[69] Proper rule demanded an elite capable of exuding a wisdom that scientific knowledge could not provide. Niebuhr sanctioned the role of the religious-political prophet who acted outside of government but advised the powerful. The intuitive insight of such a person transcended the grasp of the ordinary layman. Self-chosen prophets are not comfortably reconciled with elective democratic politics. Niebuhr's tendencies ran counter to Dewey's goals of popular enlightenment and cooperative community.

During and after World War II, Dewey and Hook confronted this challenge to pragmatic liberalism. Niebuhr was victimized by a new failure of nerve. He sought to escape within an obscurantist supernaturalism at a time when people were seeking security in a "quick-fix" faith. Instead of Western civilization decaying due to its neglect of spiritual values, the failure to apply the scientific method to all areas of social life was to blame. Hook replied that "against Niebuhr's myth of a private and mysterious absolute we counterpoise the public and self-critical absolute of scientific method."[70] Hook disapproved of efforts by the federal government to consecrate the war by appealing to the "principles of Christianity." Hebrew-Christianity was the source of feudalism not democracy. Democracy enfranchised both a set of rules so that men could live peacefully with their provisional differences and a technique to resolve the differences into a civic consensus. Instead of being stigmatized by original sin, men were neither basically good nor evil. Dewey attributed the "degraded" view of human nature to the passive conviction that men could only be saved by divine intervention.[71]

Historically, liberalism acknowledges both the power of the passions and the destruction that evil men instigate. Rather than searching for some religious dogma or ultimate cause of human actions, social problems could be managed better by specific institutional arrangements and not appeals to moral virtue. However, institutional arrangements alone were not sufficient; they required attentiveness to method and the nurturing democratic habits of mind.[72] George Geiger questioned Dewey directly about pragmatic liberalism's efficacy in times of crisis. Could it not be argued that liberal tentativeness forecloses action when violence is mandated? How could liberalism inspire emotional commitment after studiously examining all elements in a situation, admitting its own weaknesses and the partial soundness of the enemy? Dewey responded by reaffirming that the world was confronted with a radical choice. The choice was not intelligence versus action, but intelligent action versus irrationalism.[73] Crises demanded an even more acute analysis and patient gradualism, not utopian one-step solutions. He now held that democracy seemed preferable under even these desperate conditions. The belief that rules had to be eternal in order to be efficacious was "childish." Maintaining absolute ends and customs independent of their consequences would doom mankind. A piecemeal approach, rather than a quest for universal salvation, could lead mankind out of its malaise.

Dewey was alarmed at the post-war revolt against science and the rise of European existentialism. Sanctioning ethical commitments created "ex nihilo," existentialism transmitted an unrestrained subjectivism and escapism, neither of which could establish an adequate basis for society. Literary intellectuals utilized the wartime destruction, typified by the atomic bomb, as a basis for the wholesale criticism of the scientific project. Science itself was evil, a projection of man's *hubris*. Mortals could not be trusted with such awesome power. Instead of assailing science, man had only himself to blame for his mistakes, according to Dewey.[74] This revolt against modernity was deeply rooted.

In 1948, Julien Benda renewed his attack on "the treason of the intellectuals." He indicted pragmatic relativism for undermining the values of the Western world. Benda conjoined pragmatism and Marxism-Leninism as doctrines all of which endeavored to be rigorously practical. The intellectual had descended from the lofty glorification of disinterested intelligence and eternal values to a crude expediency and political activism. He also stated that William James's support for the Spanish-American War exemplified his intellectual bankruptcy. Dewey effectively replied by indicating that James was actually a member of the Anti-Imperialist League. Benda's misreading of James represented an act of intellectual irresponsibility. Bolshevism was a creed as absolutistic as Benda's dogmatism. Not pragmatism but absolutism rationalized the status quo and implemented Machiavellian means to obtain a predetermined, fanatical goal. The real Socratic tradition signified the application of critical intelligence and not blind customs to human problems.[75]

Though Dewey's politico-philosophical critics generally attacked strawman caricatures, they did effectively place pragmatic liberalism on the defensive. In 1944, Jacques Barzun remarked that "today it is rather Dewey's 'Reconstruction in Philosophy' (purely scientific instrumentalism) that seems on the other brink of the gulf.'"[76] The intellectuals, who should be the most enlightened social group, often manifested the worst rancor, bias, opportunism, and sheer dishonesty. Dewey's faith in open inquiry was never shattered. He continued to defend and clarify his outlook until his death. The Mumford-Frank-MacLeish literary axis collectively made the metamorphosis from pacifism to popular frontism to war propagandism. MacLeish served in the prestigious post of Librarian of Congress, while Lewis Mumford was knighted by Queen Elizabeth. As Nietzsche remarked in *Human All-Too-Human*: "To scholars who become politicians the comic role is usually assigned; they have to be the good conscience of a state policy."

NOTES

1. John Dewey, "Anti-Naturalism in Extremis," *Partisan Review* (Jan.–Feb., 1943):39.

2. Brand Blanshard, "Metaphysics and Social Attitudes," *SF* (Dec., 1937):79–81.

3. Sidney Hook, "Metaphysics and Social Attitudes: A Reply," *SF* (Feb., 1938):154.

4. Sidney Hook, "Scientific Method on the Defensive," *Commentary* (June, 1946):85–90.

5. John Dewey, "President Hutchins' Proposals to Remake Higher Education," *SF* (Jan., 1937):103.

6. Robert M. Hutchins, "Grammar, Rhetoric, and Mr. Dewey," *SF* (Feb., 1937):138. Dewey, "The Higher Learning in America," *SF* (March, 1937):167.

7. Mortimer Adler, "God and the Professors," *Vital Speeches* (Dec. 1, 1940):98. Apparently, Adler blamed Dewey for his failure to obtain a job in the philosophy department at Columbia University, though Dewey had been retired from that institution for ten years. Earlier, as a student of Dewey, Adler peppered him with a running critical commentary on each Dewey lecture. Dewey condemned Adler's "unabashed dogmatism" as early as 1935. Dewey to Otto (May 8, 1935), Max Otto Collection, Wisconsin Historical Society, Madison, Wisconsin. See Sidney Hook, *Pragmatism and the Tragic Sense of Life* (New York: Basic Books, 1974), p. 105.

8. Sidney Hook, "The New Medievalism," *NR* (Oct. 28, 1940):602–606.

9. Mortimer Adler, "This Pre-War Generation," *Harper's* (Oct., 1940):532.

10. Robert Hutchins, "Education for Freedom," *Harper's* (Oct., 1941):517–526. *School and Society* ran a series of articles which purported to demonstrate a conjugal relation between pragmatism and fascism. Hans Elias argued that the German and Italian youth movements were the result of liberal education, not authoritarianism. By juxtaposing quotes from Hitler and Dewey, Ernest Oertel attempted to establish that experimentalism bred fascism. Hans Elias, "Liberalistic Education as a Cause of Fascism," *School and Society* (May 11, 1940): 593–98. Ernest Oertel, "Experimentalism Begets Fascism," *School and Society* (Aug. 13, 1940): 76. John Brubaker attempted to rescue Deweyan pragmatism from the charge of irresoluteness by claiming that it was actually absolutist. Democracy provided a "frame of reference" for society. By establishing the absolutism of democracy, Brubaker hoped to engender in the schools a crusading zeal comparable to that of the fascists and the communists. William Sanders replied that absolutizing democracy would transform it into a static symbol, blunting social criticism. See John Brubaker, "The Absolutism of Progressive and Democratic Education," *School and Society* (Jan. 4, 1941):9. William Sanders, "Toward a New Educational Despotism," *School and Society* (April 5, 1941):441–43.

11. Sidney Hook, "The Counter-Reformation in American Education," *Antioch Review* (1941):109–116.

12. Robert Hutchins, "The Path to War," *Vital Speeches* (Feb. 15, 1941):261. See also: "The Proposition Is Peace," *Vital Speeches* (April 15, 1941):391.

13. Walter Lippmann, "Education vs. Western Civilization," *American Scholar* (Dec. 1940):185.

14. Sidney Hook, "Thirteen Arrows Against Progressive Education," *The Humanist* (Spring, 1944):1–10. Hook, "Letter to Editor," *The Humanist* (Spring, 1943):32–38.

15. John Dewey, "S. 2499, Its Anti-Democratic Implications," *The Nation's Schools* (March, 1947):20–21; "Sectarian Education," *New York Times* (Oct. 1, 1947), p. 28. Dewey signed a letter opposing public aid to parochial schools.

16. Alexander Meicklejohn, *Education Betweeen Two Worlds* (New York: Harper & Brothers, 1942), p. 283.

17. John Dewey, "A Challenge to Liberal Thought," *Fortune* (Aug., 1944):155-7. Alexander Meicklejohn, "A Reply to John Dewey," *Fortune* (Jan., 1945):207-8. "Rejoinders by Dewey and Meicklejohn," *Fortune* (March, 1945):10, 14.

18. Ernest Nagel, "Are Dr. Meicklejohn's Views Totalitarian?" *The Humanist* (Autumn, 1943):120-123.

19. Harry Gideonese, "The Coming Showdown in the Schools," *SRL* (Feb. 3, 1945):6.

20. Harry Gideonese, *The City of Man* (New York: Viking Press, 1941), p. 66.

21. Lewis Mumford, *The Pentagon of Power* (New York: Harcourt, Brace & Jovanovitch, 1974), p. 279.

22. Lewis Mumford, *Faith for Living* (New York: Harcourt, Brace & World, 1940), p. 86.

23. Lewis Mumford, "The Corruption of Liberalism," *NR* (April 29, 1940):368.

24. "Kallen vs. Mumford," *NR* (Dec. 5, 1934):104.

25. Lewis Mumford, "A Call to Arms," *NR* (May 18, 1938):39.

26. George Fielding Eliot, "An Open Letter to Mr. Lewis Mumford," *NR* (June 15, 1938): 164-5. "What Is the Enemy?" *NR* (May 18, 1938):32-33. *NR* (Nov. 2, 1938):355-6.

27. George Spiller, ed., *Mumford—Brooks Letters* (New York: Dutton, 1970), p. 86.

28. Lewis Mumford, *Faith for Living,* p. 105.

29. Lewis Mumford, "America and the Next War," *NR* (June 28, 1939):209.

30. Lewis Mumford, "The Corruption of Liberalism," *NR* (April 29, 1940):373.

31. Lewis Mumford, *Faith for Living,* p. 88.

32. Lewis Mumford, "F.D.R. Loses First Pacific Battle by Failing to Use U.S. Navy, Air Force on Japs," *NL* (Sept. 6, 1941):4. Lewis Mumford, "Demand for Peace Terms Is Maneuver to Break Britain," *NL* (March 15, 1941):7.

33. Sidney Hook, "Metaphysics, War, and the Intellectuals," *Menorah Journal* (Oct., 1940):330-31. During the thirties, Mumford joined Popular Front groups, including the League of American Writers. After the "Stalinazi Pact," he conceded that his suspended judgment about the Purge Trials almost became "a noose around his neck." George Spiller, ed., *Mumford—Brooks Letters,* p. 166.

34. "Mr. Mumford and the Liberals," *NR* (April 29, 1940):563.

35. "Letters on Mumford," *NR* (May 13, 1940):643-4.

36. Fleming MacLeish, "The Assault on Liberalism," *CS* (June 1940):10-13.

37. James T. Farrell, "The Faith of Lewis Mumford," *Southern Review* (Winter, 1940): 417-38.

38. Malcolm Cowley, "Shipwreck," *NR* (Sept. 9, 1940):357. Richard Rovere, "Mumford Review," *CS* (Oct., 1940):26.

39. Reinhold Niebuhr, "Review of Mumford," *N* (Sept. 14, 1940):221-2. For another lavish review, see Frederick Redefer, "Family, Life, and Self," *SF* (Oct., 1940):26.

40. John Dewey to Max Otto (Sept. 16, 1940), Max Otto Collection, Wisconsin Historical Society, Madison, Wisconsin.

41. Waldo Frank, "Our Guilt in Fascism," *NR* (May 6, 1940):665.

42. "Resignations Accepted," *NR* (June 10, 1940):695-6.

43. Lewis Mumford, "Save the Seed Corn," *NR* (Feb. 16, 1942):228.

44. Lewis Mumford, *Values for Survival* (New York: Harcourt, Brace & World, 1946), p. 101.

45. Lewis Mumford, "German Apologetics and the German Record," *SRL* (Aug. 11, 1945):5-6.

46. George Spiller, ed., *Mumford—Brooks Letters,* pp. 273-77.

47. Lewis Mumford, "Mr. Beard and His Basic History," *SRL* (Dec. 2, 1944):27.

48. George Spiller, ed., *Mumford—Brooks Letters,* pp. 321, 323.

49. Reinhold Niebuhr, "The Blindness of Liberalism," *Radical Religion* (Autumn, 1936):4.

50. Reinhold Niebuhr, "Optimism and Utopianism," *World Tomorrow* (Feb. 22, 1933): 179.

51. Reinhold Niebuhr, *The Nature and Destiny of Man* (New York: Scribner's Sons, 1943), pp. 110-111.

52. Hans Morgenthau, *Scientific Man vs. Power Politics* (Chicago: University of Chicago Press, 1948), p. 36.

53. See Paul Merkley, *Reinhold Niebuhr* (Montreal: McGill-Queen's University Press, 1975), pp. 101-103.

54. John Dewey, "Unity and Progress," *WT* (March 8, 1933):232.

55. Reinhold Niebuhr, "Is Social Conflict Inevitable?" *Scribner's Magazine* (Sept., 1935): 166-69.

56. Reinhold Niebuhr, "Shall We Seek World Peace or the Peace of America?" *WT* (March 15, 1934):133.

57. Reinhold Niebuhr, "Why I Leave the F.O.R.," *CC* (June, 1934):17.

58. Reinhold Niebuhr, "Spanish Problems," *Radical Religion* (Fall, 1937):1.

59. Reinhold Niebuhr, "The War in China," *Radical Religion* (Fall, 1937):27-30. Reinhold Niebuhr, "America and the War in China," *CC* (Sept. 29, 1937):1196.

60. Reinhold Niebuhr, "Must Democracy Use Force?" *N* (Jan. 28, 1939):117. Reinhold Niebuhr, "After Munich," *Radical Religion* (Winter, 1938):2.

61. Reinhold Niebuhr, "The British Conscience," *N* (July 26, 1939):219-221.

62. Reinhold Niebuhr, "An End to Illusions," *N* (June 2, 1940):778–79.

63. Reinhold Niebuhr, *Christianity and Power Politics* (New York: Scribners, 1940), p. 72.

64. Reinhold Niebuhr, "American Neutrality," *Radical Religion* (Jan., 1940):6.

65. Reinhold Niebuhr, "Whosoever Will Save His Life," *Christianity and Crisis* (Feb. 24, 1941):1. Reinhold Niebuhr, "Union for Democratic Action," *Radical Religion* (Summer, 1941):6.

66. Reinhold Niebuhr, "The Mirage of Mediation," *Christianity and Crisis* (July 28, 1941): 1–2. Reinhold Niebuhr, "American Doldrums," *Christianity and Crisis* (Sept. 22, 1941):9.

67. *SF* (Nov. 15, 1941):43.

68. Editorial, "Christmas Light on History," *Christianity and Crisis* (Dec. 29, 1941):2.

69. Paul Merkley, *Reinhold Niebuhr,* p. 111.

70. Sidney Hook, "The New Failure of Nerve," *Partisan Review* (Jan.–Feb., 1943):4. Dewey, "The Democratic Faith and Education," *Antioch Review* (June, 1944):274–83.

71. John Dewey, "Anti-Naturalism in Extremis," *PR* (Jan.–Feb., 1943):33.

72. Sidney Hook, "Intelligence and Evil in Human History," *Commentary* (Jan.–June, 1947):210–221.

73. George Geiger, "Dewey's Social and Political Philosophy," in Paul Schilpp, ed., *The Philosophy of John Dewey,* Library of Living Philosophers, vol. 1 (Evanston, Ill.: Northwestern University Press, 1939), pp. 364, 593.

74. John Dewey, "The Penning-In of Natural Science," *The Humanist* (Summer, 1944): 157–59. Dewey, "The Crisis in Human History," *Commentary* (March, 1946):6. Dewey, "Are Naturalists Materialists?" *Journal of Philosophy* (Sept. 13, 1945):515–30. Dewey, "Philosophy's Future in Our Scientific Age," *Commentary* (Oct., 1949):388–94. Sidney Hook, "The Scientific Method on the Defensive," *Commentary* (June, 1946):85–90.

75. Julien Benda, "The Attack on Western Morality," *Commentary* (Nov., 1947):416–22. Dewey, "William James' Morals and Julien Benda's," *Commentary* (Jan., 1948):46–50.

76. Jacques Barzun, "The Literature of Ideas," *SRL* (Aug. 5, 1944):27.

11

The Anti-Stalinist Left

After Pearl Harbor, Dewey joined the war effort but vigilantly protested the implementation of totalitarian practices. He did not debauch his intellectual integrity. Dewey again faulted the narrow isolationism and materialism of "America First," which had contributed to the world's desperate condition. Totalitarianism was a spreading cancer that simultaneously betrayed both opportunism and militaristic expansionism. Superior force was needed to curb its designs. Dewey offered the following observation regarding the military threat posed by totalitarianism:

> War with a totalitarian power is war against an aggressive way of life that can maintain itself in existence only by a constant extension of its sphere of aggression. It is war against the invasion of organized force in every aspect and phase of life—an invasion which regards its success within Germany as the promise of greater success throughout the world.[1]

Totalitarianism could not be appeased. He reissued *German Philosophy and Politics* with a new introduction entitled, "The One-World of Hitler's National Socialism." Explaining the sources of Hitler's appeal, Dewey's account was devoid of the "devil race" rhetoric that induced Clifton Fadiman, Rex Stout, and Lord Vansittart to propose extermination plans for Germany. War propagandists, like Norman Cousins, insisted that one had to hate the enemy in order to prosecute the war effectively.[2] This blind hysteria could have stampeded the public toward a self-defeating unconditional surrender policy; and Dewey did not desire to defeat Nazi totalitarianism only to have it replaced with a Soviet totalitarian threat.

Dewey attributed Hitler's success to the latter's ability to unify disparate elements of German life. Bereft of philosophical training, Hitler raised opportunism to a fine art. However, his rambling particularism transcended the German dualism between inner and outer life. Through the spiritual strength of will, the German mission and solidarity could be magically

191

achieved. Hitler did not deify the state or politics; instead, he emphasized a mystical volkish community, a revolt against modernity.[3] Since both nationalism and socialism sought to displace atomistic individualism, Hitler synthesized the two by enforcing a fanatical and selfless patriotism through work. Unlike the Marxists, Dewey did not mince words when calling Nazism a brand of socialism. He acknowledged that millions of socialists had been converted to Nazism. Hitler scorned the petty, self-interested, and private life of bourgeois-capitalist society. Productivity was not primary for Hitler: economic rationality was secondary to the molding of totally committed true believers. The fixation upon blood, race, and soil nurtured a submergence of the intellect within a collective consciousness that revealed an Hegelian truth higher than that of cold reason. If fear and hate provided the tools for Hitler's demonic mass manipulation, apathy was his greatest enemy. He generated a continuous excitement possessing the intensity of a religious rite. Not a reactionary hierarchy but a brutish mass democratization occurred. Dewey's account stressed (1) how Nazism was a reaction to universal conditions of modern life, (2) how propaganda could easily manipulate the masses, (3) how German culture and history had bred conditions amenable to Hitler. Within the intellectual climate of 1942, Dewey's analysis was remarkably temperate.

The wartime alliance with the Soviet Union stimulated a predictable reflex to resurrect the Popular Front mythology. In a letter to the *New York Times,* written on January 11, 1942, Dewey sharply rebuked Joseph Davies's book, *Mission to Moscow.* The book justified the blood purges and "show trials" as a necessary strategy if Stalin was to liquidate a "fifth column" within the Soviet Union. Davies, a former American ambassador to Moscow, still maintained close affiliations with the Roosevelt Administration. His book voiced a well-tuned apology for Stalinism. Dewey urged that one could engage in an expedient alliance with Stalin and yet deplore the Soviet government's terrorism. However, this would ultimately imperil firm convictions about America's commitment to precious domestic freedoms. Dewey reminded readers that Stalin's pact with Hitler had launched the war. The Soviet leader had made no effort to glorify his new Allies, and a large network of Soviet agents still operated in the Western democracies. Stalin knew that totalitarianism and democracy were totally incompatible. Dewey charged that Davies's book constituted but one example of a one-sided Soviet love affair being cultivated in the United States.[4]

John Childs, editor of *Social Frontier,* objected to Dewey's characterization of Soviet cooperation as wartime expediency. Childs was confident that America and Russia could cooperate in post-war reconstruction and that the Soviet Union would outgrow the folly of training foreign subversives. How Russia behaved depended upon how we treated her. Isolation only deepened Soviet hostility and suspicions. Besides, Russia would be so preoccupied with domestic problems that its efforts to engage in foreign adventures would be severely restricted. The Soviet system had achieved sensational economic progress, while the United States and Britain lagged far short of "true democracy."[5] Childs's exemplary indulgence toward the Soviet Union articulated a thought pattern having perennial appeal. This appeal has been only temporarily sobered by grim revelations about Soviet activities.

Dewey replied by attacking those "weak-kneed" liberals who credulously refused to acknowledge Stalin's true designs, even after all that had transpired during the thirties. Negotiations between Britain and Russia about the sacrifice of the Baltic states and Poland were already underway. America must not be cornered into accepting peace on Stalin's terms. Dewey advocated a sane and critical policy appraisal, one that would obviate the dangers of Soviet hegemony. If Russia was to cooperate after the war, its liberation from the yoke of totalitarianism was prescribed. The propitious time to discuss war aims was when Stalin depended upon American help and evinced vulnerability. This process should ensue immediately. Dewey's advice went unheeded. Childs was astounded by Dewey's suggestion of a war against Stalinist totalitarianism before genuine peace could be established.[6] The boundaries of the cold war debate among liberals were already coming into focus.

When *Mission to Moscow* resurfaced as a film, Dewey repeated that the movie offered totalitarian propaganda for mass consumption.[7] Stalinesque productions like *The North Star* and *Song of Russia* were released shortly thereafter. The film advisor to *Mission to Moscow* was Jay Leyda. He was actually a former employee of Moscow's International Bureau of Revolutionary Literature and was reputed to be an outstanding communist propagandist.[8] Kremlin efforts to sell a positive image of the Soviet Union through Hollywood movies and other media achieved some success in rehabilitating both Stalin and Soviet life. With the help of a huge promotional campaign, *Mission to Moscow* broke box-office records in New York and was circulated widely. Corliss Lamont's National Council of Soviet-American Friendship presented certificates of appreciation to Davies and the film's producers at a Madison Square Garden rally.[9] The *Washington Post* announced a special preview of the film for newsmen and government officials under the sponsorship of the National Press Club. According to the article: "There was a deep and almost reverent silence through most of the showing. . . . At the end there was a great burst of applause which ended only when the orchestra of the theatre drowned it out with the finale."[10] Dewey's untimely disrobing of the film ruffled fashionable sensitivities.

Arthur Pope, chairman of the Committee on National Morale, responded that *Mission to Moscow* was acclaimed by the New York press as "brilliant, informative, and lively." He deemed the question of Soviet tyranny to be virtually a dead issue. He characterized Dewey's Trotsky Commission as "without competence, status, or authority." Pope ridiculed Dewey, saying

> . . . he [Dewey] can hardly be so naive as not to know that the success of their [the Soviet's] effort is due not merely to their courage, but also to farsighted planning, powerful organization, discipline, and a spontaneous loyalty, engendered

in no small measure by the very government of which he is so contemptuous, while solid achievements and human ideals have, after many years, given the Russian people a common rallying point.[11]

Stalin was their leader by overwhelming popular choice and confidence. While Pope defended the film's use of a simplifying fictional technique, Davies introduced the film candidly as "the truth about Russia." All that the American people wanted to know was whether they could trust the Russians, and the answer was a resounding "yes." Pope argued that Allied morale would be subverted if citizens could freely malign leaders of Allied nations. Everyone's freedom of speech had to be curtailed in wartime to avoid divisive conflicts. Pope accused Dewey of treason: promoting fear and hatred of Russia aided and abetted Hitler.[12]

During this second honeymoon period with Stalin, Dewey steadfastly refused to be intimidated. He replied that the film itself impugned the gallantry of the British, fomented dissension, and concocted a litany of historical fabrications. Why did Stalin sabotage Hitler's enemies if he was merely buying time? Why were Polish army troops still in Soviet concentration camps? What was Soviet policy on India? Defense of the film was tantamount to proposing that democracy take an extended vacation during the war.[13]

The avalanche of pro-Soviet propaganda in major newspapers, magazines, radio, and motion pictures conditioned the American public to swallow the belief that a fortuitous wartime partnership could blossom into a lasting peace. *Life* magazine published a special 116-page issue that pictured Stalin warmly kissing peasant babies. The *New Republic* asserted that Russia could live fraternally with nations of good will if America would just let her. Cordiality was strained due to American rather than Soviet intransigence.[14] American correspondents in Moscow accepted their censorship benignly and churned out dispatches scarcely distinguishable from those of *Pravda*.[15] Calls to define Allied war aims beyond unconditional surrender were considered collaboration with the enemy. When pacifist George Hartmann, formerly of Teachers College, requested a negotiated peace, the *New Republic* and the *Nation* called for him to be investigated by the FBI.[16]

Only the *New Leader* with Dewey as a contributing editor, Eugene Lyons's *American Mercury,* the *Partisan Review,* and *Common Sense* voiced suspicions about Soviet intentions. David Dallin declared that the Soviet Union really had not disguised its plans for post-war Europe. Stalin offered Hitler a conditional peace in 1943. Bertram Wolfe insisted that there were actually two wars rather than one: democracy against totalitarianism, on the one hand, and the Allies versus Hitler on the other. Stalin wanted to drive out Hitler but refused to permit American use of land or naval bases to fight Japan. The Soviet role in the Katyn forest massacre of Polish officers was suppressed, the slaughter was brushed aside as nothing more than Nazi propaganda.[17] Neither the *New Republic* nor the *Nation* even mentioned the story. Despite Eleanor Roosevelt's appeal, the Soviet Union executed

Polish, Jewish-socialist leaders Victor Alter and Henryk Ehrlich for spreading defeatist propaganda, though neither had the slightest pro-Nazi sympathy. After a momentary uneasiness about the executions, the *New Republic* dismissed any action by the West as intervention into Russia's internal affairs.[18] The editors sighed that it would have been so simple for Stalin to release the dissidents to the custody of the West. The Office of War Information and the War Writer's Board continued to pump the American public with a steady stream of pro-Soviet literature. Dewey was amazed at the number of fellow-travelers to be found in the publishing industry and how they tended to maneuver into strategic positions.[19]

The *New Republic* typified the operative mentality of totalitarian liberals in World War II. The journal printed and supported Vice-President Henry Wallace's speech "Beyond the Atlantic Charter." Wallace noted that the Russians had detected some of the excesses in political democracy.[20] Defending a convergence theory between communism and Americanism, Wallace applauded the Soviet Union for its world leadership in practicing ethnic democracy. The editors feared that reactionary forces in the West would instigate a war against Russia. They concluded that "such a war of political democracy against social democracy would be fatal to our civilization as well as freedom."[21] Stalin's outlook was, objectively speaking, more democratic than Churchill's.[22] The editors hailed Stalin's new attitude toward the Orthodox Church. Earnestly analyzing the Soviet constitutional change toward more autonomy in the constituent republics, the *New Republic* contemplated the implications of this new federalism for foreign policy. How could they have imagined that Stalin would decentralize the government in the middle of a war?[23] After Truman dropped him from his post as Secretary of Commerce, due to disagreements over Soviet policy, Wallace became editor of the *New Republic* on October 12, 1946.

When the Kremlin claimed the Baltic states and Bessarabia, the journal scoffed at self-determination as "wishful thinking." Only a naive person could entertain the idea that the Russians would not propose territorial claims.[24] Yet, fears of Russian armies in eastern Europe were both "unjustified and ungenerous" since the Red Army had saved America from extinction. All that the Russians really wanted was national security. The editors explained: "It is perfectly clear that Russia's policy is defensive, not aggressive. [The Soviets] will interfere in European affairs only to the extent they believe necessary to protect themselves from attack."[25] The Allies, therefore, were not at odds over a post-war Europe, because all were committed to democratic government. The journal conceded, however, that there might be variances over the interpretation of democracy.[26] It perceived no signs that Soviet plans would be displeasing. Besides, since the United States could not stop Soviet power in eastern Europe, the decision to postpone boundary settlements until after the war made "good sense." The *New Republic* simultaneously advocated a policy of weakness and appeasement toward the Soviet Union; later it took refuge in the fact that America was powerless to oppose Stalin in any case.

When the Soviet Union and Czechoslovakia signed a peace treaty in 1943, the editors exuberantly cast off their "inner doubts." They announced that "the treaty is a clear indication that Russia has no imperialist design on the territory of her neighbors and does not insist that they accept anything farther to the Left than a genuinely democratic rule."[27] With Frederick Schuman's assistance, the journal discredited the Polish government-in-exile, while describing Stalin's handpicked Lublin regime as "representative."[28] The Soviet Union had a legitimate sphere of interest and deserved friendly governments on its borders.[29]

Dewey endorsed Roosevelt for president in 1944. He distrusted Republican isolationism and was pessimistic about the prospects for a permanent peace.[30] The war would not end all wars but, hopefully, it would secure the basis for a generation of peace. After Trotsky's assassination by a Stalinist agent, Dewey signed a letter to the president of Mexico pleading for better protection of anti-Stalinist refugees in that country. Despite the prominence of its sponsors, the New York City dailies, with the exception of the *New York Times,* failed to print a single line about the story.[31] In the same year, Dewey also joined the Tresca Memorial Committee. Carlo Tresca was an anti-communist anarchist who was a good friend of Dewey. The committee suspected that Tresca had been assassinated by Stalinists; Alan Cranston, then in the Office of War Information, and Walter Cronkite blamed it on the Mafia.[32] The committee had great difficulty in getting the police to investigate the case during the war.

In 1944, Dewey became a member of the Liberal Party of New York, a group that included among its members Reinhold Niebuhr, George Counts, and David Dubinsky.[33] Niebuhr opposed the unconditional surrender policy and advocated a positive peace designed to reintegrate a democratic Germany into the European community. He rejected schemes like the Morgenthau Plan, which attempted to wreak vengeance on the German people.[34] Dewey helped to organize the Council for a Democratic Germany. In 1946, together with Sidney Hook, Robert MacIver, and Norman Thomas, he protested the deportation of Sudeten Germans and Hungarians from Czechoslovakia.[35] Later, he resigned from the Roosevelt Committee for the Arts and Sciences because he recognized too many fellow-travelers within its ranks.[36]

Shortly after the war, Dewey and other anti-Stalinist liberals exposed intellectuals who were massaging American public opinion with the Soviet line.[37] As the grim evidence of Russian imperialism mounted, the editors of the *New Leader, Commentary,* and the *Partisan Review* struggled to defend democracy in a war ravaged world. In March 1945, Dewey pointed out how ironic it was that those who vilified attempts to appease the Nazis, since it led to a wider war, were now advocating appeasement toward Stalin in an effort to avoid war at all costs.[38] Arthur Schlesinger, Jr., referred to the official liberal of the era as a "fellow-traveler," as evidenced by the columns of the *Nation,* the *New Republic,* and Max Lerner's *PM.* Schlesinger remarked that for the most chivalrous reasons totalitarian liberals could not believe that ugly facts would underlie fair words. However the Soviet Union was viewed, it kept appearing as "a kind of enlarged Brook Farm Community, complete with folk dancing in native costumes, joyous work in the fields, and progressive kindergartens."[39] The *New Republic* refused to review either Schlesinger's *Vital Center* or Irvin Ross's *Strategy for Liberals*.[40] In a short letter to the *Partisan Review,* Dewey praised its editorial "The Liberal Fifth Column."[41] The article examined the role of Soviet apologists who concocted heady rationalizations for each new Soviet aggression. The fear of war was used to promote appeasement. As long as American policy remained weak, democratic peoples in Europe could be intimidated into capitulation.

Indications of a new Popular Front were ubiquitous. On April 22, 1946, the *New Republic* proclaimed, "it is time that the United States awoke to the truth that nothing is gained for us vis-à-vis Russia by getting tough."[42] The U.S. State Department, it was thought, jeopardized peace far more than did the Kremlin. Soviet apologist Frederick Schuman was conveniently selected to review Victor Kravchenko's *I Choose Freedom.* I. F. Stone was livid over Churchill's Iron Curtain speech; Stone opposed the "counter-revolution" in Greece, termed the presence of the Red Army in Iran a false rumor, and held that the Dardanelles in all fairness should be Soviet.[43] Though admitting that the Soviet Union was totalitarian, Lewis Mumford did not issue another call to arms. He urged American leaders to "disarm Soviet Russia's justifiable suspicions and to remove every conceivable reason for distrustful belligerence."[44] This policy was not appeasement but a "candid confession of our sins." Mumford proposed that the United States withdraw from any Pacific or Atlantic base that the Soviets considered a danger to their security. He rejected the doctrine of containment as a self-imposed problem, and he favored unilateral disarmament. In 1946 the *New Republic* ran a series of articles by Earl Browder. Not surprisingly, the editors endorsed his plan for a massive American loan to the USSR.[45] The *Nation,* conceding that it had no corroborating evidence, condoned the execution of Chetnik leader Draga Mihailovitch for fear of making him a Soviet martyr.[46] Dewey sponsored a cable to Ernest Bevin, British Labour prime minister, indicating that Americans did not support any new appeasement program.[47] The Henry Wallace position represented only a small minority comprised of communists, fellow-travelers, and totalitarian liberals. The cry of imperialism against Britain and America was designed merely to divert attention from an expanding imperialism on the part of the Soviets. The cable encouraged Bevin to resist this imperialism resolutely.

Dewey, Hook, and Niebuhr molded a coherent foreign policy that anticipated and influenced many of the initiatives of the Truman Administration. In a letter to President Truman (July 21, 1945), both Dewey and Herbert Hoover pleaded with him not to sell out Poland. The letter appealed for the institution of truly free elections, the withdrawal of Soviet troops, freedom for anti-communist political prisoners, and the right of correspondents to travel freely in Poland. The war, it was argued, would have been fought largely in vain if America condoned in Russia what had been roundly condemned in Nazi Germany. A firm nonappeasement policy would prevent war.[48] After visiting Germany in 1946, Niebuhr condemned Wallacite apologetics. Niebuhr was convinced that Stalin wanted to conquer the whole of Europe. For this reason, Niebuhr cooperated with George Kennan to formulate the doctrine of containment.[49] Hook agreed that the United States should do everything possible to rally democratic elements in Europe. This required sufficient military security to thwart Soviet intimidation along with economic recovery to ensure the allegiance of the working classes. Without necessary economic aid, Hook feared a communist triumph. Regarding the platform for a new party, he advised more emphasis upon international collective security. National disarmament was quixotic until all nations were political democracies.[50] Hook proposed a broad, international front of democratic loyalists, particularly organized labor. Neither Hook nor Niebuhr advocated a preventive war against Stalin. However, the world could not remain forever divided between freedom and tyranny. Until the Soviet Union became a genuine democracy, the United States must remain steadfast. Socialists should subordinate radical economic programs to the maintenance of democratic freedoms. A piecemeal approach to this goal was advisable. Soviet imperialism was the paramount concern.

Dewey vigorously endorsed the Truman Doctrine. He failed to comprehend how any intelligent person could not recognize the threat of world war, especially when appeasement invited aggression. Dewey was heartened that both major parties endorsed an international, bipartisan view that accepted America's world responsibilities. Though Russia was at that time too weak to prosecute a war, Dewey offered the following warning: "If Russia got the Near East under its control, the Arab countries would probably follow, and then probably Italy, France, and Germany. Under these conditions, Russia would be powerful and its rulers would be in a position to carry out their plan of bolshevizing the whole world."[51] Reviewing David Dallin's book *Forced Labor in Soviet Russia,* Dewey agreed that the subjugation of ten to fourteen million lives through slave labor was an inherent part of Soviet policy.[52] He dismissed as "incredibly gullible" the thesis that the Soviet Union behaved aggressively because it felt insecure. Was Iran a threat to the Soviet Union? The Kremlin copied Hitler's tactics of the big lie, disguising wholesale repression with idealistic subterfuge. For example, Vyacheslav Molotov charged that unemployed Americans would envy the working conditions in Soviet labor camps. The Soviet Union officially denounced Dewey's "fascist" philosophy and termed him "the most vicious enemy of the American laboring masses."[53]

When Henry Wallace resigned from his editorship of the *New Republic* in order to launch his bid for the presidency in 1948 on the Progressive Party ticket, Dewey adamantly opposed him. He identified Wallace as a candidate who had "the active support of Communists and fellow-travelers both in and outside of labor organizations."[54] Wallace opposed the Marshall

Plan, objected to Greek and Turkish aid, defended the communist coup in Czechoslovakia as an act of self-defense against a right-wing American plot, and fought the Berlin airlift. Dewey accused Wallace of abandoning the democratic peoples of Europe to the world's "most reactionary imperialist" government. The European Recovery Act constituted the best hope for a free Europe. Wallace could no more promote world peace than he could guarantee civil rights in eastern Europe. Dewey rejected any "moral fission" of the world into Soviet and American spheres; these would callously ignore the peoples already shackled by Soviet tyranny. Along with Reinhold Niebuhr, he warned: "There can be no compromise, no matter how temporary, with totalitarianism. Compromise with totalitarianism means stamping an imprimatur on the drive for a Pax Sovietica."[55] Like the Nazi-Soviet Pact, the events in Czechoslovakia temporarily awakened many naive liberals who now abandoned Wallace. Not even the *New Republic* or the *Nation* could endorse him; his credibility had dissolved almost completely.[56]

Dewey offered qualified approval of the United Nations; however, he insisted that the right to a veto for those in the Security Council had to be repealed.[57] In contrast to the post-World War I era, Dewey insisted that a viable world organization had to be initiated from the political side.[58] He criticized Republican-isolationist efforts to smear Dean Acheson, and he defended the Marshall Plan. Witnessing Soviet thrusts in Asia, Dewey congratulated Acheson on obtaining United Nations support for the Korean War.[59] Dewey joined the Iron Curtain Refugee Campaign Committee as well as the Congress for Cultural Freedom.[60] The latter promoted democratic ideals in academic circles throughout the world.

Dewey sought to offset the threat of communist subversion by voicing concern for civil liberties. Communist activities should be investigated by judicial authorities. Toward this end, he joined the Committee of One-Thousand to Abolish the House Committee on Un-American Activities.[61] Having previously been a target of the committee himself, Dewey feared that congressional investigatory powers were being abused for demagogic political reasons. Liberals were now paying the political price for failing to police their own ranks years ago. Eugene Lyons contended that the communists were fortunate to be investigated by incompetents like Senator Joseph McCarthy and Martin Dies, Jr.[62] The *New Leader* applauded Alger Hiss's conviction because his activity symbolized Soviet infiltration in high places.[63] Editor William Bohn noted ominously how many of Hiss's apologists had been former government employees. The journal published documented evidence on Owen Lattimore and the Institute of Pacific Relations revealing that the agency had been infiltrated by Soviet agents and had shaped America's China policy.[64] The *Nation* sued the *New Leader* for libel in an effort to protect its frontist writer Alfredo del Vayo. Reinhold Niebuhr resigned as a contributor to the *Nation* due to its persistent Soviet apologetics and fellow-traveling.[65] Leslie Fiedler argued that mere leftist sentiment was no guarantee against evil or ignorance. Alger Hiss shared the illusions of so many who had defended his right to hide behind the smoke-screen of the Fifth Amendment. Irving Kristol declared that this immunity conceded a right to conspiracy, which no viable government could sustain.[66] Sidney Hook insisted that a Fifth Amendment plea exposed the utter moral bankruptcy of radicals who refused to defend and publicize their ideas and actions. Social democrats, along with Leslie Fiedler, called upon liberals to escape from innocence to political responsibility.

Freda Kirchwey, editor of the *Nation,* maintained that the threat McCarthyism posed to American liberty was as grave as communism. Many liberals were again seduced by this line of reasoning. They crusaded against the phantom threat of McCarthyism in comparison to the impending danger of Stalinism.[67] (But how many of McCarthy's victims ended up in concentration camps?) Sidney Hook reasoned that the expression of communist ideas should not be punished; rather, it should be participation in the communist movement. Dewey did not believe that Communist Party members should be automatically excluded from teaching. These members were no subversive threat since they had no cover. Fellow-travelers could be more dangerous. Each case should be adjudicated individually. Sidney Hook agreed that the issue of communist teachers was overblown since very few existed. However, party members were an ultimate threat to academic freedom. Democracy must be allowed to protect itself from the intrigues of a small disciplined cadre. Communists were obliged to distort, conspire, and propagandize; all of which were actions that disqualified them from teaching on grounds of professional ethics. Conspiracy could be meaningfully separated from intellectual heresy. While party members were "prima facie" liable for dismissal, faculties ought to control disciplinary actions. Hook conceded that allowances should be made for discretion, even in cases that involved self-professed members. Fellow-travelers, on the other hand, were a more elusive threat. Their ideas should be openly criticized and discredited but not disciplined. The positions of Dewey and Hook converged on the Communists as a teachers' issue. Both remained sensitized to democratic procedures.[68]

On October 20, 1949, Dewey celebrated his ninetieth birthday.[69] The Kremlin responded by denouncing him three days later as a "philosophical lackey of American imperialism and a war-mongering Winston Churchill of philosophy."[70] Through an extended political education, he grappled with the dilemmas confronting democracy in a world plagued by despotism. Though he loathed war, Dewey understood that it might be forced upon us as a lesser moral evil to prevent the triumph of tyranny. Accepting the lesser evil is the substance of political realism. His intellectual integrity, openness, and courage permitted him to rethink his political approach in lieu of new evidence. The political debates during Dewey's lifetime possess a familiar, contemporary ring. The struggle for human liberty is incessant. Though his message has been neglected and perverted, who has done more to clarify and give coherent meaning to the practices of American democratic life? Dewey served as both a scholar and political activist. To tread this delicate tightrope required a strength of character that could abstain from ideological fixations. While many intellectuals fall short of this ideal, their political role is inescapable. Ultimately, democracy requires that truth and politics must be compatible.

NOTES

1. John Dewey, *German Philosophy and Politics,* 2nd. ed. (New York: G.P. Putnam's Sons, 1942), p. 47.

2. Norman Cousins, "The Time for Hate Is Now," *SRL* (July 4, 1942):13. Cousins, "An Open Letter to Clifton Fadiman," *SRL* (Nov. 7, 1942):10. *Common Sense* objected to the war bond advertisement captioned, "It Costs Plenty to Kill a Jap." The ad pictured the face of a Japanese soldier looking like Pithocanthropus Erectus and had rattlesnakes with the head of a Japanese. *CS* (July, 1945):30.

3. Dewey, *German Philosophy and Politics* (1942), p. 35. See Dewey, "Techniques of Reconstruction," *SRL* (August, 1940):110.

4. Dewey and Childs, "Can We Work With Russia?" *SF* (March 15, 1942):79–80.

5. Ibid.

6. "Dr. Dewey on Our Relations With Russia," *SF* (April 15, 1942):194.

7. John Dewey and Suzanne La Follette, "Several Faults Are Found in 'Mission to Moscow' Film," *New York Times* (May 9, 1943), p. 8E.

8. T. R. Greene, "'Mission to Moscow' Advisor Was Soviet Film Propagandist," *NL* (Oct. 3, 1942):1.

9. *NR* (Nov. 8, 1943):662. Harold Ickes, Claude Pepper, Joseph Davies, Corliss Lamont, and General Stillwell appeared at these Soviet-American friendship rallies.

10. *Washington Post* (April 29, 1943).

11. *New York Times* (May 11, 1943), p. E14.

12. *New York Times* (June 12, 1943), p. 12.

13. *New York Times* (June 19, 1943), p. 12.

14. *NR* (April 5, 1943):429.

15. Marhooska Fischer, "American Correspondents in Russia," *CS* (Dec., 1945):33–35. "Those Moscow Correspondents," *Time* (Dec. 17, 1945):61–62.

16. "Peace Now," *NR* (Feb. 7, 1944):164–5. *N* (Feb. 5, 1944):146–7.

17. David Dallin, "Russia's Aims in Europe," *American Mercury* (July, 1943):391–402. Bertram Wolfe, "Stalin at the Peace Table," *CS* (May, 1943):160–2.

18. *NR* (April 5, 1943):428.

19. John Dewey to Walter Houston (April 25, 1945), John Dewey Papers, Morris Library, Southern Illinois University.

20. Henry Wallace, "Beyond the Atlantic Charter," *NR* (Nov. 23, 1942):668.

21. "Must We Fight Another War?" *NR* (Dec. 21, 1942):812.

22. *NR* (Aug. 23, 1943):238.

23. *NR* (Feb. 14, 1944):198.

24. *NR* (Feb. 22, 1945):235.

25. *NR* (Sept. 20, 1943):320.

26. *NR* (Nov. 1, 1943):603.

27. *NR* (Dec. 27, 1943):900.

28. Frederick Schuman, "The Polish Frontier," *NR* (Jan. 15, 1944):138–41.

29. *NR* (Feb. 21, 1944):230–31.

30. *New York Times* (Oct. 30, 1944), p. 32. Dewey expressed his early support for Roosevelt by joining the Independent Citizen's Committee for the Re-Election of Dean Alfange, a New Dealer. Reinhold Niebuhr, George Counts, and John Childs were other members. See *NR* (Oct. 19, 1942):503.

31. "Letter to the President of Mexico," *PR* (1942):174–75. The *New Masses* blasted this committee as pro-fascist. "The Background," *New Masses* (March 24, 1942):13.

32. John Diggins, *Mussolini and Fascism: The View From America*, pp. 411–443.

33. John Childs to John Dewey (Oct. 20, 1944), John Dewey Papers, Morris Library, Southern Illinois University.

34. Reinhold Niebuhr, "Victor's Justice," *CS* (Jan., 1946):6–9.

35. "Hitler's Spirit Still Lives: Introduction," John Dewey et al. in *Tragedy of a People: Racialism in Czechoslovakia* (New York: American Friends of Democratic Sudetens, 1946), pp. 3–6.

36. John Dewey to Albert Barnes (April 27, 1947), John Dewey Papers, Morris Library, Southern Illinois University.

37. Ferdinand Lundberg, "The *PM* Camouflage," *NL* (July 20, 1946):5. Arnold Beichman, "The Unprofitability of Cults," *NL* (May 5, 1948):8–9. Beichman worked for *PM* from 1941–1946. The American Newspaper Guild nearly elected a communist-backed candidate in 1947. See Jeane Harmon, *Such Is Life* (London: Hammond, Hammond & Co., 1959), ch. 12. "Crimea, A Cynic's Peace," *CS* (March, 1945):3–4. Philip Rahv, "Review of Koestler's *Yogi and the Commissar*," *PR* (Summer, 1945):398–402. James Burnham, "Lenin's Heir," *PR* (Winter, 1945):60–72. Dewey praised *Commentary* for being an authentic voice of liberalism. See Dewey, "*Commentary* and Liberalism," *Commentary* (Nov., 1948):485.

38. John Dewey to Sidney Hook (March 8, 1945), Sidney Hook Collection, Center for Dewey Studies, Carbondale, Illinois.

39. Arthur Schlesinger, Jr., *The Vital Center* (Boston: Houghton, Mifflin Co., 1949), p. 37.

40. "Heard from the Left," *NL* (March 11, 1950):8.

41. John Dewey, "Letter to Editor," *PR* (1946):285. The article noted that employees at the Soviet embassy were allowed to read only the *Daily Worker, PM*, the *Nation*, and the *New Republic*, "The Liberal 'Fifth Column,'" *PR* (1946):291.

42. "Wanted: A Policy," *NR* (April 22, 1946):563.

43. I. F. Stone, "U.S. and USSR," *N* (March 16, 1946):306–7.

44. Lewis Mumford, *Values for Survival* (New York: Harcourt, Brace and World, 1946), pp. 58–59.

45. Earl Browder, "American Loan to USSR," *NR* (Aug. 26, 1946):222–25.

46. "The Michailovitch Trial," *N* (May 25, 1946):615.

47. "A Cable to Bevin," *NL* (Jan. 28, 1947):1. The letter was also signed by Sidney Hook, A. A. Berle, Dorothy Thompson, Stewart Alsop, and Henry Luce.

48. "Appeasement Imperils Peace," *NL* (July 21, 1945):1, 16.

49. Reinhold Niebuhr, "Fight for Germany," *Life* (October 21, 1946):65–72. Niebuhr, "For Peace We Must Risk War," *Life* (September 20, 1948):38–39.

50. Sidney Hook, "The Future of Socialism," *PR* (Jan.-Feb., 1947):24–36. Hook, "Ideas For a New Party," *Antioch Review* (1947):305. Dewey became Honorary Chairman of the National Educational Committee for a New Party. See Alonzo Hamby, "Henry A. Wallace, the Liberals, and the Soviet Union," *Review of Politics* (1969):157–69.

51. "John Dewey Applauds Truman Doctrine," *NL* (May 3, 1947):5.

52. John Dewey, "Behind the Iron Bars," *NL* (Sept. 13, 1947):1.

53. Sidney Hook, "The USSR Views of American Philosophy," *Modern Review* (November, 1947):649–52, 655–660. Sponsored by the American Labor Conference on International Affairs, this journal attempted to encourage anti-communist trade unionism on both sides of the Atlantic. Dewey was listed as a contributor, while Hook was on the editorial board.

54. John Dewey, "Henry Wallace and the 1948 Elections," *NL* (Dec. 27, 1947):1.

55. John Dewey, "Wallace vs. a New Party," *NL* (Oct. 30, 1948):14. Cold war-revisionist, Norman Markowitz, attempted to wrap Henry Wallace around John Dewey's image of a democratic socialist America. Nothing could be further from the truth. See Norman Markowitz, *The Rise and Fall of the People's Century* (New York: Free Press, 1973), pp. 18, 162, 328.

56. Freda Kirchwey, "Prague—A Lesson for Liberals," *N* (March 6, 1948):205–6. Michael Straight, "There Are Great Fears," *NR* (March 22, 1948):6–7.

57. Albert Einstein to John Dewey (Sept. 4, 1947), John Dewey Papers, Morris Library, Southern Illinois University. Einstein lent his name to an assortment of communist causes. See "Einstein Flunks Out," *NL* (June 22, 1953):22–23.

58. John Dewey to Sidney Hook (Sept. 1, 1945), Sidney Hook Collection, The Center for Dewey Studies, Carbondale, Illinois.

59. *New York Times* (Nov. 19, 1950): p. E14.

60. *NL* (Dec. 31, 1949):14. See William Barrett, "Cultural Conference at the Waldorf," *Commentary* (May, 1949):487–93. The article describes Hook's activities at the communist-inspired Cultural and Scientific Conference for World Peace.

61. "Committee of One Thousand," *N* (Oct. 2, 1948):2.

62. Eugene Lyons, "Communists Lucky to Be Investigated by Dies, McCarthy," *NL* (April 1, 1950):1, 6.

63. William Henry Chamberlain, "The Conviction of Alger Hiss," *NL* (Feb. 4, 1950):16.

64. William Bohn, "Hiss Perjury Conviction Sign of Maturity," *NL* (Jan. 25, 1949):1. Richard Walker, "Lattimore and the IPR," *NL* (March 31, 1952):52–516.

65. "Fellow Associates," *NL* (April 28, 1952):30–31.

66. Leslie Fiedler, "Hiss, Chambers, and the Age of Innocence," *Commentary* (Aug., 1951):109–119. Irving Kristol, "Civil Liberties, 1952—A Study in Confusion," *Commentary* (March, 1952):228–236.

67. See Norbert Muhlen, "The Phantom of McCarthyism," *NL* (May 21, 1951):16–18.

68. John Dewey, "Communists as Teachers," *New York Times* (June 21, 1949), p. L24. See Sidney Hook to John Dewey (June 22, 1949; June 27, 1949; July 11, 1949) and John Dewey to Sidney Hook (June 23, 1949; July 2, 1949), Sidney Hook Collection, The Center for Dewey Studies, Carbondale, Illinois. Hook, "Academic Integrity and Academic Freedom," *Commentary* (October, 1949):329–339. Hook, "Communists in the Colleges," *NL* (May 6, 1950):16–18.

69. Both the *New Republic* (Oct. 17, 1949) and the *Saturday Review* (Oct. 22, 1949) dedicated an entire issue to John Dewey.

70. "Moscow Denounces Dewey," *New York Times* (Oct. 23, 1949), p. 62.

Epilogue

The first step toward revitalizing interest in Dewey's political philosophy is to dissolve the malignant encrustation of those interpretations which have over the years clouded his legacy. Synthesizing humanism and naturalism with staunch anti-Communism, Sidney Hook has carried forward the mantle of pragmatic liberalism. There is some evidence that a rediscovery of the pragmatic temper is underway.[1] However, far from merely being intellectually fashionable, a more enduring recognition of Dewey's life and work can be obtained by comprehending his sophisticated philosophical defense of the democratic way of life. In the midst of an ominous climate of world politics and cultural nihilism, Dewey's outlook offers an urgently needed avenue toward political civility. Indeed, the issues he addressed remain pivotal today.

What are some of the misconceptions which contort and discredit Dewey's social philosophy? One standard criticism charges him with being incurably optimistic, possessing a naive faith in the goodness of human nature, and harboring the unfounded belief that science and technology could resolve every source of human conflict. Dewey's philosophy is that of a meliorist; he insists that progress is possible but by no means inevitable. Human nature is neither intrinsically good nor inherently evil, but through proper educational training humane social habits can be cultivated. The scientific project can help to relieve the human estate and, in addition, it can offer expanded cultural opportunities for the common man. However, Dewey also warns that scientific-technological power can quite easily be utilized for diabolical purposes if society is not rooted in those civilized values which he vigilantly defended. Nor does Dewey neglect the artistic and spiritual dimensions of life in favor of a crude mass philistinism. He believes that an industrial civilization could be constructed that would offer the required material foundation for a dynamic democratic culture.

Dewey has also been linked to the interest group liberalism exemplified by such noted political scientists as Robert Dahl and David Truman. Critics argue that Dewey was preoccupied with the process and mechanics of democracy,

205

allowing for the free play of conflicting predatory groups, while remaining value neutral toward the results of the process. Only one response seems appropriate here: Dewey's entire political career is the strongest possible testimony against such an allegation. He advised in favor of social cooperation rather than social conflict, insisting that ethical values were the basis of politics. Scientific investigation could provide the public with the evidence necessary to formulate enlightened policies. These policies would not be determined by a scientific elite of experts but by the public at large.

During World War I, Dewey did not become a morally blind servant of power. Defending Wilsonian ideals, Dewey sought an enduring peace through an international environment capable of nurturing democracy. Unlike Randolph Bourne's impressionistic view, Dewey did not believe that war necessarily precluded the possibility for intelligent action. In certain circumstances, war might well be the only intelligent action possible. Along with the *New Republic* editors, Dewey was an internationalist liberal who recognized that democratic goals required "a long period of struggle." He realized that Germany had become the world's chief menace to peace and democracy, thereby posing a direct threat to America's interests and security if it were to emerge triumphant. In addition to war as a lesser of evils, Dewey defended democratic goals as "objects of fair adventure." These goals were not guaranteed in any way; instead, they constituted a renewed possibility if the Allies were victorious. During the war, Dewey staunchly protected civil liberties and academic freedom. He was not prone to brush aside such concerns in the fever of battle. In order to promote a benign peace, Dewey persistently called for a clarification of Allied war aims. The *New Republic* retained a critical autonomy from the Wilson Administration and sought to rally liberal forces world-wide toward a reconciling, non-Carthaginian peace. Even after the Treaty of Versailles, Dewey defended American involvement by reminding his readers that a German victory, virtually imminent without America's participation, would have been far worse. The Treaty of Brest-Litovsk had given the world a fearful glimpse of a Ludendorff-dictated peace.

Dewey never became an absolute pacifist. Pacifism was incompatible with his experimentalism. Indeed, he formulated a classic critique of pacifism during World War I. The tactic of nonresistance could be justified only on the basis that it would be more effective in attaining justice than the alternative of utilizing force to deter aggression. As a proponent of the Outlawry of War Movement, Dewey hoped to mobilize world opinion against a system of international law that legitimized war. He recognized that years, if not decades, of painstaking education would be required before public opinion could ever constitute an effective instrument in world affairs. Actually, the Outlawry proposal was designed as a tool to enable people throughout the world to exert democratic control over their respective governments. Its success was tantamount to establishing international democracy. Dewey conceded that the right to self-defense could never be abrogated. A weird constellation of the Lindbergh flight, peace fever, and diplomatic intrigue culminated in the signing of the Kellogg-Briand Pact on August 27, 1928. Dewey was not a naive political enthusiast. He realized that, far from being the result of irresistible public demand, the pact was little more than diplomatic maneuvering. On the day that the pact was enacted, he indicated that it hindered rather than helped the objectives of the Outlawry of War Movement. Dewey's efforts on behalf of the Outlawry of War can best be conceived as a means to promote worldwide democracy rather than as a lobby for pacifism.

As a resolute opponent of Stalinism, Dewey demonstrated exemplary moral courage and integrity by championing the unfashionable belief that communism and democracy were incompatible He vigilantly resisted the escapist siren of totalitarianism, which had seduced many intellectuals into a fatal self-corruption. No one did more to undermine the position of the Popular Front within the academic-artistic community. While initially opposing America's entry into World War II, largely as a result of his disdain for the Popular Front, Dewey did not remain locked into past commitments, as has been alleged. On the contary, he was responsive to the constantly evolving predicament of the war crisis. He argued that totalitarianism was an aggressive way of life, one that could be maintained only by continuous expansion. Superior force, not appeasement, could curb its acquisitive designs.

Dewey's approach to economics is conditioned by an increased estrangement from state socialism. Even during the Great Depression, when emergency government action was mandated, his remedies were rooted in democratic guild socialism. He recognized the totalitarian danger embedded within state socialism and therefore advocated a more flexible, voluntaristic approach. Focusing upon results rather than abstract social blueprints, Dewey embraced a mixed economy as the best experimental means to obtain economic security, productivity, and political freedom. Democracy must take precedence over any economic scheme. Dewey knew that in the complex corporate age, the role of government must be adjusted in order to cope with the crises confronting society. No attempt was made to preordain any eternal ratio between the public and private sector; government ought to be a flexible instrument responsive to public needs, while resisting efforts to transform it into an imperial self-perpetuating bureaucracy. He chastised the defenders of *laissez faire* capitalism who sought to minimize government. Canonizing the private pursuit of profit not only promoted material philistinism but transformed individual freedom into libertinism and eradicated the bonds of a moral community, one animated by an acknowledgment that individual welfare is ultimately dependent upon the strength and virtue of the entire society.

When compared to the politicized intellectuals of his era, Dewey discussed politics with a refreshing sobriety. He resisted the temptation to create utopian one-step solutions or to engage in sensationalist public posturing and malicious personal attacks upon opponents. He held that scholars had the obligation to raise the level of public discourse. However, professional academics persistently discarded the caution, prudence, and sense of evidence that governed their scholarly vocation. While by no means infallible in his political judgments, Dewey's record certainly compares very favorably with his intellectual rivals. Twenty years ago, Morton White concluded that when compared to Niebuhr and Lippmann among democratic theorists, he preferred Dewey.[2] Since White's interpretation of Dewey involved some unwarranted criticism, the evidence to reinforce his initial judgment is even more compelling today.

Instead of dogmatic platitudes, Dewey argued that political policies should be judged on the basis of their consequences. Politics addresses itself to the concrete question of how men can live together in peace, justice, prosperity, and freedom. It seeks proximate justice, not a millennial transfiguration of man that would regiment the alleged reign of universal love and brotherhood. This utopian impulse harbors the seeds of totalitarianism within a frantic quest to transcend the human condition. Dewey warned that the amalgamation of politics and theology foments dangerous aberrations within the democratic polity. By seeking divine sanction for specific social policies, political theologians engage in an obscurantism that initiates a war of absolutes, not empirical analysis. Politics and religion are distinguishable social institutions. While theologians may properly address social issues, their political advice should be evaluated on the basis of the common good and not by private divine revelations or appeals to strict biblical literalism. Along with White, the question still remains today: what other political technique is there besides the scrupulous examination of consequences?

Pragmatism retains a set of principles but nurtures an openness to the evidence that would enable society to cope with the complex, indeterminate problems that demand action. Dewey advised that attention be paid to the context of problems. The pragmatic framework establishes both the means and the disposition to foster the qualities of discreteness, truthfulness, and compromise, all of which are necessary for the strength of democracy. This framework does not eliminate political debate but creates the foundation for constructive change among both conservatives and liberals. For example, Edmund Burke ridiculed the ideological predilection for abstract theories, while urging the prudential policy of adapting transitional institutions to meet new contingencies. Like Aristotle, political wisdom and statesmanship consists of synthesizing inherited experience with critical intelligence. Specific circumstances will determine whether social experimentation or social preservation should gain emphasis. Dewey was as opposed to ritualistic liberalism as he was to avaricious social Darwinism. His democratic vision is not a symptom of a tired, outmoded, milque-toast liberalism, but a challenge for each new generation.

NOTES

1. For example, see Michael Levin, "Why Not Pragmatism?" *Commentary* (Jan., 1983):43–48.
2. Morton White, *Social Thought in America* (Boston: Beacon Press, 1957), p. 263.

Selected Bibliography

Blewett, John, ed. *John Dewey: His Thought and Influence*. With a Foreword by John Brubacher. New York: Fordham University Press, 1960.

Boydston, Jo Ann, ed. *Guide to the Works of John Dewey*. Carbondale: Southern Illinois University Press, 1970.

Dykhuizen, George. *The Life and Mind of John Dewey*. Carbondale: Southern Illinois University Press, 1970.

Hook, Sidney. *John Dewey: An Intellectual Portrait*. New York: John Day Co., 1939.

————. *John Dewey: Philosopher of Science and Freedom*. New York: The Dial Press, 1950.

Howlett, Charles. *Troubled Philosopher*. Port Washington, N.Y.: Kennikat Press, 1977.

Keenan, Barry. *The Dewey Experiment in China*. Cambridge, Mass.: Harvard University Press, 1977.

Lamont, Corliss. *Dialogue on John Dewey*. New York: Horizon Press, 1959.

Marcell, Charles. *Progress and Pragmatism. James, Dewey, Beard, and the American Idea of Progress*. Westport, Conn.: Greenwood Press, 1974.

Nathanson, Jerome. *John Dewey, The Reconstruction of the Democratic Life*. New York: Ungar, 1967.

Novak, George. *Pragmatism vs. Marxism*. New York: Pathfinder Press, 1975.

Roth, Robert. *John Dewey and Self-Realization*. Englewood Cliffs, N.J.: Prentice-Hall, 1963.

Related Works

Addams, Jane. *Peace and Bread in Time of War*. New York: MacMillan Co., 1922.

Adler, Selig. *The Isolationist Impulse.* New York: Free Press, 1966.

Barnes, Harry Elmer. *World Politics and Modern Civilization.* New York: A.A. Knopf, 1930.

Beard, Charles. *Open Door at Home.* With G. H. E. Smith. New York: MacMillan Co., 1934.

———. *Giddy Minds and Foreign Quarrels.* New York: MacMillan Co., 1939.

———. *President Roosevelt and the Coming of the War, 1941.* New Haven: Yale University Press, 1948.

Bingham, Alfred. *Insurgent America.* New York: W.W. Norton Co., 1938.

Bourne, Randolph. *War and the Intellectuals.* Edited by Carl Resek. New York: Harper & Row, 1964.

Bowers, C. A. *The Progressive Educators and the Depression.* New York: Random House, 1969.

Brooks, Van Wyck. *Letters and Leadership.* New York: B.W. Heubsch, 1918.

Caute, David. *The Fellow Travelers.* New York: MacMillan, 1973.

Chatfield, Charles. *For Peace and Justice: Pacifism in America, 1914-1944.* Knoxville: University of Tennessee Press, 1971.

Cohen, Warren. *The American Revisionists.* Chicago: University of Chicago Press, 1967.

———. *America's Response to China.* New York: Wiley Co., 1971.

Croly, Herbert. *The Promise of American Life.* New York: MacMillan, 1909.

Diggins, John. *Mussolini and Fascism: The View From America.* Princeton: Princeton University Press, 1972.

Divine, Robert. *The Illusion of Neutrality.* Chicago: Quadrangle Books, 1968.

Elliott, William. *The Pragmatic Revolt in Politics.* New York: MacMillan, 1926.

Ferrell, Robert H. *Peace in Their Time.* New York: W.W. Norton Co., 1969.

Forcey, Charles. *The Crossroads of Liberalism: Croly, Weyl, and Lippmann, and the Progressive Era, 1900-1925.* New York: Oxford University Press, 1961.

Hook, Sidney. *Reason, Social Myths, and Democracy.* New York: John Day Co., 1940.

———. *Education and the Taming of Power.* New York: Open Court, 1973.

Shih, Hu. *The Chinese Renaissance.* Chicago: University of Chicago Press, 1934.

Israel, Jerry. *Student Nationalism in China, 1927-1937.* Stanford: Stanford University Press, 1966.

Jonas, Manfred. *Isolationism in America, 1915-1941.* Ithaca: Cornell University Press, 1966.

Keynes, John Maynard. *The Economic Consequences of the Peace.* New York: Harcourt, Brace, and World, 1920.

Lasch, Christopher. *The New Radicalism in America.* New York: Vintage Books, 1965.

Lawson, R. Alan. *The Failure of Independent Liberalism.* New York: Capricorn Books, 1971.

Link, Arthur. *Woodrow Wilson and the Progressive Era.* New York: Harper & Row, 1963.

Lippmann, Walter. *Drift & Mastery.* New York: M. Kennerley Co., 1914.

———. *Public Opinion.* New York: Harcourt, Brace & Co., 1922.

———. *The Phantom Public.* New York: Harcourt, Brace & Co., 1925.

———. *The Good Society.* Boston: Little, Brown & Co., 1937.

MacLeish, Archibald. *The Irresponsibles.* New York: Duell, Sloan & Pearce Co., 1940.

Martin, James J. *American Liberalism and World Politics, 1931–1941.* New York: Devin-Adair, 1964.

Meicklejohn, Alexander. *Education Between Two Worlds.* New York: Harper & Bros., 1942.

Mills, C. Wright. *Sociology and Pragmatism.* New York: Oxford University Press, 1966.

Mumford, Lewis. *The Golden Day.* New York: Boni & Liveright, 1926.

———. *Faith for Living.* New York: Harcourt, Brace & World, 1940.

———. *The Condition of Man.* New York: Harcourt, Brace & World, 1944.

———. *Values for Survival.* New York: Harcourt, Brace & World, 1946.

Niebuhr, Reinhold. *Moral Man and Immoral Society.* New York: Scribners, 1932.

———. *Christianity and Power Politics.* New York: Scribners, 1940.

———. *The Irony of American History.* New York: Scribners, 1952.

Noble, David. *The Paradox of Progressive Thought.* Minneapolis: University of Minnesota Press, 1958.

Osgood, Robert. *Ideals and Self-interest in America's Foreign Relations.* Chicago: University of Chicago Press, 1953.

Pells, Richard. *Radical Visions and American Dreams.* New York: Harper & Row, 1973.

Schneider, Herbert. *Making the Fascist State.* New York: Oxford University Press, 1928.

Stoner, John. *S. O. Levinson and the Pact of Paris.* Chicago: University of Chicago Press, 1943.

Strout, Cushing. *The Pragmatic Revolt in American History: Carl Becker and Charles Beard.* New Haven: Yale University Press, 1958.

Warren, Frank. *Liberals and Communism.* Bloomington: Indiana University Press, 1966.

White, Morton. *Social Thought in America: The Revolt Against Formalism.* Boston: Beacon Press, 1970.

Index